THE ETHICS OF PREV

In this book, eleven leading theorists debate the normative challenges of preventive war through the lens of important public and political issues of war and peace in the twenty-first century. Their discussion covers complex and topical subjects including terrorism, the "Bush doctrine" and the invasion of Iraq, Iran's nuclear capabilities, super-power unilateralism, and international war tribunals. They examine the moral conundrum of preventive intervention, and emphasize the need for a stronger and more effective international legal and political order and a corresponding re-evaluation of the normative status of international law. Together their essays form a challenging and timely volume that will be of interest to scholars in ethics and political philosophy, political theory, international relations, international law, and peace studies, and to general readers interested in the broader issues of peace and justice in the new world order.

DEEN K. CHATTERJEE is Senior Advisor and Professorial Fellow in the S. J. Quinney College of Law at the University of Utah and the editor-in-chief of the two-volume *Encyclopedia of Global Justice* (2011) and the series editor of Studies in Global Justice. His publications include *Democracy in a Global World: Human Rights and Political Participation in the 21st Century* (2007); *Ethics of Assistance: Morality and the Distant Needy* (2004); and with Don E. Scheid, *Ethics and Foreign Intervention* (2003).

THE ETHICS OF PREVENTIVE WAR

EDITED BY

DEEN K. CHATTERJEE

CAMBRIDGE
UNIVERSITY PRESS

CAMBRIDGE UNIVERSITY PRESS
Cambridge, New York, Melbourne, Madrid, Cape Town,
Singapore, São Paulo, Delhi, Mexico City

Cambridge University Press
The Edinburgh Building, Cambridge CB2 8RU, UK

Published in the United States of America by Cambridge University Press, New York

www.cambridge.org
Information on this title: www.cambridge.org/9780521154789

First published 2013

Printed and bound in the United Kingdom by the MPG Books Group

A catalogue record for this publication is available from the British Library

Library of Congress Cataloguing in Publication data CIP

The ethics of preventive war / edited by Deen K. Chatterjee.
pages   cm
Includes bibliographical references and index.
ISBN 978-0-521-76568-8 (Hardback) – ISBN 978-0-521-15478-9 (Paperback)
1. Aggression (International law)   2. Just war doctrine   3. Self-defense (International law)
I. Chatterjee, Deen K., editor of compilation
KZ6396.E87 2013
172′.42–dc23
2012034436

ISBN 978-0-521-76568-8 Hardback
ISBN 978-0-521-15478-9 Paperback

To my beloved sister Archana,
for her love, wisdom, and unfailing support

Contents

Contributors

MICHAEL BLAKE is Professor of Philosophy and Public Affairs at the University of Washington, and Director of the Program on Values in Society. Previously he taught at the Kennedy School of Government and in the philosophy department at Harvard University, and was a Laurance S. Rockefeller Fellow at the Center for Human Values at Princeton University. He received his bachelor degree in Philosophy and Economics from the University of Toronto, legal training at Yale Law School, and his doctorate in Philosophy from Stanford University. He specializes in Social and Political Philosophy, Philosophy of Law, and International Ethics. He has previously published articles in *Philosophy and Public Affairs*, *Journal of International Affairs*, *Public Affairs Quarterly*, *Canadian Journal of Philosophy*, and *Philosophical Topics*.

CHRIS BROWN is Professor of International Relations at the London School of Economics and Political Science. He is the author of numerous articles in international political theory and of *Practical Judgement in International Political Theory: Selected Essays* (2010); *Sovereignty, Rights and Justice* (2002); *International Relations Theory: New Normative Approaches* (1992); editor of *Political Restructuring in Europe: Ethical Perspectives* (1994); and co-editor (with Terry Nardin and N. J. Rengger) of *International Relations in Political Thought: Texts from the Greeks to the First World War* (2002). His textbook *Understanding International Relations* (2009) is now in its fourth edition and has been translated into Arabic, Turkish, and Chinese.

DEEN K. CHATTERJEE is Senior Advisor and Professorial Fellow in the S. J. Quinney College of Law at the University of Utah and the editor-in-chief of the two-volume *Encyclopedia of Global Justice* (2011) and the series editor of Studies in Global Justice. His areas of specialization are justice and global initiative, ethics of war and peace, and philosophy of religion and culture.

C. A. J. (TONY) COADY is an Australian philosopher with an outstanding international reputation for his writings on epistemology and on political violence and political ethics. His book *Testimony: A Philosophical Study* (1992) was widely praised as a ground-breaking work in epistemology, and his more recent books, *Morality and Political Violence* (2008) and *Messy Morality: The Challenge of Politics* (2008) have received enthusiastic reviews. The latter book embodies the Uehiro Lectures on Practical Ethics that he delivered at the University of Oxford in 2005. He was founding Director of the Centre for Philosophy and Public Issues at the University of Melbourne in 1990 and was later Deputy Director of its successor body, the Centre for Applied Philosophy and Public Ethics. His most recent appointments have been as a Vice Chancellor's Fellow at the University of Melbourne from 2009 and as a Leverhulme Visiting Professor at the University of Oxford in 2012.

JEAN BETHKE ELSHTAIN is the Laura Spelman Rockefeller Professor of Social and Political Ethics at the University of Chicago. She has also been a Visiting Professor at Harvard and Yale. Professor Elshtain holds nine honorary degrees and in 1996, she was elected a Fellow of the American Academy of Arts and Sciences. Her publications include *Public Man, Private Woman: Women in Social and Political Thought* (1981); *Women and War* (1987); *Democracy on Trial* (1993); *Jane Addams and the Dream of American Democracy* (2002); *Just War Against Terror: The Burden of American Power in a Violent World* (2003); *Sovereignty: God, State, and Self* (2008); and *The Gifford Lectures* (2005–06). Professor Elshtain is a contributing editor for *The New Republic*. She has been a Fellow at the Institute for Advanced Study, Princeton; a Scholar in Residence, Bellagio Conference and Study Center, Como Italy; a Guggenhein Fellow; a Fellow of the National Humanities Center; and in 2003–04, she held the Maguire Chair in Ethics at the Library of Congress. Professor Elshtain also serves on the Scholars Council, The Library of Congress; on the Board of Trustees of the James Madison Program in American Constitutional Ideals at Princeton University; the Board of Trustees of the National Humanities Center; and the Board of the National Endowment for Democracy. Professor Elshtain was a Phi Beta Kappa Scholar for 1997–98 and served as Vice President of the American Political Science Association for 1998–99. She was also appointed by President George W. Bush to the National Council for Humanities.

RICHARD FALK is Albert G. Milbank Professor Emeritus of International Law at Princeton University and since 2002 Research Professor in Global and International Studies at the University of California, Santa Barbara. He is Chair of the Board of the Nuclear Age Peace Foundation. His most recent books are *Achieving Human* Rights (2009); The *Declining World Order* (2004); and *The Great Terror War* (2003). The latter considers the American response to September 11, including its relationship to the patriotic duties of American citizens. Since 2008 he has been Special Rapporteur on Occupied Palestine for the UN Human Rights Council, and previously, served as a member of the Independent International Commission on Kosovo. He is the author or co-author of numerous books, including *Religion and Humane Global Governance*; *Human Rights Horizons*; *On Humane Governance: Toward a New Global Politics*; *Explorations at the Edge of Time*; *Revolutionaries and Functionaries*; *The Promise of World Order*; *Indefensible Weapons*; *Human Rights and State Sovereignty*; *A Study of Future Worlds*; *This Endangered Planet*; and co-editor of *Crimes of War*.

GEORGE R. LUCAS, JR. holds the Distinguished Chair in Ethics in the Vice Admiral James B. Stockdale Center for Ethical Leadership at the United States Naval Academy (Annapolis), and is also Professor of Ethics and Public Policy (tenured) at the Graduate School of Public Policy at the Naval Postgraduate School (Monterey, CA). He has taught at Georgetown University; Emory University; Randolph-Macon College; the French Military Academy (Saint-Cyr); the Catholic University of Louvain, Belgium; and served as Philosophy Department Chairman at the University of Santa Clara in California. He has received research fellowships from the Fulbright Commission and the American Council of Learned Societies. Professor Lucas is the author of five books, more than forty journal articles, translations, and book reviews, and has also edited eight book-length collections of articles in philosophy and ethics. Among these titles are *Anthropologists in Arms: The Ethics of Military Anthropology* (2009), *Perspectives on Humanitarian Military Intervention* (2001), and a special issue of the *Journal of Military Ethics*, "New Warriors and New Weapons: Ethics and Emerging Military Technologies" (JME 9/4, December 2010). His most recent essays are "Permissible Preventive Cyber Warfare" (forthcoming) and "The Industrial Challenges of Military Robotics" (2011). He is also co-editor (with Capt. Rick Rubel, US navy, retired) of the textbook, *Ethics and the Military Profession: The Moral Foundations of Leadership*, and a companion volume, *Case Studies in Military Ethics* (2004). These texts are used in core courses devoted to ethical leadership at the United States Naval Academy, the United States Air Force Academy, and at Naval ROTC units at over fifty-seven colleges and universities throughout the nation.

LARRY MAY is a political philosopher who has written on conceptual issues in collective and shared responsibility, as well as normative issues in international criminal law. He has also written on professional ethics and on the just-war tradition. He is currently W. Alton Jones Professor of Philosophy and Professor of Law at Vanderbilt University. He is also a Professorial Fellow at the Centre for Applied Philosophy and Public Ethics, Charles Sturt University as well as Visiting Fellow at the Australian National University. He has previously taught at Washington University; Purdue University; University of Wisconsin; and University of Connecticut. He has a BS in international affairs from Georgetown University, and a Ph.D. in philosophy from the New School for Social Research, where he was Hannah Arendt's last research assistant. He also has a JD in law from Washington University. Professor May has published twenty-five books, ten of which are single-authored monographs. The most recent books have won awards from the American Philosophical Association; the North American Society for Social Philosophy; the International Association of Penal Law; the American Society of International Law; and the American Library Association. His writings have been translated into French, German, Spanish, Italian, Polish, Serbian, Japanese, Chinese, and Korean. Professor May's work on legal ethics and international law has led to invitations to advise such groups as: the Indiana State Senate, the US State Department, the CIA, as well as members of the Australian High Court. He also served on the board of directors of the American Philosophical Association and is past president of AMINTAPHIL, the American section of the International Society for Philosophy of Law.

JEFF MCMAHAN is Professor of Philosophy at Rutgers University. He is the author of *The Ethics of Killing: Problems at the Margins of Life* (2002) and *Killing in War* (2009). He has three other books forthcoming: a collection of essays called *The Values of Lives*, a book on war called *The Right Way to Fight* that is intended for both academic and non-academic readers, and a sequel to his 2002 book called *The Ethics of Killing: Self-Defense, War, and Punishment.*

STEPHEN NATHANSON is Professor of Philosophy at Northeastern University, Boston, Massachusetts. His most recent book is *Terrorism and the Ethics of War* (2010). In addition, he is the author of *Patriotism, Morality and Peace* (1993); *Economic Justice* (1998); *An Eye for an Eye? The Immorality of Punishing by Death* (2nd edn., 2001); *Should We Consent to be Governed?* (2nd edn., 2001), and numerous articles on issues in ethics and political philosophy.

ALEX NEWTON is a senior adviser in Australia's Department of the Prime Minister and Cabinet. Her main areas of interest are human rights and business, social investment, and international relations policy. She holds a Master of Laws from Columbia University where she was a Harlan Fiske Stone Scholar and Bachelors of Arts and Laws degrees from Sydney University. Alex lectures in transnational business and human rights in the Australian National University's graduate law program. She previously worked with the UN Secretary General's Strategic Planning Unit, New York, as a consultant to UN-HABITAT and as a lawyer with the Australian Human Rights Commission. Her articles are published in a number of professional and other publications, including the *Law Society Journal of NSW* and *Polemic*. In addition, Alex has produced stories on a range of issues in the legal and social justice fields as a freelance producer and reporter for the Australian Broadcasting Corporation, Australia's national broadcaster.

CHAPTER I

Introduction

Deen K. Chatterjee

The increasingly common "preventive" use of military force raises difficult moral and legal issues that seriously challenge prevailing international law. Despite the justifying rhetoric alleging that these anticipatory wars aim to increase or ensure peace and security, such wars pose both moral and political dilemmas. Even when a war is declared in self-defense in response to an actual or imminent show of aggression, it is possible to take a principled pacifist or utilitarian stance instead of resorting to violence. While the long-standing just-war doctrine sanctions military self-defense, and international law endorses it, preventive wars in the name of self-defense when the danger is not actual or imminent raise moral conundrums and lead to problematic outcomes. Also, moral and military hazards of "rescue" wars are compounded when they are preventive wars against anticipated evils. The recent trend of justifying preventive war by blurring the distinction between preemption and prevention with epithets like "gathering threats" does little to clarify the important issues that arise.

The conundrum of whether nations should adhere to existing international law or carry out illegal but morally justified intervention is not new in the context of egregious violation of negative human rights by certain regimes. For instance, illegal intervention in the name of an urgent humanitarian cause occurred in the NATO bombing of Yugoslavia in 1999. But nations hide behind international law in their reluctance to undertake military intervention to enforce basic rights of subsistence. Certainly it is true that raising high barriers to intervention and respecting sovereignty minimizes self-serving military interventions couched in moral rhetoric. If interventions were permitted in inept or failed states in response to their ineptitude, then there would be no limit to military operations, posing a grave threat to the stability of world order. Consequently, "non-interventionism" is the standard thrust of international law, with "reluctant interventionism" being the practice only in exceptional cases.

With the changing nature of warfare in the twenty-first century, the permissibility of preventive war with a broader mandate of intervention has become a major focus of controversy. The bar against preventive use of force is much higher than that for preemption due to the greater odds of mistakes in assessing the severity and likelihood of danger, the extent of harm to non-combatants, and the probability of high incidence of preventive wars resulting from baseless fear or false pretense. Nonetheless, the blurring of the distinction between preemption and prevention in matters of peace and security due to the likely scenario of certain unstable regimes and hostile non-state actors acquiring weapons of mass destruction (WMD) has contributed to a more open attitude toward preventive war. Scholars also point out that a permissive interpretation of preventive measures can be found in the later just-war tradition of Grotius/Hobbes as part of reasonable self-defense, and also in Chapter 7 of the United Nations Charter pertaining to the Security Council in matters of international peace and security. Sovereignty and non-intervention might be the accepted norms, but stipulated measures suggestive of preventive intervention are permissible with Security Council authorization, thus making preventive war legal under current international law.

Nonetheless, matters of legality and morality related to preventive war are far from settled, as the chapters in this volume amply attest. In particular, the self-proclaimed authority of the United States to use unilateral preventive military measures for self-defense under the broad rubric of global security has generated intense controversy. Critics cite the US war on terror as an example of what could go wrong with a permissive policy of preventive war. Since the Bush doctrine of 2002, largely in response to the terrorist attacks on the United States on September 11, 2001, along with the recent wars in Iraq and Afghanistan (with an Iran conflict looming on the horizon), preventive war with a global mandate has apparently become part of official United States policy or doctrine. The thrust of this new direction is framed in terms of national defense and security, though humanitarian preventive intervention remains a policy option, as evident in the recent intervention in Libya (though it is debatable whether the Libya operation was really a case of preventive intervention and whether it could be called a humanitarian mission, given the fact that the Libyan conflict at that time had the appearance of a civil war). The potential for the global mandate of a nation's military, along with all other trends of globalization, has profound implications for international law, international relations, and overall peace and security. The permissibility of preventive war is a central issue in this debate.

The primary focus of this volume is on the moral, legal, and practical viability of preventive war for self-defense and security, though some chapters discuss the moral implications of anticipatory "rescue" wars, mainly for contrast and comparison. Most contributors examine preventive war via analysis of just-war thinking and through the lens of the important public and political issues of war and peace in the twenty-first century.

In Part I, Jean Bethke Elshtain, Chris Brown, and George Lucas examine the conceptual, normative, and methodological terrains of preventive war, both in the context of the just-war tradition and in view of the challenges of the twenty-first-century military conflicts and terrorist threats. Elshtain begins her discussion by exploring whether preventive war is an entirely new and unacceptable idea, as many critics of the Bush administration have charged, and whether preventive war cuts against the grain of American history, which is another common complaint. She asserts that the United States has taken actions in the past that can reasonably be called preemptive if not preventive, and that the Iraq war, if construed as a security decision by the United States (a move that Elshtain finds not unreasonable) can have prima facie justification in view of the failure of the United Nations as a credible organization for collective security. She also contends that due to the ambiguity in many aspects of the just-war theory, it is an open question whether preventive war is justifiable within the just-war tradition. Though the barrier to preventive war is higher than that to preemptive use of force, Elshtain notes that given the changing nature of modern warfare, with the rise of non-state actors and certain regimes posing grave threats to national and collective security, the idea of imminence in estimating the severity of threat should be understood in an expanded sense, making the preventive use of force a viable option in cases of dire emergency.

In his chapter, Chris Brown points out the need for a serious discussion of preemption and prevention in view of the novel and unconventional security threats posed by terrorism and rogue states today. For him, such a discussion is needed on its own merit, regardless of the ill-planned invasion of Iraq and the broad resistance to the Bush administration's National Security Strategy of 2002 – the so-called Bush doctrine. In fact, Brown notes that the importance of examining the ethical and legal implications of preemption is underscored by the fact that the Bush doctrine, though widely critiqued, is still largely in effect as part of current United States policy. In supporting the Bush doctrine of preemption, Brown points out that the doctrine's expanded notion of preemption, which blurs the distinction between preemption and prevention, is justified in today's world, though he admits that perhaps the reason the doctrine aroused so much skepticism is because it conveyed the impression that it could effectively provide absolute security or be successful in promoting freedom and democracy. In speculating what could replace the conventional distinction between preemption and prevention, Brown proposes a somewhat Aristotelian approach, drawing insights from classical realism and noting that a rule-based justification for preemption is not likely to be feasible in today's uncertain world.

George Lucas offers yet another angle on the normative and methodological debate surrounding preventive war. Declaring that the "case against preventive war is far from clear," he investigates the "methodological chaos" in the debate on the morality of preventive war, concluding that several competing paradigms of prevention and preemption have unduly clouded the case for a limited justification for preventive war. For instance, contemporary international law prohibits unilateral preventive war even in self-defense, but the classical just-war theorists were less clear on this issue. Lucas points out that the classical paradigm not only differs in its methodological stance from the mode of today's legal discourse on the justification of preventive war, it contained ambiguities and indeterminacy in the formulation and interpretation of some of the key provisions of the just-war doctrine, such as just cause, proportionality, legitimate authority, and right intention. In addition, these conditions were not put forth in a consistent and uniform manner, thereby leaving them open to varying interpretations regarding their relative importance or priorities. Thus the crucial notion of self-defense as a just cause, or whether other considerations besides self-defense could count as just cause, were left open-ended in the just-war tradition; yet so much of the debate on preemption and prevention depends on a clear and consistent articulation and application of these terms. All this prompts Lucas to consider the classical just-war doctrine less a coherent theory and more a form of ideal speech – a normative discourse "on the moral constraints on the resort to deadly force." For him, this explains the contrast (and the apparent confusion) between the morality of war and its presumed legality in today's debate. Not unlike Brown's approach in the previous chapter toward addressing the moral dilemmas arising from the conundrum of preemption and prevention, Lucas claims that the classical tradition is better suited to respond to such conundrums in today's complex world than is a rule-bound legalist paradigm that is getting progressively inept in framing the vexing moral issues of war and peace in our post-Westphalian global order.

In his chapter, Lucas writes: "How can law-abiding peoples and nations avoid recourse to the destruction of war, while yet responsibly acting to protect themselves against legitimate threats to their security, welfare, and even to the rule of law itself? This question deserves careful scrutiny on its own terms (as the remaining contributors to this volume attest)." Indeed they do! The conceptual, normative, and policy issues raised in the first part of the volume require a closer scrutiny of the legal and moral dilemmas of preventive use of force and an assessment of these dimensions in a world order that is juridically horizontal (interactions of sovereign states) and geopolitically vertical (shaped by doctrines of exception and unilateralism). With that objective, in Part II, Michael Blake, Richard Falk, and Larry May discuss the moral dilemmas of preventive war by focusing on international legal norms and institutions, while later chapters take up the task of critical moral assessment of prevention.

Michael Blake begins his chapter by noting that there is both a right and wrong way of explaining our intuitive disapprobation of preventive war. The wrong way begins with the negative consequences of the acceptance of a doctrine of preventive war, and proceeds to condemn the doctrine itself. This equation is incorrect, Blake suggests, because it confuses the validity of the doctrine with the empirical consequences of widespread endorsement of the doctrine. A better way of explaining our hostility toward preventive war, he argues, accepts that preventive war can be morally justifiable where serious threats to national self-interest may be found, but that a legal principle condemning the unilateral pursuit of such wars might nonetheless be defensible. Such legal principles might be grounded not directly in the moral status of the war itself, but indirectly in the beneficial consequences of demanding that individual states articulate their cases to an impartial international community. This conclusion requires us to rearticulate the moral status of international law. We should not, Blake concludes, think of international law as itself providing authority for a war, but rather giving a legitimate demand for provision of evidence that the moral authority for warfare already exists.

In an interesting twist to the logic of preventive use of force, Richard Falk discusses the challenges of preventive use of threat, or what he calls "threat diplomacy" in world politics, specifically against the backdrop of ongoing confrontation with Iran. He finds it revealing that while the global discourse has been focused on the perceived Iranian threat, almost no attention has been paid to the legality or propriety of the dire threat directed against Iran. Article 2(4) of the United Nations Charter prohibits threat or use of force in a most unconditional language – it does not distinguish between threat and international uses of force in its "war prevention goal" after the Second World War. Thus a threat to use force against the territorial integrity and security interests of any state is against international law and morality as mandated by the United Nations Charter. Accordingly, Falk finds it surprising that the Security Council has rarely been criticized for failing to come forward on behalf of the weaker states in the face of ongoing and illegal threats directed at them, for instance in the years leading up to 2003 against Iraq and the current confrontation against Iran. For Falk, this asymmetry in global perception is indicative of the geopolitical hegemony by powerful states over the legitimate rights of weaker states.

In the course of discussing whether it is realistic or legitimate to prohibit all threat to use force, and whether threat diplomacy can be effectively used to bring the parties to negotiation, Falk looks squarely at evolving concerns surrounding threat diplomacy. He spells out five dimensions where the issues merit careful scrutiny: international law, deterrence, the long war after the 9/11 attacks on the United States, countering nuclear proliferation, and nuclear terrorism. Falk shows that in each case the reliance on threats has the potential to make matters worse, while not using threats can improve a situation. In sum, reliance on coercive diplomacy paves the way toward unilateralism and non-accountability of the hegemonic powers, which is not good for world peace and is also counterproductive and imprudent for the countries themselves relying on such measures.

In probing the nature of aggression and international criminal responsibility, Larry May's primary concern in his contributed chapter is whether those who undertake preventive war where there are serious human rights violations should be prosecuted in an international tribunal for such wars. Is the fact that the war was preventive a defense against the charge of aggression or at least a mitigating factor concerning punishment in such cases? For May, this is an especially pressing issue in international criminal law, as the International Criminal Court debates whether to begin prosecuting cases of the crime of aggression along with the other three crimes under the Court's jurisdiction, namely crimes against humanity, genocide, and war crimes.

May proceeds first to distinguish preventive wars from preemptive and anticipatory wars. For that, he turns for guidance to the just-war tradition of Gentili and Grotius. While for Gentili first strike as anticipatory defense is justifiable even if there is little evidence that a danger is imminent, Grotius is more cautious in arguing that an offensive war is hard to justify in anticipation of an attack that may not materialize, and the premise can be used as a pretext for a self-serving and unjust war. May points out that this idea still forms the norm in current international law. Accordingly, for May, the Bush doctrine's provision for not precluding uncertainty and lack of evidence in engaging in warfare is closer to Gentili's view. It goes beyond "interceptive" or even anticipatory use of force and departs from the accepted international norm.

In deciding which international institution should determine what is aggressive war and which state has engaged in it, the issues of fairness and proper authority come to the fore. In the absence of any binding institutional jurisdiction in world affairs, the most obvious institutions that would have a legitimate claim of authority to decide which state is an aggressor are the ones that were set up by large multilateral treaties. According to May, the United Nations or one of the international courts are the most obvious institutions having such authority. In matters of determining aggression, the United Nations has the advantage since it was established to put an end to aggressive war, though May notes that there is dispute about which part of the United Nations should have the proper authority to decide on aggression: the Security Council, the General Assembly, or the Secretary General, each having serious drawbacks. May claims that the International Criminal Court, on the whole, should be the most likely body to decide on state aggression, though he notes that the ICC too has its problems.

In initiating trials of aggression after a preventive war, there are competing considerations ranging from deterrence and retribution to reconciliation and fairness. International trials for aggressive wars, including preventive wars, are held for discouraging military and political leaders from engaging in this type of war, as well as holding them accountable if they do. On the other hand, considerations of reconciliation for the sake of peaceful resolution of war may take precedence over deterrence and retribution in the aftermath of preventive war. But, most importantly, fairness considerations may prevail against prosecuting leaders of preventive war because such wars are often not clear-cut cases of aggression. Most military and political leaders engage in preventive wars because of their good-faith commitment to the safety and security of their own people. Thus, for May, while states may be condemned and even sanctioned for waging aggressive wars of prevention, in general it may not be fair to bring state leaders to trial for pursuing such wars. He argues that we should be more cautious in cases of individuals than in the case of states. He finds the bifurcation between Grotius and Gentili instructive here: Grotius' criteria for aggression should be construed as standards for state aggression, for which states should be held liable, and Gentili's expanded standards should be used for determining when state aggression may have constituted crimes of aggression, for which individuals should be liable for prosecution.

Part III contains three critiques of preventive war: Jeff McMahan's specter of moral conundrum, Stephen Nathanson's observation that both just-war theory and rule consequentialism lead to a rejection of preventive war, and Alex Newton's demonstration, though not a critique of preventive use of force *per se*, of how a policy of anticipatory prevention can go gravely wrong. McMahan notes that one moral objection to preventive war is not extensively discussed: the fact that preventive war generally requires attacking military personnel who may not have done anything, individually or collectively, to make themselves morally liable to attack. Preventive war, in other words, may involve large-scale intentional killing of innocent people. One response to this objection is that people who voluntarily join the military thereby make themselves strictly liable to attack, and even to preventive attack, if their government engages in planning and preparation for an unjust war. Consenting to join the military in the knowledge that this involves a risk of being used as an instrument of wrongdoing is sufficient to make a person liable to attack if he or she later has the misfortune to serve a government that begins to prepare for aggressive war. For McMahan, however, there are at least two concerns about this response. First, to prevent this claim from collapsing into a doctrine of pure collective liability, whereby soldiers are held liable to attack merely by virtue of group membership, it is necessary to distinguish between voluntary and non-voluntary membership. Yet this is a difficult normative rather than straightforwardly factual issue, since there is usually some element of choice in being or remaining in the military. But, second, if we concede that membership as a result of extreme coercive pressure counts as non-voluntary, it might follow that countries with universal conscription and draconian penalties for refusal to serve could not be morally liable to preventive attack while countries with volunteer armies could – an unsettling conclusion.

Stephen Nathanson's chapter begins with Michael Walzer's well-known case against preventive war. He argues that Walzer's approach is weakened because of his acceptance of a highly truncated version of just-war theory, a version that deprives him of important grounds for rejecting preventive war. Given Walzer's claim that just cause is sufficient for a just war and his dismissive remarks about proportionality and last resort, he has little basis for critiquing a preventive war that is motivated by the goal of defending a nation from a (perhaps distant) future attack. In contrast, Nathanson aims to defend the view that preventive wars are not justified and finds support in the multiple criteria of traditional just-war theory's *jus ad bellum* framework. For him, the one criterion that is especially impossible for preventive wars to satisfy is last resort – a criterion that he claims is "extremely plausible." In addition, even if any one criterion can be construed as a justification for going to war in anticipatory self-defense, the theory's multiple criteria collectively impose constraints on such a move. In essence, the *jus ad bellum* criteria provide us with a nuanced, balanced, rational, and impartial framework for evaluating a broad range of complex issues that mitigates partial, rash, and narrow perspectives. Nathanson finds this approach consistent with the cost/benefit evaluative framework used by the consequentialists for promoting overall human well-being. He argues that rule consequentialists might in fact adopt a version of the traditional *jus ad bellum* criteria in objecting to preventive war. However, Nathanson suggests that often in actual cases, a simple, rough-and-ready best case/worst case analysis can be psychologically compelling in spite of its evident defects. This is why he finds preventive war so dangerous as an option.

Alex Newton's chapter on the confrontation between Iran and the United States is a case study of the current situation from the perspectives of international law, international relations, and the morality of warfare. Through careful examination of the international trends and practices, the evolving uncertainties and ambiguities of the situation in Iran on the nuclear front, and especially the past and current policies and guidelines of the United Nations, along with the pronouncements of leading authors on international relations and ethics, Newton concludes that any preventive military strike by the United States on the Iranian nuclear facilities would be gravely mistaken and patently illegitimate, both legally and morally. Her chapter is not a critique of preventive war *per se* but addresses the moral and practical hazards of a preventive strike against Iran at a time when such a course of action is openly contemplated in influential political circles. She makes her case vivid through analogies with the mistakes of the 2003 invasion of Iraq. However, relying heavily on Michael Doyle's "jurisprudence of prevention" that draws on the just-war criteria and supports unilateral prevention in rare cases, Newton seems to leave open the possibility of a justified preventive use of force against Iran if and when Iran is deemed by credible evidence to be a sufficient and unacceptable threat.

In the fourth and final part, Tony Coady and Deen Chatterjee look beyond the option of preventive war to seek durable peace and security.

Contrary to the viewpoints presented in earlier sections, where some authors elucidate the need for a suitable policy of preventive use of force in response to the conditions of the twenty-first century, Coady sees no legitimate application of such a policy in today's world and finds the just-war prohibition of preventive war entirely valid. Chatterjee substantiates the traditional just-war resistance to preventive war by articulating the notion of "just peace." Both he and Coady favor diplomacy and proactive measures such as institutional reforms for a durable global civil society in order to eliminate the need for preventive use of force in the name of peace and security.

Coady notes that the arguments for preventive war are basically those encapsulated in the slogan "prevention is better than cure," the idea being that preventing something bad from happening is less costly and more effective than dealing with it after it has happened. For Coady, the slogan's benefits depend heavily upon the sort of prevention in question and the likely incidence of the harm being forestalled. Information campaigns about the advantages of exercise and a healthy diet in the cause of preventing heart disease, strokes, and diabetes are one thing; bringing massive, lethal violence to bear upon foreign populations in the hope of preventing their doing something horrific is quite another matter. Coady's chapter addresses the problems of preventive war and argues that the slogan has no legitimate application to warfare in the world as it presently is or is likely to be in the foreseeable future. He examines certain arguments that seek to show the need to abandon traditional just-war objections to preventive war, especially those that use analogies from domestic law enforcement, such as laws against conspiracy and attempted criminal activity. These arguments seek to bring anticipated crimes within the ambit of just cause, but Coady argues that they are unsuccessful. He specifically directs his objections to those preventive wars that are targeted against potential terrorism and anticipated persecution of citizens by their own governments, arguing that these cases of preventive military measures face overwhelming difficulties. Coady then points out effective non-military alternatives, for instance, in the case of terrorism: policing, surveillance, diplomacy, education, international cooperation, recognizing and meeting genuine grievances; in the case of government persecution of its citizens: diplomatic pressure, non-violent coercive measures including carefully developed sanctions aimed at the rulers rather than the ruled, economic and financial measures aimed at dictators, and legal sanctions against powerful persecutors. Coady notes that these methods, though likely to be effective, are not guaranteed to fully succeed and are not easy to implement in practice, but he reminds us that the same is even more true with preventive war.

Chatterjee's chapter complements Coady's in exploring options other than preventive war. Placing the debate on just war in the wider discourse of global justice and invoking the concept of just peace, this final contribution to the volume discusses the idea of prevention from a non-interventionist perspective and shows how it can be an effective measure for national security as well as humanitarian policies. Chatterjee notes that a slippery transition from preemption to prevention has been present in the writings of prominent political and legal theorists. For many of them, a general ban on preventive war is relaxed if there is credible evidence of "sufficient threat," leading to the permissibility of preventive use of force in the name of self-defense or humanitarian intervention. In contrast, Chatterjee claims that his normative directive of justice, when applied to the global order, takes us in the direction of just peace. From this perspective, he stipulates that the provision for even a limited permissibility of preventive war is ill-conceived. If one does not place a principled premium on a proactive and comprehensive non-interventionist policy of global justice, then the option of preventive war, however constrained, could gain undue legitimacy.

Taken together, the chapters in this book examine the complex and contested moral and legal issues of preventive war through analyses of contemporary key topics. They reflect the latest ideas of the authors on this urgent question, which is a pressing international issue and will likely be more so in the near future. As the chapters examine the moral conundrum of preventive intervention, they emphasize the need for a stronger and more effective international legal and political order and a corresponding re-evaluation of the normative status of international law. In addition to suggesting new perspectives, the contributors use the current debate to shed light on enduring questions about war and peace. Given the complex challenges of modern warfare to the issues of peace and justice, the authors show sensitivity to the distinctive demands of an interdisciplinary approach that blends empirical research with normative pronouncements. This is a timely and compelling discourse on a critical topic of global importance.

PART I

Conceptual, normative, and methodological terrains

CHAPTER 2

Prevention, preemption, and other conundrums

Jean Bethke Elshtain

In the early days of the second Iraq war, we heard cries of "illegal" repeatedly. The commencement of hostilities against Saddam Hussein's "Republic of Fear" was said to violate established norms of international law; to make the United States an outlaw among nations; and to constitute a disastrous precedent. We were told that the United States had *never* before in its history engaged in preventive or preemptive action against a hostile foe and that, therefore, the administration of George W. Bush was *sui generis* in its arrogant violation of law and its besmirching of American foreign policy. These sorts of claims are subject to empirical investigation, of course, and such investigation shows them to be false. The United States has, indeed, engaged external foes in the absence of official declarations of war and in a manner that can reasonably be called preemptive if not preventive.[1] This may or may not be a good thing, of course, but it does belie the charge of notorious originality on the part of the Bush administration at that time. Different words may be used – as, for example, the locution "anticipatory self-defense" deployed by the Kennedy administration in the days of the Cuban missile crisis – but the reality is that the United States has taken action in the past that can reasonably be called preemptive.

As to "illegality," which will not be my primary focus, for every critic there were less vocal defenders who insisted, and continue to insist, that international law lined up with the Bush administration rather than against it where the Iraq conflict was concerned. One basic truth, encoded in the United Nations Charter itself, is that no state abrogates its sovereignty when it becomes a member of that organization. It follows that each state remains the judge of its own interests and security needs. A conundrum, to be sure, for one sees, in the establishment of the United Nations, the

---

[1] See Max Boot, *The Savage Wars Of Peace: Small Wars And The Rise Of American Power* (New York: Basic Books, 2003).

phenomenon of an international "community" composed of sovereign entities who are not bound by that "community" in their security decisions – not really. Given that the United Nations has largely failed as an instrument for collective security, it is unsurprising that the United States, while determinedly seeking UN authorization, would, if necessary, build a coalition and act absent that authorization. There is nothing "illegal" about this. One can argue against such steps on legal grounds or political desiderata, but *per se* ruled out of bounds: no.

For the just-war thinker, these are important considerations, but legal or illegal is not a trump card in just-war argument. The legal and the moral cannot be equated, although one hopes they are not in conflict. The illegal and the immoral do not map onto one another precisely although one hopes and anticipates that they run more or less parallel to one another. That this likely happens most of the time testifies to the fact that our notions of what counts as "law" in the international realm – and it is a notoriously slippery and under-developed enterprise – are deeply indebted to the tradition of discourse called "just-war thinking." The just-war tradition did not emerge in a historic vacuum, of course, so it is not surprising that it is shaped, in part, by the historic cirumstances of a given era. That said, there are basic commitments and norms that are solid – on both the *ad bellum* and *in bello* ends of the scale – in just-war thinking. That means they have stood the test of time and endured for centuries. Here one thinks about the principle of non-combatant immunity, for example, or discrimination as it is often called: one is not permitted to make civilians the explicit target of military action. Or, on the *ad bellum* side of the ledger, the insistence that the use of force should, ideally, be a response to an act of aggression by another party, remains the guiding rule of thumb.

But matters do not end there and many aspects of just-war thinking are highly contested. What rises to the fore as most exigent depends very much on the historic moment and its politics. For example: in the 1980s the overriding concern was the possibility of a strategic nuclear exchange between the two great super-powers, the US and the USSR. It is unsurprising that just-war discourse – like the United States Catholic Bishops' *Challenge of Peace* issued in 1983 – had, as its preeminent concern, the nuclear question.

How times have changed! Matters that were off to the side in the 1980s now loom as the heart of the matter. I refer to questions of humanitarian intervention and contending with "non-state actors" in the international arena who are, in practice, dedicated to terroristic ends using terroristic means. How does one deal with such foes, foes lacking international standing in a de jure sense? What is the right and wrong of it? When the Bush administration declared a global "war on terror," it was widely derided in the dominant media both here and abroad and this for a variety of reasons I cannot here rehearse. But one major concern was whether or not the term "war" can ever appropriately be deployed when a sovereign state battles a non-state entity or entities? Given that such entities may be sponsored by, or given sanctuary by, state actors – like Al-Qaeda in Taliban-controlled Afghanistan, can action be taken against that state or states as a means to defeat the purposes of terrorists? Terms like "preemption" and "prevention" bubbled to the surface as hot button, overriding preoccupations. What is the difference between preemption and prevention? Is either ever justifiable within the just-war tradition?

PREEMPTION OR PREVENTION: WHAT IS THE DIFFERENCE?

The terms "preemption" or "prevention" are sometimes used interchangeably. They are not, however, synonyms and one invites serious misunderstanding by failing to discriminate between the two. The barrier to preventive use of force is higher than that for preemption, although both have to make a strong case. Some just-war thinkers, especially those tied to legalistic argumentation, fall back on the Westphalian presuppositions concerning the nigh absolute inviolability of state sovereignty: a curious move if one thinks about it. The just-war tradition predates Westphalia by centuries and, within just-war reasoning, state sovereignty has a relative but not an absolute value. One suspects, in many cases, that hiding behind the cover of state sovereignty is a way to express a political position and to do so in a manner that strains or distorts just-war norms. To be sure – and to be fair – state sovereignty occupies something of a "given" status or assumption in Michael Walzer's classic, *Just and Unjust Wars*, first published in 1977.[2] Walzer operates within the framework of what he calls "the legalist paradigm." His presuppositions are Westphalian insofar as he takes the sovereign state as his basic unit of exploration and examination. Other just-war thinkers begin in "another place," so to speak, seeing in state sovereignty a value, but not necessarily the highest value; and certainly not a secure trump card in argumentation.

Why is this important? Well, where one locates the state and the value one assigns to it help to determine just how formidable will be the barrier

---

[2] Michael Walzer, *Just and Unjust Wars*, 4th edn. (New York: Basic Books, 2006).

to preemptive or preventive action. One can set that barrier so high that no course of preemption ever meets the standard of what is justifiable within the just-war tradition.[3] And prevention is ruled out of court so peremptorily that it is not even worthy of sustained discussion. Others will lower the barrier, at least somewhat, as state sovereignty is measured against other values that one endorses and cherishes, especially if those values incorporate an explicit anthropology, or understanding of the human person. For example: a just-war thinker who measures his or her position against the value of "the dignity of the human person," may find that state sovereignty can and should be trumped on certain occasions in the name of an overriding "common good." The example that comes most readily to mind for most contemporaries is genocide. Is one permitted to stand by and do nothing, if one has the capacity to do something, as a people or identifiable group is targeted for systematic slaughter? Do we resort to the inviolability of state sovereignty at such junctures? How do we override state sovereignty, if we decide it is not the only or the highest good in such a situation?

As I already indicated, a few years ago such questions were largely of "academic" interest as the Cold War dominated thinking about international affairs and the use of force. But with the break-up of the Soviet Union, questions that had lain relatively quiescent suddenly loomed. It seemed, and seems, as if we are bombarded daily with cries of distress and calls for some action of some sort to stop an atrocity here or an out-of-control state there. It behooves us, therefore, to be clear about the rough and ready meanings of preemption and prevention respectively, keeping in mind throughout that there is no one settled stipulative definition of either of these concepts. In general, however, preemption refers to action taken in light of a threat of immediate provenance. The threat is here and now. If we do not act, claim responsible public officials, we will surely be overrun, attacked, even decimated tomorrow. Walzer discusses preemption in *Just and Unjust Wars*. His example is not a slamdunk in the minds of many and remains controversial. But his reasoning is clear and helps us to take our bearings where preemption is concerned. Whatever one makes of Walzer's case study, he clarifies for us what preemption is all about: *an immediate threat*.

Prevention is distinguished from preemption by the more distant nature of the threat. In the case of prevention, a state acts in such a way as to

---

[3] See, for example, John Howard Yoder's highly legalistic analysis, *When War is Unjust: Being Honest in Just-War Thinking* (Minneapolis: Augsburg Press, 1984; revised edn., New York: Orbis Books, 1996).

prevent the emergence of an immediate threat in the future and does so given its assessment that the threat, once it develops fully, will be nearly impossible to contain or defeat without significant cost in blood and treasure. Better, then, to nip this threat in the bud rather than to permit it to flower fully. This way of thinking is clearly visible in current debates about Iran and its nuclear program. The debate demonstrates for us the "fog" of thinking about war, not just war itself. Judgments must be made in the absence of transparent, unassailable evidence. Evidence is interpreted; intelligence is gathered. There is, at present, general concurrence that the bellicose Iranian regime is moving at break-neck speed to develop useable nuclear weapons and the capacity to deliver them.

The regime, in the person of its inflamed president, Mahmoud Ahmadinejad, has already issued threats based on the presupposition that Iran will have functioning nuclear weapons in the near term. The relevant questions, then, turn in part on just how imminent the threat is: do we have two years? Ten? And, more importantly, how do we act? Is acting to prevent Iran from completing its nuclear weapons program ever justifiable within just-war thinking? This takes us to the heart of prevention, namely, *a threat in situ that, if it is allowed to continue, will constitute a clear and present danger in the future.* The Bush administration's National Security Strategy document of 2002, although loathe to use the language of preemption, spoke of the lawful use of military force in the case of an imminent danger of attack.[4] Critics of this document insisted that it egregiously violated just-war teaching; supporters argued that it did not and that, although the proof turned on concrete cases and examples, there was no a priori interdiction on preventive use of force. There the matter stands.

As if all this were not complicated enough, one must add another feature to this heady brew, namely, the articulated norm called "Responsibility to Protect" or R2P. First issued under the imprimatur of the International Commission on Intervention and State Sovereignty in the fall of 2001 and much overshadowed by the aftermath of the attacks of 9/11, R2P has gained considerable headway in debates in Western Europe although it is less in play in the United States. One way or the other, the principle is that the United Nations has a responsibility to act in instances where the horrors being perpetrated are substantial, egregious, and

---

[4] National Security Strategy of the United States of America (NSS 2002), issued in September 2002. The aim of NSS 2002 is to set forth criteria for American international relations and the use of military force in an era characterized by what the document sees as unprecedented events and situations.

continuing – my characterization – and where the "international community" has a responsibility to interdict in order to protect the innocent.
Should the United Nations fail to act – and that is a high probability – a
member state or coalition of states may take this responsibility upon
themselves.

I have discussed this responsibility to act under the rubric of international justice, arguing that a claim on the use of force in one's behalf if
one is the victim of systematic, egregious, and continuing violence is a
fundamental right, if you will, a rock-bottom claim that an aggrieved
group may make upon the "international community."[5] Of course, the
burden to act will fall most heavily on those who are capable of projecting
their power, like the United States, but that is neither here nor there as one
sorts the matter through just-war criteria – at least not until one comes to
the prudential criterion and asks whether one's intervention is likely to
succeed or not. It makes little sense to expend human lives in an effort that
is doomed to failure – even in the name of sparing lives now being lost. If
one's action will add to the loss of life, it is better to demur, even as one
acknowledges the nature of the horror and the fact that basic human
dignity is under siege.

Clearly, in the case of NATO intervention in Libya, the Obama
administration determined on behalf of the United States that the prudential criterion had been met – certainly one hopes this was aired fully – and
that intervention under the aegis of NATO would meet the norms of right
authority as well as an exigent emergency and "right," namely, the right of
peoples to be spared systematic assault and slaughter – one of the themes of
international justice as I unpack it. To be sure, this is no "slamdunk" case,
as the intervention was based on *anticipated* harm, since systematic and
egregious slaughter was not then taking place – although many nasty
things were and they seemed a harbinger of things to come, at least if
Ghadafi's rhetoric was to be believed. Those pushing for intervention
within the Obama administration were liberal interventionists, including
Secretary of State, Hillary Clinton. This position overlaps in many essen-
tials with the articulated doctrine of the previous Bush administration:
despite the claims of partisans to the contrary, there is more continuity
than difference in the policies of the two administrations.

With the distinctions between prevention and preemption now clearly
in mind, then, let's turn to whether or not just-war thinking affords a

---

[5] See Jean Bethke Elshtain, "International Justice as Equal Regard and the Use of Force," *Ethics and
International Affairs* 17:2 (September 2003), 63–75.

powerful, clear, and coherent way of reasoning about these matters or whether, as critics of just war claim frequently, just-war criteria matter not at all in the final analysis, for each and every state will act in ways best suited to defend its own interests, whatever the right and wrong of it may be.

JUSTIFYING PREEMPTION AND PREVENTION

Walzer's analysis is cast within the frame of the international system of sovereign states. Walzer indicates that a major way in which his thinking has changed since the original publication of his classic text is in the matter of humanitarian intervention or "rescue," hence where preemption may well be concerned. In a recent visit to my course on "Just War Thinking" at the University of Chicago, Walzer indicated in direct response to a student question how his thinking had changed on these topics: they now occupy a central role in his thinking, by sharp contrast to the late 1970s, when these issues were not of primary concern. He has, he told the class, set the bar rather lower where preemptive intervention is concerned. Prevention is another matter – there the bar is higher – but does it remain forbidden, as he once insisted?[6]

Is there instead, perhaps, another way to reason about preemption? Bear in mind that there is no legal right – none – of humanitarian intervention in the United Nations Charter. Indeed, the UN Charter, as I noted earlier, leaves the full presuppositions of state sovereignty intact, prohibiting intervention in situations under the legal jurisdiction of any given state. R2P – the Responsibility to Protect – although it does not have the normative force of the UN Charter, is a way to "soften" the prohibition on intervention without creating an essentially permissive regime where such intervention is concerned. The bar against intervention within a sovereign state member of the UN (and one must be a de jure recognized state to be a full-fledged member of the UN) remains high but it is not unassailable. That is, intervention cannot *by definition* be ruled out of court and counted more or less automatically as a wrongful act of aggression. It may or may not be such.

The norm and its overriding turns on the occasion and its seriousness, its gravity. A border skirmish between contending parties within a state does not rise to the level of serious consideration of the use of force by an outside party. On the other hand, a program of slaughter, systematic rapes,

---

[6] Michael Walzer, class lecture, University of Chicago Divinity School, Winter Term 2010.

rounding up children as child soldiers, and the like, clearly does rise to that level. (One example might be the actions of the notorious butcher, Charles Taylor, when he ruled Liberia and fomented internal strife in Sierra Leone that involved mass killings, mass raping, kidnapping children and turning some 200,000 of them into youthful, drugged-out brain-washed killers, and created tens of thousands of displaced refugees). In cases such as these, consideration of preemption must begin in earnest, as I have argued under the rubric of "international justice and the use of force." My basic claim, beginning with a presupposition of the dignity of the person and equal moral regard for all persons, is that those being violated in systematic, continuing, and egregious ways, have a claim on the international community to intervene with force, if necessary, on their behalf. This does not trigger an automatic resort to force but opens it as a real possibility, indeed a moral necessity, in some situations.[7]

What lies behind this general approach is a set of Augustinian presumptions concerning the functioning of *caritas* or charity in the world of political entities. One may well have a responsibility to one's neighbor, a responsibility to protect the innocent from certain harm. This pre-Westphalian argument locates political bodies as a feature of a fallen world but does not infuse them with the normativity later granted by the Westphalian settlement. To be sure, Augustine understood full well the need for rule and governance. Anarchy is a horror to be avoided. So no one should scorn the creation and sustaining of "empires" or polities. At the same time, the good that political entities do needs to be kept in perspective: the city of man is not and can never be the city of God. It follows that God's creatures, or some of them, may be called upon to fight and even to die to protect other of God's creatures who have come into harm's way. It will, in other words, be somewhat easier within this Augustinian ambience to arrive at justification for preemption where "rescue" is concerned, rather than Walzer's legal paradigm – but intervention is not automatic. Augustine was well aware of the fact that rulers can deploy moral argument when the motive for force is, instead, aggrandizement. There are ways to assess this, of course. Does the ruler intervene and then seize territory? Does he

---

[7] See Elshtain, "International Justice as Equal Regard and the Use of Force." In the essay I attempt to answer the questions: what does it mean to make a claim under the equal regard norm? And: who can be called upon to use coercive force on behalf of justice? The upshot of the argument is that the states, or state, with the greatest capabilities to project their power will bear the lion's share of responsibility for enforcing an equal regard norm. I acknowledge the difficulties of articulating a strong universal justice claim while assigning to a particular state or states a disproportionate enforcement burden. But that is the simple reality of our current situation.

perpetrate his own egregious cruelties? And so on: the proof is in the pudding.

To sum up: for just-war thinkers save, perhaps, the most narrowly legalistic – and here one is more likely to run into this among highly legalistic critics of just war rather than among just-war thinkers themselves – preemption can be justified but a rigorous argument is required and the decision arrived at will always be, or should always be, articulated with some regret that such "rescue" or humanitarian intervention or, alternatively, measure or measures to forestall an imminent attack, are necessary. In other words, one makes it clear that preemption is not just "another day at the office" but is, instead, undertaken in a specific moment of crisis.

Prevention is another matter, however, and here the barrier to action is set higher. Some just-war thinkers make that barrier unscaleable: prevention can never be justified. Others lower it somewhat, arguing that there are "new things" in the world that just-war thinkers must now contend with.[8]

DOES PREVENTION UNDERMINE INTERNATIONAL NORMS?

An argument deployed frequently against the possibility of prevention – remember that prevention means dealing with a threat before it is fully realized and imminent – is that it will set off a cascading series of "preventive" attacks or interventions, a kind of domino effect. If prevention is resorted to by the United States, say, does that not set a precedent for a small state in sub-Saharan African to attack its neighbor under the pretext that it will soon be a preeminent threat to themselves? (As if such states required any such pretext or argument – they seem to have no trouble at all attacking and attempting to destroy one another, although such continuing violence is most often meted out most brutally to one's own people, or portions of one's people.) We hear such arguments frequently: for example, in the discussion of "enhanced interrogation," a common theme or critique was that if the United States violated certain Geneva rules for prisoners of war – and here I will simply bracket the distinction between legal and illegal combatants and what force such a distinction has – it would follow as a matter of course that when Al-Qaeda or some group of Iraq "insurgents" grabbed one of our soldiers, they would follow suit.

---

[8] This is the general approach taken by George Weigel in "The Development of Just War Thinking in the Post-Cold War World: An American Perspective," in Charles Reed and David Ryall, eds., *The Price of Peace: Just War in the Twenty-First Century* (Cambridge University Press, 2007), 19–36.

This was not a persuasive argument as everyone knew that it mattered not to terrorist groups what we did or did not do: they would terrorize and behead prisoners as they saw fit. Be that as it may, and leaving aside the "domino effect" argument, a strong and persuasive argument could be cast more forthrightly and in a manner that does not turn on prudential criteria, namely, that the United States has a stake in building up an international culture of "equal moral regard" and, therefore, that we must demur at times even if, or when, our actions might be justifiable.

Similarly, for those functioning largely outside a morally exigent just-war tradition, whether preventive action is engaged in or not will turn primarily on a set of calculations of benefits to be gained and losses to be endured. Within just-war teaching, as we have already learned, the matter is not reducible to such calculations: do we locate state sovereignty so high that the barrier to violating it cannot be breached? Or, instead, are there urgencies that may justify prevention?

In my view, prevention should have a status not unlike that of supreme emergency in Walzer's *Just and Unjust Wars*. By that I mean it should be resorted to with considerable trepidation and regret, and only when there is no reasonable alternative. I fear, however, that this statement may mislead somewhat. Walzer's supreme emergency, the overriding of the norm of discrimination in a situation where whole peoples – and not just states – hang in the balance, is highly controversial as in effect, he creates a new category. The basic criteria of just-war discourse and tradition do not include an official, normative "override" like "supreme emergency." In Walzer's hands, this override is not altogether unlike the traditional notion of "executive privilege" or "the exception" in political theory and the history of political thought. The point is that the category is not a stipulated normative rule but, rather, a temporary exception to that rule.

Many have argued – or did – that this also invites the domino effect. Walzer can reasonably claim at this juncture that one can detect no such thing in the actions of policy-makers since the publication of his book in 1977. Those who are going to embark on a course of outright aggression and killing – like Saddam Hussein against the Kurds, for example – are unlikely to find it necessary to make the case on moral grounds and to deploy the criterion of supreme emergency; rather, it is a simple case of "the mighty do what they will and the weak suffer what they must."

Prevention is not as innately controversial as supreme emergency, although some may well see it differently. My reason for associating the two is that prevention should be quite rare, not normative, and can be justified *only* when the developing threat is of such a dire nature that we cannot – we simply cannot – take the chance that it will become imminent. And the "we" here is likely not to be one nation alone. Let's return to my example of Iran's nuclear program. The European Union agrees it would be a catastrophe by any measure were Iran to go nuclear. Arab states in the Middle East shake in their boots as they contemplate that possible "reality." Israel's life as a polity is at stake if one takes Ahmadinejad's words seriously: he will obliterate the Zionist entity at first opportunity. Sure, tens of thousands of Muslims may die but they would die a glorious death as martyrs so it is an occasion for rejoicing. Is this just so much hot air? Will no such thing happen? We do not know, do we? So how do we act? Do we pretend not to hear any of this? Do we regard it automatically as rhetorical hyperbole and downgrade its importance? Or do we take it very seriously indeed and, running worst case scenarios, determine that we must act before the threat is actualized?

This matter becomes ever more fraught in situations of dramatic uncertainty of the sort that pertains as of this writing – the summer of 2012. Democratic revolts have broken out throughout the Arab world, including its most powerful state, Egypt. What the outcome over the long term will be, nobody knows. It is possible that democratization will take place without liberalization and that dangerously reactionary or radical groups will be voted into positions of power. This outcome would, possibly, shift the balance of power ever more against Israel and generate even more uncertainty into an already precarious situation.

Given these possibilities, the temptation to preempt may well increase – depending, of course, in which direction the rearrangement of forces in the Middle East goes forward.

As I indicated, this will be rare – this sort of situation – for it is certainly not the stuff of day-to-day "international relations." The state system works to maintain a kind of homeostasis most of the time – the famous "balancing" business that is the stuff of "realist discourse" – and there is something to that. So prevention will be rare, as such threats are going to be rare. Now, there are many who would say: why strain so mightily to arrive at some "thin" justification for what so obviously needs to be done in the name of state security – the security of one's own people if not the security of others? A nuclearized Iran may not present an immediate threat – once it is achieved – but it will directly threaten the stability of the Middle East, hence the world, and of our own security. Thus, both raison d'état and "reasons of the system," if you will, dictate prevention.

This argument has great force but the just-war thinker would fret that it bodes to make prevention more normative or common than it ought to be.

Thus, he or she insists that just-war prohibition on prevention must be considered: can it be overridden? And, if not prohibition, then a high barrier? There, too, can it be overriden? I would argue "yes," but with great temerity and caution as one in no way wants such arguments to become commonplace. I actually do not think they will become such. No one, including the United States, wants to run around trying to nip every possible future threat in the bud: that would be an impossible way to conduct foreign policy in light of the realities of such policy. One is always dealing with a finite number of soldiers and a finite, not infinite, budget. One must triage the threats and it will be only a very few, I suspect, that will rise to the level that would justify prevention.

CONCLUSION

Just-war thinking has many strengths. It is normative without generating a set of unyielding Kantian legalisms. It is prudent without falling into crude realpolitik. It speaks to a general yearning for a world in which people are treated with minimal decency. It recognizes both necessity and responsibility. Thus, preemptive and preventive use of force, as refracted through just-war thinking, will display a greater measure of gravity, being the result of serious moral reasoning, than conclusions arrived at using various shortcuts of either a narrowly legalistic or crudely reductionist sort.

CHAPTER 3

After 'Caroline': NSS 2002, practical judgment, and the politics and ethics of preemption

Chris Brown

INTRODUCTION

Few subjects are as potentially important for the study of international political theory in the twenty-first century as the ethical implications of the notion of preemptive war, and the putative distinction between preemption and prevention, and yet, in the post-9/11 environment, few subjects are as difficult to approach in a calm, rational manner. The reason for this strange state of affairs is, I suggest, clear. In most writer's minds preemption is associated with two reference points; the US National Security Strategy of 2002 (hereafter NSS 2002), which appeared to legitimate a very strong, and perhaps indefensible, doctrine of preemption, and the Iraq war of 2003, which was partly justified in terms of preempting a threat from weapons of mass destruction (WMD) which, in the event, proved not to exist, or at least not there and then.[1] Because of these two commonly understood reference points, the issue of preemption has become indelibly associated with the foreign policy of the late administration of President George W. Bush, and the assumption is that to take any attitude to preemption which does not simply involve condemning the notion out of hand is morally equivalent to endorsing that foreign policy – a position which most writers on international ethics are very unwilling to adopt. I share this latter unwillingness, but it seems to me to be a mistake to take this to mean that the issue of preemption is out of bounds for all time. As the presidency of George W. Bush recedes into the past and at least some elements of his foreign policy have been reversed, it is to be hoped that the issue of preemption can be approached without the political baggage it carried up

---

An earlier version of this chapter was presented at the International Studies Association's Annual Convention in 2007, and appears as "Practical Judegment and the Ethics of Preemption," in Chris Brown, *Practical Judgement in International Political Theory: Selected Essays* (London: Routledge, 2010), 236–249.

[1] NSS 2002 cited here from a PDF download at www.whitehouse.gov/nsc/nss.pdf.

until January 2009. After all, indiscriminate attacks designed to kill Western civilians predate both 9/11 and the Bush administration and are continuing now that Bush has left office.[2] Since one possible response to such attacks may involve the preemptive use of force against the terrorists and those who give them sanctuary, there is a need to develop an ethically acceptable approach to preemption, which is the aim of this chapter.[3]

In what follows I intend to examine the conventional ethical and legal distinction between preemption and prevention, and to examine reasons why this distinction is difficult to sustain under twenty-first-century conditions. I will then suggest that the attempt to replace this traditional distinction with a new, rule-based, definition of the circumstances under which preemption is justified is unlikely to succeed. Instead, we must approach the subject from a different, more Aristotelian, direction – and in so doing we will be able to link up with, and build on, some of the insights of classical realism, *pace* the argument of most contemporary realists that preemption is not part of their intellectual toolkit. However, before proceeding with this task, it is necessary to examine, briefly, NSS 2002 and the run-up to the Iraq war, in order to explain why we should not allow the controversy provoked thereby to prevent a serious discussion of preemption – and, although the political context which produced NSS 2002 is now in the past, the document itself has never been officially disavowed, so is, in a sense, still current.

NSS 2002 AND THE IRAQ WAR

What, exactly, is wrong with the way in which NSS 2002 handles the issue of preemption? I put the question in this way, because although right-thinking people agree that there is something wrong with the doctrine, they are less clear on exactly what it is. I suggest here that what is wrong with NSS 2002 is *not* the thoughts on preemption laid out in that document, but the apparent belief that, via a successful doctrine of preemption, something close to absolute security can be obtained – this is a version of the "one per cent doctrine," originally articulated by then Vice-President Cheney and

---

[2] US readers will be familiar with the unsuccessful attack on the World Trade Center in 1993, but may be less familiar with the campaign launched by Algerian Islamists against French civilians in the 1990s, or the attacks on European tourists in Egypt in that decade; for the post-Bush era, consider the so-called "under-pants" bomber in December 2009, and the aborted attack on Times Square in April 2010 as well as various attempts to bring down airliners over the Atlantic.

[3] To preempt (as it were) an unfruitful discussion, I use the term terrorism to describe the deliberate targeting of the innocent, and am happy (although that is not the right word) to acknowledge that such acts are often carried out by governments, including some whose policies I broadly support.

described so ably by Ron Suskind in the book of that name, which states that even a threat to the United States of this low magnitude must be eliminated.[4]

NSS 2002 is a complex document, and the section which deals with preemption is nuanced and sensible in the way in which it sets up the problem. The authors present a brief version of the conventional account of legitimate preemption, and a reasoned explanation of why this conventional account is no longer wholly adequate:

> [For] centuries, international law recognised that nations need not suffer an attack before they can lawfully defend themselves against forces that present an imminent danger of attack. Legal scholars and international jurists often conditioned the legitimacy of preemption on the existence of an imminent threat – most often a visible mobilisation of armies, navies and air forces preparing to attack.
>
> We must adapt the concept of imminent attack to the capabilities and objectives of today's adversaries. (NSS 2002, 15)

These capabilities and objectives are spelt out in the document in language that is neither extremist nor alarmist, and indeed is close to that employed in a later section of this chapter, which is why I will not discuss it further here, but merely point out that the authors go on to stress that the US has always maintained the option of preemptive action and to caution against using the doctrine improperly as a pretext for aggression. In short, this is a temperate and balanced discussion of the issue – why then is NSS 2002 regarded with such hostility by both left-wing and realist critics of the Bush administration?

The answer, I think, lies not in the detail of the argument, but in the atmospherics of the document, the mood-music that accompanies the discussion of the issues. There is the commitment to "freedom" and "democracy promotion," which is expressed in language more commonly heard from Human Rights Watch or Amnesty International than found in an official document:

> [People] everywhere want to be able to speak freely; choose who will govern them; worship as they please; educate their children – male and female; own property; and enjoy the benefits of their labor. These values of freedom are right and true for every person in every society – and the duty of protecting these values against their enemies is the common calling of freedom loving peoples across the globe and across the ages. (NSS 2002, Preamble)

---

[4] Ron Suskind, *The One Percent Doctrine: Deep Inside America's Pursuit of its Enemies Since 9/11* (New York: Simon and Schuster, 2006).

The language here is that of a particularly activist version of Wilsonian internationalism, which is regarded with disdain by both realists and the modern left, albeit for rather different reasons. The latter regard this kind of language as a smokescreen behind which the interests of the ruling elite are pursued, while the former are more worried that the national interests of the US might actually be distorted by such idealism. In the next paragraph of the Preamble there is a reference to creating "a balance of power that favors human freedom," but this incoherent nod towards the language of conventional diplomacy hardly undermines the force of the rhetoric. The impression is that the US will use its power to promote freedom and democracy and the thought that preemptive action might be part of this strategy is difficult to dismiss – especially when the various sections of the NSS are headed by some rather unfortunate *obiter dicta* of President Bush. The president's extraordinary promise to "rid the world of evil" might have been understandable when he delivered it five days after 9/11 during his address in Washington DC at the National Cathedral on 14 September 2001, but to repeat it a year later in an official document positively invites the thought that this was an administration that accepts no goal short of absolute security.[5]

There is only one reference to Iraq in NSS 2002, and that to the war of 1990/91, but the association of the issue of preemption with the Iraq war of 2003 is another reason for the neglect of the subject. The 2003 war was largely justified to the public in terms of the need to act preemptively in the face of the threat posed by Saddam's alleged cache of WMD.[6] When no such weapons were found, this was taken by many commentators not only to impugn the integrity of President Bush and Prime Minister Blair, but also to undermine the notion of preemption. Whether Bush and Blair deliberately misled the public is open to question (both leaders appear to have been genuinely surprised when no WMD turned up in Iraq, which argues against deliberate deception) but as far as the issue of preemption is concerned, the outcome in Iraq did not undermine the doctrine set out in

---

[5] David C. Hendrickson, "Towards Universal Empire: The Dangerous Quest for Absolute Security," *World Policy Journal* 19:3 (2002), 2–10, is one of the earliest and best discussions of the implications of this position.

[6] Largely, but not exclusively. In Britain, it is commonly held that Prime Minister Blair defended participation in the war solely in terms of the need to destroy Saddam's WMD; this is not the case – the prime minister also presented the humanitarian case for action on a number of occasions, although perhaps without enough emphasis. For chapter and verse, see Christoph Bluth, "The British Road to War: Blair, Bush and the Decision to Invade Iraq," *International Affairs* 80:5 (2004), 871–892. US administration references to the need for "regime change" independent of the WMD issue are more extensive.

NSS 2002. The latter refers specifically to the need for "better, more integrated, intelligence capabilities, to provide timely, accurate information on threats, wherever they may emerge" and to the importance of close co-ordination with allies "to form a common assessment of the most dangerous threats."[7] In so far as the Iraq war was based on an intelligence failure and opposed by the majority of the US's most important allies, it looks, in retrospect, more of a vindication of NSS 2002 than a refutation.

AGGRESSION, PREVENTION, AND PREEMPTION

The conventional account of legitimate preemption, referred to above, involves a contrast between the preemptive and the preventive use of force. Prevention involves an attack on a putative enemy not currently posing a direct threat, but deemed likely to do so in the future; such action, it is said, cannot be understood as justifiable in terms of self-defense.[8] Preemption, on the other hand, involves a response to an immediate, imminent threat and *is* potentially justifiable as an act of self-defense. It is this distinction that the Bush administration was accused of blurring both in principle and in practice.[9] Much turns here on the notion of imminence. The classic statement defining "imminent" in international law derives from the *Caroline* case. The *Caroline* was an American steamer operating on the Niagara River, which was attacked on December 20, 1837 in US waters by British forces based on the Canadian side of the river. The British claimed that they acted in self-defense on the basis that the boat was carrying armed supporters of the then-current insurrection in Canada, which latter fact was not disputed by the US authorities. In 1842 a Special Minister, Lord Ashburton, was sent to Washington to negotiate a settlement to this and other Anglo-American disputes; American Secretary of State Daniel Webster proposed to Ashburton that Britain could only justify its actions by demonstrating "a necessity of self-defence, instant, overwhelming, leaving no choice of means and no moment for deliberation." Without admitting fault, Ashburton accepted these conditions as consistent with general principles of international law, and the *Caroline* criteria are now regularly referred to by international lawyers as defining

---

[7] NSS 2002, 16.

[8] Rugby players and supporters will be familiar with the notion of "getting your retaliation in first."

[9] Sometimes the term "anticipatory" war is employed by analysts or politicians. I take "anticipation" to cover both preemption and prevention, i.e., to mean, very simply, shooting first.

how imminent an imminent threat has to be before action is justified.[10] The key issue as between the US government and its critics is whether these criteria are appropriate for twenty-first-century conditions – but before investigating this issue it might be helpful to draw out some of the unspoken assumptions behind the distinction between preemption and prevention.

The central point here is that this distinction takes for granted that "aggression" is both morally wrong and a criminal act, and, more important, that aggression is generally defined in temporal terms, that is in terms of who fired the first shot. There is here to be seen a strong presumption against the use of force in international relations, and an even stronger presumption against the first use of force – hence the requirement that the stringent *Caroline* conditions be met before a claim of self-defense can be allowed. Of course, and quite right too, it might be said – but, in fact, these presumptions are nowhere near as morally self-evident as they are sometimes taken to be, and, in any event they describe an international order that is barely sixty years old. As to the latter, the notion that to make war for reasons other than self-defense is to engage in a criminal act is a recent development, reaching back to 1945 or, perhaps, the 1920s. Certainly, prior to the First World War, the legal right of the state to make war for whatever reason it thought fit was generally recognized; it is worth noting that the *Caroline* criteria were about what could be considered as an act of *self-defense*, and neither side to the dispute assumed that self-defense was the only legal basis on which states could use force. Realist writers argued then, and continue to argue now, that, regardless of post-1945 international law, in a "self-help" system the decision to use force is ultimately a political decision, albeit one with moral and legal implications.

As to those moral implications, it is certainly the case that ethical thought on war has generally rejected the idea that the use of force is simply one tool in the locker of statecraft, but it is not the case that the moral verdict on war is quite as committed to the presumption against the first use of force as those who would make much of the preemption/prevention distinction would wish it to be. As James Turner Johnson has recently argued, the just-war tradition is *not* committed to the view that the only just use of force is in self-defense; a (slightly qualified) version of this latter proposition is set out in Michael Walzer's justly influential work

---

[10] For details of the case and correspondence see "The Webster-Ashburton Treaty and the Caroline Case" at the Yale Law School Avalon Project website www.yale.edu/lawweb/avalon/diplomacy/britain/br-1842d.htm#web1.

on *Just and Unjust Wars*, but Walzer's "legalist paradigm," while it may summarize accurately the contemporary legal regime, does not reflect the just-war tradition as a whole.[11] Medieval and early modern writers on just war required that force be used only in pursuit of a "just cause"; the assumption of the tradition was that a just and orderly peace was the norm of human affairs (or at least was what God intended for us), and that when this peace was violently disrupted it might be necessary to use force to restore it. This necessity cannot simply be defined in terms of self-defense; sometimes righting a wrong will involve the first use of force – what is crucial here is that wrong has been done to someone, and those who respond to this wrong should be public authorities, should act proportionally, with right intention, protecting as far as possible the rights of the innocent, and with a reasonable belief of success. These are the classic criteria for the just use of force and they are not restricted to self-defense.

It might be held that in the twenty-first century warfare has potentially more terrible consequences than in the past and that this justifies redefining the just-war tradition to the point where it becomes indistinguishable from pacifism; such seems to be the current position of the Vatican, although it is by no means clear that the empirical proposition on which this shift in meaning is based is accurate. The presumption against the first use of force in international relations is usually employed to oppose humanitarian interventions, but the logic of the argument here is quite closely related to the logic of anticipation. To argue that the first use of force is never morally justifiable rules out both humanitarian actions and preventive actions; make this the central moral prescription is, in effect, to decide that the current state of the world is sufficiently just such that any attempt to change it by force would be unacceptable – this is, I think, a contestable proposition.

This is a digression, although, I think, an important one, and I will return to the analogy between anticipatory war and humanitarian actions later, but the main issue remains; are the *Caroline* criteria still relevant, and if not, why not? The NSS 2002 presents two reasons for thinking that imminence nowadays has to mean something different from what it meant in the past, both of which are contestable, but certainly not without merit. The first point focuses on technology, and has two dimensions, speed and destructiveness. It is often argued that the pace of twenty-first-century

---

[11] James Turner Johnson, *The War to Oust Saddam Hussein: Just War and the New Face of Conflict* (Massachussetts: Rowman and Littlefield, 2005); Michael Walzer, *Just and Unjust Wars* (4th edn., New York: Basic Books, 2006).

events is simply a great deal faster than was common in the nineteenth century. On the face of it, this seems obviously true but, in fact, in the *Caroline* case, quite short time periods were actually involved because crossing the Niagara River in a steamboat did not take very long; indeed, the British envoy was prepared to accept Webster's criteria for "imminence," precisely because he thought that the action of the British forces was indeed taken in a context that left "no moment for deliberation." Rather, what is different today is the *combination* of speed and destructiveness; in the *Caroline* case a decision had to be taken very quickly by the man on the spot, but although the volunteers carried by the *Caroline* would have been a nuisance had they landed on the Canadian side of the river, they did not pose an existential threat to large numbers of civilians, or to the colony or, *a fortiori* to Britain itself. The stakes today are potentially a great deal higher. 9/11 killed nearly 3,000 people and could easily have killed more; the use of some form of WMD could push the death toll much higher, and there is no reason to think that potential terrorists would be loath to cause such mayhem. The central point is that although "instant, overwhelming . . . [leaving] no time for deliberation" sound like absolute criteria they are in fact, and must be, relative terms – a second was, in practice, a meaningless unit of time in 1839, but in 2007, the average laptop can carry out a billion or more "instructions per second." Similarly, the potential costs of making a type 2 error, and not acting when one should have acted, are of a different order of magnitude to those that might be expected in the mid-nineteenth century.

Speed and destructiveness are matters of capability: what of intentions or objectives? NSS 2002 argues that today's enemies are no longer status-quo oriented, risk-averse states, but "rogue" states that are prepared to use their capabilities actively rather than simply defensively, or non-state actors who are similarly averse to recognizing limits on their behavior, and who are prepared to use extreme tactics, including the mass killing of civilians, and to sacrifice themselves in so doing. As a consequence, so it is argued, the US and its allies need to be prepared, if the circumstances are favorable, to be proactive, attacking terrorist groups and the states that harbor them and disarming rogue states.

Leaving aside, for the moment, the important issue of favorable circumstances, what can be said about the wider points being made here? First, the definition of a rogue state is obviously contestable, and the judgment that a state is risk-averse as opposed to status-quo oriented is pretty much in the eye of the beholder; the desire of states such as Iran and North Korea to obtain nuclear weapons may look "offensive" from the perspective of the

US or local rivals, but the rulers of those countries may see things rather differently.[12] Second, the threat posed by non-state actors is, again, not a new phenomenon; in the *Caroline* case the US denied any involvement in the activities of the volunteers, although the British authorities felt the US could have done more to restrain them. Third, the extremism of modern terrorist groups as opposed to their equivalents in the past is also debatable; the anarchist groups who carried out assassinations around the world in the twenty-five years before 1914 were also careless of human life, including their own, although, admittedly, they rarely targeted civilians as such, as opposed to crowned heads, or ministers of state. Even the issue of states harboring terrorist groups is not without precedent. Just as continental Europeans raged about "Londonistan" in the 1990s and accused the British of providing a refuge for terrorists, so a hundred or more years ago the same states leveled the same charge at Victorian Britain.

All these points suggest that the authors of NSS 2002 exaggerated the changes that have taken place in the post-Cold War years – but, still, it is difficult to avoid the thought that some things actually are different. Nationalist movements in the nineteenth century – and their twentieth-century successors such as the IRA – did not generally wish to cause mass civilian casualties, partly because they knew that such tactics would be, from their point of view, counterproductive. The anarchist bomb-throwers of the 1890s (the nearest past equivalent of the modern suicide bomber) were never a mass movement and their tactics were rejected by the worker's movement and its socialist ideologues. By way of contrast, the religious foundation of the most dangerous of modern terrorist movements is, I think, genuinely new – the existence of very large numbers of people willing to carry out, or, at least, sanction, on religious grounds the murder of innocents in terrorist attacks does present a genuine and new problem, especially when so many people are willing themselves to die in carrying out such deeds. The overlap between state and non-state actors is also, if not new, then at least newly significant. The paradigm case here is that of the relationship between the Taliban and Al-Qaeda; although the former were an Afghan movement who had taken over Afghanistan and had at least some claim to international legitimacy, and the latter a multinational group most of whose members were from the Gulf or Egypt, i.e., foreign

---

[12] This is, of course, a standard point made by realists of all stripes; security dilemmas occur precisely because of the difficulty in deciding whether capabilities are offensive or defensive in nature – offensive realists such as John Mearsheimer make this the core feature of international relations; John Mearsheimer, *The Tragedy of Great Power Politics* (New York: W. W. Norton, 2001).

to Afghanistan, it is clear that the distinction here between native and foreigner is by no means as significant to the parties concerned as it might be to an international lawyer. Mullah Omar and Osama bin Laden appear to have seen themselves as partners in the same enterprise, and it was not unreasonable of the US and its allies to treat them accordingly.

In summary, although the new world in which we have to live is not quite as different from the old as it might, at first sight, seem to be, nonetheless there are organizations (state and non-state) in the world whose ideological foundations make them difficult to deter, and whose potential capacity to deliver serious damage to the infrastructure of industrial societies and to their populations make them difficult to ignore. It does seem plausible that some kind of rethinking of the notion of preemption is required – but what sort of rules might replace the *Caroline* criteria?

RULES, DOUBLE STANDARDS, AND POLITICAL JUDGMENT

The problem here is nicely (if unintentionally) summarized in NSS 2002. Having spelled out the case for loosening somewhat traditional restraints on preemption, the authors go on to say: "[The] United States will not use force *in all cases* to preempt emerging threats, nor should nations use preemption as a pretext for aggression" (15 – emphasis added). At one level, this is a statement of the obvious (of course the US will not react with force to *all* possible threats), followed by an example of routine finger-wagging, but at another level it reveals a genuine problem. If one acknowledges that preemption is sometimes justified in circumstances where the conventional notion of immediacy is inappropriate – which, I have argued, is not an unreasonable position – how is one to distinguish those circumstances from circumstances when preemption is *not* justified? The point is that selectivity as to which cases will be subjected to preemptive action is endorsed, but without any attempt to provide principles or rules for distinguishing one case from another; the result is to leave the clear impression that double standards are at work here. The implication of the second half of the above sentence could be that it is unjustified when nations other than the US preempt, but this clearly will not do, unless one believes that the US is uniquely virtuous in the conduct of its international relations, a position as absurd as its opposite, that the US is uniquely wicked.

How do we negotiate our way out of this dilemma? Can the *Caroline* criteria be redrafted to make them appropriate for modern circumstances? The authors of NSS 2002 do not make the attempt; this might be seen as unfortunate, but is, I would argue, perfectly sensible given the near impossibility of the task. The problem here is a special case of a more general phenomenon – the difficulty of drawing up rules to govern behavior in an anarchic world, when the behavior in question touches upon issues states have regarded as central to their sovereignty and political identity. An analogous case brings us back to the issue of "humanitarian intervention." For the last decade or more, the majority of scholars who have considered the matter have acknowledged that while the general norm of non-intervention is of key importance to international order, there are some circumstances where it may be overridden for humanitarian reasons. What circumstances? Numerous attempts have been made to draw up check-lists of criteria which have to be met before humanitarian interventions can take place, but with no success; either the criteria are so tightly drawn that it is clear they will never be met, or they are so loosely drawn that they could not actually restrain state behaviour.[13] The central point is that a rule-based approach to this problem cannot succeed.[14] The only rule that is clear and unambiguous is "don't intervene," but this is unhelpful if the reason one has approached the issue in the first place is because of the belief that sometimes intervention is necessary and just. The same logics apply in the case of preemption. The only rule that is clear and unambiguous is "don't preempt" – but, as argued above, this simply will not do. There are potentially real-world circumstances where preemptive action is both necessary and just. The problem is that defining these circumstances in concrete terms such that they might form the basis of rules that would determine the morality of any particular act of preemption seems to be impossible. As we have seen, even the *Caroline* rule requires interpretation, its apparent absolutism always giving way to nuances in practice.

What we have here, I suggest, is a general problem with rule-based moral reasoning, which may seem particularly obvious when it comes to humanitarian intervention and preemption, but which actually applies to many other, less fraught, areas of human existence. We are, I suggest, accustomed to the idea that moral reasoning most frequently involves reference to some kind of rule – the Ten Commandments, Kant's

[13] See, for a recent example, the "Roundtable: Humanitarian Intervention after 9/11" based on Tom Farer's attempt to draw up such criteria – *International Relations* 19:2 (2005), 211–250. Farer's respondents (Daniele Archibugi, Neta Crawford, Thomas Weiss, Nicholas Wheeler, and the present author) agree on nothing other than that his criteria do not work.

[14] See the discussion in Chris Brown, "Selective Humanitarianism: In Defence of Inconsistency," in Deen Chatterjee and Don Scheid, eds., *Ethics and Foreign Intervention* (Cambridge University Press, 2003), 31–50.

Categorical Imperative or whatever – and that this is the only way to avoid arbitrariness, inconsistency, and "double standards," all of which are thought of as undesirable. But is this so? And are arbitrariness and inconsistency quite as undesirable as they are often taken to be? I think not, and, in any event, they are pretty well unavoidable in ordinary life as well as in matters of high politics.[15]

What is important here is to remember that rule-based moral reasoning is not the only way to approach ethical issues. Rather, what we need, I suggest, is to look beyond this approach, and back to the kind of ethical reasoning that follows the Aristotelian injunction, summarized by Stephen Toulmin, that "sound moral judgment always respects the detailed circumstances of specific kinds of cases."[16] Rule-based moral reasoning attempts to produce an algorithm that will give a general answer to the question of what is right and what is wrong; in the case of preemption as in the case of humanitarian intervention, this approach is unlikely to succeed. An Aristotelian – or more generally classical – approach to ethics is, I will argue, more promising. Toulmin's version of Aristotle's ethics is particularly helpful in this respect. On his account, in the seventeenth century the moral insights of renaissance humanism and the classical world were put aside. Under the influence of Descartes and Hobbes, along with many lesser talents, formal logic came to displace rhetoric, general principles and abstract axioms were privileged over particular cases and concrete diversity, and the establishment of rules (or "laws") that were deemed of permanent, as opposed to transitory, applicability came to be seen as the task of the theorist. Toulmin suggests that at this time moral reasoning became "theory-centered" rather than "practically-minded."[17] Moral reasoning became a matter of following a theoretically validated rule, rather than of making a practical judgment; he suggests, plausibly, that this shift was part of a yearning for certainty that accompanied what was a very turbulent period in European history – but the result was to impoverish moral reasoning.

The point is that, in dealing with complex situations, such as deciding whether it is right that one state should preemptively use force against

---

[15] A moment's introspection will confirm the truth of the first part of this observation. In ordinary life we face repeated minor moral dilemmas which we very rarely resolve by reference to a rule; e.g., what rule are we applying when we give money to one *Big Issue* seller and not another? More on this in "Selective Humanitarianism" (see note 14 above).

[16] Stephen Toulmin, *Cosmopolis: The Hidden Agenda of Modernity* (University of Chicago Press, 1990), 32.

[17] Ibid., 34. To my mind the paradigm case of a practical-minded moralist is Montaigne, but Rabelais and Shakespeare would do.

another, or against terrorists based within the jurisdiction of another, there is no substitute for a form of moral reasoning that involves a judgment that takes into account the totality of circumstances, rather than seeks for a rule to apply. Sometimes preemption would be morally justified but politically disastrous; sometimes preemption would be cost-free in political terms, but morally quite unjustified; more usually, the particular circumstances will be more ambiguous than such extreme cases. Moreover, the information upon which judgments are made as to both political and moral justification is always going to be inadequate. Uncertainty is part of the human condition – we do what we can with what we have, but we never can be sure that we are right. Given the nature of the kind of decisions that need to be made in today's world, which quite closely mirrors the chaos of seventeenth-century Europe, it is not surprising that – now as then – there should be a desire for clear-cut rules and criteria, but – now as then – such a search will be in vain, and, insofar as it dulls our critical faculties, positively harmful. We need our leaders to cultivate the habits of political judgment and we should not seek refuge in the illusion that there can be moral rules that can substitute for such judgment. Fear of accusations of inconsistency and double standards need to be put aside – what is usually, and wrongly, described as inconsistency arises not from treating similar cases differently, but from recognizing differences in particular circumstances which are invisible to those who put their trust in universal rules.

REALISM, RISK, AND PRACTICAL JUDGMENT

The importance of practical judgment was a consistent theme of classical realism – certainly as espoused by Hans J. Morgenthau[18]– and one might have expected contemporary realists to approach the issue of preemption in the same spirit. On the whole, this has not happened; most modern realists have been rather dogmatically opposed to the notion of preemption.[19] Why is this? For two reasons I think, one good, but not wholly appropriate, and the other rather more ambiguous. The former has been alluded to above – the notion of preemption has become attached in many people's minds to the search for absolute security, and, as David Hendrickson has argued, and all other realists would agree, such a quest is

---

[18] I discuss Morgenthau as a "practice theorist" in Chris Brown, "The 'Practice Turn', *Phronesis* and Classical Realism: Towards a *Phronetic* International Political Theory," *Millennium: Journal of International Studies* 40:3 (2012), 439–456.

[19] See, for a very good example, Richard K. Betts, "Striking First: A History of Thankfully Lost Opportunities," *Ethics and International Affairs* 17:1 (2003), 17–24.

both doomed to failure and likely to generate errors along the way.[20] However, I would argue that this association between the quest for absolute security and the search for an acceptable doctrine of preemption is contingent rather than necessary – the latter is required even if the former goal is abandoned, as it should be.

A more ambiguous reason for opposing the notion of preemption is the commitment many (most) realists have to the importance of prudence. Prudence is often seen as the core virtue cultivated by realism, a position born out by much folk wisdom – "sufficient to the day is the evil thereof"; no need to go looking for trouble it will find you soon enough, and so on. Clearly, this is usually a sensible position, a useful corrective to rash adventurism – but to take prudence as the only important virtue is, I would argue, to misunderstand the realist tradition. The great strategists and diplomatists who shaped that tradition were prudent, but also knew when to abandon prudence and take calculated risks. Richard Betts, in his catalogue of "thankfully missed opportunities" acknowledges in passing that the failure to react early to Hitler's aggressions in the 1930s is the "best example imaginable to justify preventive war" but fails to draw the conclusion that Churchill and others who favored a policy of resistance were better realists than those, such as Carr, who supported appeasement almost to the bitter end.[21] Of course, the story of appeasement in the 1930s is used far too often to point a moral; the way in which the West – and, especially, the UK – handled the break-up of Yugoslavia is a not dissimilar tale but rather less over-used. Douglas Hurd and the other self-described realists in the British diplomatic establishment who opposed taking firm action against the Serbs in the early 1990s did not just create Britain's "unfinest hour," they also made it necessary to use more force in 1995 and 1999.[22] The genuine realists here, I suggest, were figures such as Margaret Thatcher and, from the Left, Ken Livingstone who saw clearly the dangers of excessive prudence.

Knowing when to take risks is a key component of realism, and a central task for the exercise of Aristotelian practical judgment. But how are risk assessments made in international relations? What constitutes an appropriate response to which kinds or levels of risk? One approach has been alluded to above – former Vice-President Cheney's "one percent doctrine," the original expression of which, as reported by Ron Suskind, was Cheney's opinion that "[If] there's a one percent chance that Pakistani

---

[20] See note 5 above.   [21] Betts, "Striking First," 21.
[22] Brendan Simms, *Unfinest Hour* (London: Penguin, 2002).

scientists are helping Al Qaeda to build or develop a nuclear weapon, we have to treat it as a certainty in terms of our response."[23] Most people, I imagine, would regard treating a one percent chance as the equivalent of a certainty, in terms of how one responds to it, as rather too risk-averse – although the argument that the possibility of extreme outcomes justifies regarding low actual risks as triggers for action is mirrored in a number of other places and by figures whose political position is a very long way from that of the vice-president. Consider, for example, the Precautionary Principle, much favored by environmental activists, which guides decision-making on environmental and health threats in Europe, and is summarized by Cass Sunstein as the idea that "[regulators] should take steps against potential harms, even if causal chains are unclear, and even if we do not know that those harms will come to fruition."[24] Sunstein – a critic of this principle – specifically links it to the policy of preemption, citing President Bush's defense of the Iraq war of 2003: "If we wait for threats to fully materialise, we will have waited too long."

Even more striking is the structural similarity between Cheney's argument, and a powerful case presented for nuclear disarmament by Robert E. Goodin in 1985.[25] Goodin argues that the policy of nuclear deterrence is morally unacceptable because it leaves open the remote possibility that deterrence might fail and a nuclear war take place. Such a war would be, at a minimum, an unimaginable catastrophe, but also carry the more extreme risk that life (or at least human life) on earth could be extinguished. Even if the chances of this happening are vanishingly small, Goodin argues, the stakes are so high that the risk should not be taken, and nuclear weapons should be eliminated, unilaterally if necessary. Better surrender than risk extinction. This is a "one percent doctrine" and then some, since Goodin argues even if the risk is substantially less than one percent it should not be taken.

So, the one percent doctrine is not without precedent – but it still, I believe, takes too seriously the risk of inaction and does not factor in the risks involved in responding too vigorously to threats that have not yet materialized. In the specific case cited by Cheney – aid given by Pakistani nuclear scientists to Al-Qaeda – the US response has been largely diplomatic, putting pressure on the Pakistani government to curb the activities

---

[23] Suskind, *The One Percent Doctrine*, 62.
[24] Cass R. Sunstein, *Laws of Fear: Beyond the Precautionary Principle* (Cambridge University Press, 2005).
[25] Robert E. Goodin, "Nuclear Disarmament as a Moral Certainty," *Ethics* 95:3 (1985), 641–658.

of their leading scientist A. Q. Khan, rather than military. Military action will always involve harm to innocents and if it is to be justified it ought to be on the basis of rather more than a one percent risk; prudence comes back into the picture here by mandating that military action ought to be the last resort (although, it must never be forgotten, the last resort can also be the first resort – the concept is not temporal) because of the inevitable costs involved in a violent response.

If not the one percent doctrine, then what guiding principles for helping us to make decisions on issues of preemption can be discerned? One thing is clear; the exercise of political judgment in this field, the decision to respond with violence to perceived threats, is, as NSS 2002 rightly stresses, highly dependent on good-quality intelligence – and, as NSS also stresses, allies can be helpful here in providing second opinions and helping the decision-maker to assess incoming information. Collecting such intelligence is a difficult business, and assessing it is even more difficult; to illustrate the point, consider the preemptive action against Iraq in 2003 – this is particularly interesting because the threat it was designed to neutralize turned out not to exist, and it ought to be possible to learn from such mistakes.[26]

There was a great deal of circumstantial evidence for the existence of Iraq's WMD prior to 2003 (and I see no reason to think that President Bush and Prime Minister Blair were in bad faith in asserting their belief that these weapons constituted a threat) and yet they did not exist. The failure of the intelligence agencies here illustrates first and foremost the need for the latter to continually question their own assumptions; the contrast between the piles of circumstantial evidence on the one hand, and the lack of a single hard fact on the other, ought to have set off alarm bells – perhaps it did and the alarm was turned off because the political leadership had made up its mind and did not want to read assessments that pointed against action. If this is the basic story, then clearly what happened in 2003 represents a chronic failure of political judgment, and realist critiques based on the importance of prudence are justified.

This is, I suspect, a large part of the story, but there is another angle less often explored. One of the reasons Western agencies were deceived – and most of the allies of the US and the UK shared in the intelligence failure, even if they opposed the action – was because the Iraqis deceived themselves, or rather were deceived by Saddam. Using captured documents and the results of de-briefings, Michael Gordon and Bernard Trainer suggest

---

[26] Although, as noted above, there were other reasons for the war.

that Saddam deliberately behaved as though he had WMD in order to deter Iran and menace his own population, only telling his top army leadership that there were no such weapons in December 2002, to their considerable discomfort since they could think of no other way of defending their country than by the use of WMD.[27] Saddam seems to have anticipated that the US would repeat the 1991 incursion into Iraq rather than attempt regime change, a literally fatal miscalculation. But the story becomes more complex when the reasons why Saddam had no WMD are examined – he had programs to develop these weapons in the 1990s, yet they were abandoned by 2002. Why? Here, preemption comes back into the picture, but successfully this time. Citing the work of David Kay's Post War Iraqi Survey Group, Thomas Ricks concludes that the Iraqis abandoned their WMD programs because of the success of Operation Desert Fox in 1998, when US and British warplanes delivered a sustained attack on the sites where these weapons were being developed. The attacks were successful, and the Iraqis concluded that there was no point in directing resources at re-establishing WMD programs when the US could disrupt them so easily.[28] Desert Fox was widely regarded in the West as a pointless exercise, directed mainly to drawing attention away from President Clinton's personal problems. In fact, it seems to have been an extremely successful example of anticipatory war, marred only by the failure of Western intelligence agencies to realize just how successful it had been.[29]

CONCLUSION

To stress the importance of the exercise of judgment in cases like this is to invite disappointment when it becomes clear that the author has no practical advice to add on how to make the right kind of judgments. Books have been written on political judgment, but they rarely consist of "how to" manuals; Philip Tetlock's *Expert Political Judgment* presents an excellent analysis of some of the empirical factors which necessarily feed into such judgments, and has some good advice as to how to avoid obvious errors, but this is an area where there is no substitute for having the right person in the right place to make the key decisions – and the democratic institutions of the West are not noticeably proficient at ensuring that this

[27] Michael Gordon and Bernard Trainor, *Cobra II: The Inside Story of the Invasion and Occupation of Iraq* (New York: Atlantic Books, 2006), 65.

[28] Thomas E. Ricks, *Fiasco: The American Military Adventure in Iraq* (London: Allen Lane, 2006), 21.

[29] Kay admitted to Ricks that he had been skeptical in 1998, but was convinced after interviewing Iraqis concerned with WMD development.

condition will be upheld.[30] One of the reasons why so many people look to developing rules that will constrain action is precisely because they do not trust the judgment of those who hold the great offices of state in the Western democracies – and in general they have reason for this distrust. What then must we do? The answer, I think, is that we must educate our masters, or to put the matter less dramatically, we must try to cultivate the faculty for judgment in ourselves that we hope they will also cultivate. To return to the "600 lb gorilla in the room" that has haunted this chapter, it is now clear that George W. Bush and Tony Blair made serious errors of political judgement in 2003 – their assessment of the nature of Saddam's regime and the unwillingness of the Iraqi people to fight for it was correct (there was no "Stalingrad on the Euphrates"), but their assessment of the post-war prospects for Iraq showed a chronic failure of judgment. On the other hand, all too often the critics of the Iraq war have demonstrated equal or worse judgment. From the whitewashing of Saddam's regime (happy children playing in the street before the arrival of US bombers in Michael Moore's film), to the legitimation of the murderous insurgency as a kind of modern day French Resistance, via an interminable and short-sighted post-mortem on the minutiae of the arguments in the run up to the war, the popular opposition to Bush and Blair has consistently lost sight of the main issues – and as a result the genuine failures of judgment by these two leaders have not been examined in the way they should have been.

In British media and academic circles the hatred of Tony Blair is almost visceral, which has led to an obsession with the alleged illegality of the war and a genuine desire in some quarters to see Blair indicted by the International Criminal Court. In the equivalent American circles contempt for George W. Bush is equally frequently expressed, although impeachment rather than extradition to The Hague is the preferred punishment. The obvious problem with this common mindset is that it personalizes and trivializes the failures of political judgment that took place. Instead of acknowledging the genuine dilemmas dealing with Saddam Hussein involved – the costs to the Iraqi people of a continuing sanctions regime, the costs to the region of ending that regime while Saddam remained in power – Bush is simply seen as a gun-happy "cowboy" and Blair as an American puppet. Instead of coolly assessing and criticizing the failure of both leaders to anticipate the consequences of their action, critics focus on the minutiae of the statements they made before the war, in the hope of convicting them of lying to their publics.

---

[30] Philip Tetlock, *Expert Political Judgement* (Princeton University Press, 2005).

The result is that, a decade on, the real failures of judgment that led to war in 2003 have not been exposed.

To return to a point made at the outset of this chapter, given the nature of the modern world, issues where preemption is a possible policy option are bound to arise again and this is so even if the gradual shift in US policy to a more multilateralist and magnanimous stance which was initiated by President Obama continues. There will always be people who cannot be reached by such a policy shift, or whose vision of what a magnanimous US approach would involve does not correspond to anything likely actually to emerge. Such people have posed a threat in the past, and may do so again in the future, and sometimes it may be that such a threat should be met by preemptive action. We need to think clearly about this possibility now, so that we have a decent chance of getting it right if and when it arises in the future. We cannot guarantee that our political systems will always throw up people whose judgment will be good, but we can do our best to make sure that scholars of international relations at least – and preferably a wider public – have a grasp of what is needed, and, in particular, have an aversion to knee-jerk responses whether for or against preemption. The purpose of this chapter has been to make a modest contribution to this project of public education.

CHAPTER 4

The case for preventive war

George R. Lucas, Jr.

A sovereign attacks a Nation, either to obtain something to which he lays claim or to punish the Nation for an injury he has received from it *or to forestall an injury which it is about to inflict upon him, and avert a danger which seems to threaten him* .... Must we await the danger? Must we let the storm gather strength when it might be scattered at its rising? Must we suffer a neighboring State to grow in power and await quietly until it is ready to enslave us? ... Supposing ... that no injury has been received from that State, we must have reason to think ourselves threatened with one before we may legitimately take up arms. Now, *power alone does not constitute a threat of injury; the will to injure must accompany the power* ... But the two are not necessarily inseparable; ... As soon as a State has given evidence of injustice, greed, pride, ambition, or a desire of domineering over its neighbors, it becomes an object of suspicion which they must guard against ... and, if I may borrow a geometrical expression, *one is justified in forestalling a danger in direct ratio to the degree of probability attending it, and to the seriousness of the evil with which one is threatened.*

Emer de Vattel (*c.* 1758), *The Law of Nations*[1]

Among the founding historical figures of international law, from Gentili, Vitoria, and Grotius to Montesquieu, and the Swiss jurist and "father" of contemporary international law, Emer de Vattel, the topic of "preventive war" has long provoked a lively debate. That the arguments surrounding

Early drafts of the argument in favor of preventive (and not simply "preemptive") war were originally delivered at the US Naval Academy and the US Air Force Academy in the spring of 2003, and subsequently revised and delivered as the convocation address for a National Endowment for the Humanities summer institute on "war and morality" held at the US Naval Academy (June 1–25, 2004). I am grateful to other faculty and to the participants in that institute for a number of useful suggestions incorporated in the present draft. Since then, several philosophical accounts of preventive war have been published by David Luban, Allen Buchanan and others, of which I endeavor to take account in this revised draft.

[1] Book III, Ch. 1(5); Ch. 3 (42, 44), trans. Charles G. Fenwick, in J. B. Scott, ed., *The Classics of International Law* (Washington, DC: Carnegie Institution, 1916), 280–340.

that debate are now largely forgotten owes in large part to the decisive foreclosure of that debate itself in the work of Michael Walzer in the latter part of the last century. Walzer's distinction of preventive war from "preemptive self defense" in chapter 5 of *Just and Unjust Wars*[2] broadened the latter concept by disposing of "imminence" as a criteria for preemption, and so allowed "preemption" to bear many of the legitimate moral concerns earlier ascribed to "preventive defense," as portrayed in the passage above. Moreover, Walzer's analysis of prevention itself proceeded to couch what remained of that concept wholly within the morally questionable intentions of pre-twentieth-century colonial and imperial superpowers to preserve their prerogatives within the international status quo. Such concerns (on Walzer's account, at least) consequentially seemed altogether devoid of the moral weight necessary to call nations to arms in their pursuit.[3] For the most part, scholars and (what is more important) military and policy leaders have agreed with Walzer's assessment, so much so that even a clearly preventive exercise in international security, such as the US-led invasion of Iraq in 2003, was desperately (and inaccurately) characterized by its supporters instead as an exercise in "preemptive self defense."[4]

To be sure, many early-modern moral and legal theorists do evince concerns that might properly be dismissed as merely expressions of the self-interest of powerful elites. For example, in a passage now routinely cited in

---

[2] See the preface to the first edition of Michael Walzer, *Just and Unjust Wars* (New York: Basic Books, 1977), xvii–xx, where Walzer suggests that his treatment of the topic will constitute a summary of a moral, and not a purely legal, argument with a lengthy history which it is not his explicit intention to discuss (though he makes reference to this history and its major figures from time to time). Later, in chapter 4, he describes his choice of the phrase "legalist paradigm" for the underlying conventions of this position, ". . . since it consistently reflects the conventions of law and order. It does not necessarily reflect the arguments of lawyers, though legal as well as moral debate has its starting point here" (61). More recently, Walzer explicitly defends the features of ambiguity or indeterminateness in just-war discourse that I discuss at length in this essay, while explaining his own retreat from an earlier strong presumption against wars of intervention, in the introduction to his new volume of essays on this subject, *Arguing About War* (New Haven, CT: Yale University Press, 2004).

[3] Historian Hew Strachan at Oxford recently provided a more detailed account of that history, and in the process, illustrated the underlying complexity of the case for (and against) preventive wars and "preventive strikes." See Hew Strachan, "Preemption and Prevention in Historical Perspective," in Henry Shue and David Rodin, eds., *Preemption: Military Action and Moral Justification* (Oxford University Press, 2007), 23–39. Despite its title, this collection of essays deals more with preventive than authentically preemptive war, for reasons that will become clear in my essay.

[4] Strachan likewise recognized this "policy inversion" in the discussion of foreign policy during the lead-up to the Iraq war of 2003 and since, in which preemption "does duty" for what is in fact a full-blown revival of the doctrine of preventive war. See Strachan, "Preemption and Prevention in Historical Perspective," 38–39.

current discussions of preventive war,[5] the sixteenth-century Italian legal scholar at Oxford, Alberico Gentili, writes:

> I call it a useful defense when we make war through fear that we may ourselves be attacked. No one is more quickly laid low than one who has no fear, and a sense of security is the most common cause of disaster .... we ought not to wait for violence to be offered us, if it is safer to meet it halfway .... *One ought not to delay, or wait to avenge at one's peril an injury which one has received, if one may at once strike at the root of the growing plant and check the attempts of an adversary who is meditating evil* .... No one ought to wait to be struck, unless he is a fool. One ought to *provide not only against an offense which is being committed, but also against one which may possibly be committed.* Force must be repelled and kept aloof by force.[6]

The passages from both authors that I have emphasized in italics, however, hint that much more could conceivably be at stake, and might now be at stake, than merely superpower rivalry in the sort of Darwinian international order that Walzer dismissed out of hand as an illegitimate justification for preventive war. Both jurists cited here, for example, discuss at some length the responsibilities of sovereigns and governments to provide for the security of their citizens, and to guard the state, not so much against rivals whose growing power might threaten its status, as against adversaries of whatever sort, harboring malevolent and hostile intentions that carry the very real threat of genuine harm to the populace. The commendable intention not to replicate the arrogance of bygone empires ought not, for example, to blind political leaders at present to the very real need to do their responsible utmost to protect their citizens, and the law-abiding citizens of all nations, from the very real threats presented by capricious state organizations armed with nuclear weapons, such as North Korea, and to prevent states with clearly stated hostile intentions (such as Iran) from acquiring them. Preventive war might continue to be necessary to protect those same citizens from the mischievous machinations of non-state actors like Al-Qaeda, or, on purely humanitarian grounds to indict the governments of states (such as Libya, and now, most horrendously, Syria) from turning their armies and weapons on their own citizens.

---

[5] E.g., by Strachan, "Preemption and Prevention in Historical Perspective," 24, and in Neta Crawford, "The False Promise of Preventive War," in Shue and Rodin, eds., *Preemption: Military Action and Moral Justification*, 89–125, esp. 89, 116. Gentili (but curiously, not Vattel) is discussed by others in that volume, principally Rodin.

[6] Alberico Gentili, *On the Laws of War* (c. 1612), Book I, Ch. 14, trans. John C. Rolfe, in *The Classics of International Law*, 2 vols. (Oxford: Clarendon Press, 1933), vol. II, 61–66.

When considered against these present threats in the clear light of reason, a decade after the so-called "Bush doctrine" of preemptive self-defense roiled the political landscape, the case against preventive war is far from clear. Indeed, the discussion of non-defensive but morally legitimate uses of military force exposes an underlying tension in morality and international law that has long lain dormant in the pragmatic consensus forged concerning war during the era of nuclear superpower rivalry. In 1979, for example, the eminent Catholic scholar, Bryan Hehir, called attention to the underlying tensions between what he termed the "two normative traditions" within the just-war tradition. The distinction was meant to call attention to important differences between the long history of discussion about war in traditional Roman Catholic moral philosophy, and the treatment of that topic in contemporary international law.[7] With remarkable prescience, Hehir suggested that, in the then-foreseeable future, these two distinctive approaches to the justification of resort to military force might radically diverge, and result in rival and even incompatible accounts of permissible action. During the height of the Cold War in which his essay was written, the two distinct normative traditions appeared to concur in condemning any resort to war that might involve use of nuclear force, though of course legal and moral reasoning might differ substantially in the reasons adduced. Hehir wondered, however, what might happen in other circumstances, when, for example, moral concerns for basic human rights came into conflict with legal claims of sovereignty and territorial integrity.

Hehir's prediction came to haunt us throughout the acrimonious debates, beginning in the 1990s, concerning the legal versus moral legitimacy of wars of intervention, preemption, or preventive self-defense. Offensive (or, at least, non-defensive) conflicts are treated very differently within these two contrasting traditions. International law privileges sovereignty, while morality tends to limit sovereignty on behalf of the more fundamental primacy of basic human rights.

To be sure, there are similarities as well as contrasts in what Hehir had described as the "two normative traditions" of just-war discourse. Both, for example, appear to be *compliance-based.* That is, both forms of just-war discourse resolve disputes by appealing to compliance, either with established international laws and customs, or (in the case of philosophy) with

---

[7] J. Bryan Hehir, " The Ethics of Intervention: Two Normative Traditions," in Peter G. Brown and Douglas MacLean, eds., *Human Rights and U.S. Foreign Policy* (Lexington, MA: Lexington Books, 1979), 129–139. See also G. R. Lucas, "Defense or Offense? The Two Streams of Just War Tradition," in P. French and J. A. Short, eds., *War and Border Crossings: Ethics When Cultures Clash* (Lanham, MD: Rowman & Littlefield, 2005), 45–57.

lists of necessary conditions arising from a long-standing and authoritative tradition of scholarly discourse over many centuries. By contrast, the work of more recent moral philosophers such as Walzer, and other proponents of what has come to be called "applied" moral philosophy, pursue just-war analysis by inviting readers instead to engage directly in a kind of moral casuistry: citing, describing, and analyzing specific historical cases or hypothetical examples, and then testing what might be termed their "pre-theoretic moral intuitions" on the historical cases or hypothetical examples cited.[8] From this procedure, they then elicit more general, action-guiding reasons or governing normative principles that resolve or explain the cases, or else lead to challenging or revising conventional wisdom about the meaning or application of the principles that come to guide our entry into, and conduct of war.

The application of these distinctive and sharply variant methodological approaches in the just-war tradition to the analysis of some of the most intractable of the contemporary dilemmas concerning the use of military force – what I have elsewhere termed the "methodological anarchy" of the just-war tradition[9] – yielded sharply variant conclusions about the appropriateness or legitimacy of the resort to war or other uses of military force in those instances. Practices like humanitarian intervention, for example, are almost uniformly proscribed in law and international relations, while the same practices are imposed in some instances as a moral obligation within the classical philosophical tradition, and are treated equivocally within the contemporary philosopher's analytic framework of moral casuistry.[10] Judgments or action-guiding principles – for example, that the use

---

[8] While the history of applied ethics has yet to be fully written, it developed as a distinct form of moral analysis primarily in the work of J. L. Austin at Oxford, Elizabeth Anscombe and Bernard Williams at Cambridge, and subsequently Judith Jarvis Thompson at MIT in the late 1950s and 1960s. The field mushroomed with growing interest in moral problems arising in medicine, business, and law in the 1960s and 1970s, spawning a generation of new authorities, journals, research centers, and substantial scholarship in these and other areas of "applied philosophy."

[9] See George R. Lucas, "'Methodological Anarchy': Arguing about Preventive War," in Roger Wertheimer, ed., *Empowering our Military Conscience: Transforming Just War Theory and Military Moral Education* (London: Ashgate Press, 2010), 33–55. See also George Lucas, "Methodological Anarchy: Arguing about War, and Getting it Right," *Journal of Military Ethics* 6:3 (2007), 246–252.

[10] This observation regarding the status of humanitarian military intervention in international law is the source of a good deal of misunderstanding. Contrary to widespread belief during the period of the Rwandan genocide, for example, the Genocide Convention of 1948 does not impose obligations, nor establish any substantive procedures for UN member nations regarding the use of military force to aid victims of genocide. A careful reading of the convention shows that it was a product of its time: it aimed to prohibit nations from engaging in genocide, or from sheltering individuals who had participated in genocide. That is, it aimed principally at refusing to grant quarter or safe haven to war criminals, and required nations to assist in their capture and prosecution. Thus, fears about using the "G-word" during the Rwandan crisis, for fear they would obligate armed response, were

of military force is justified only for the purpose of self-defense – may be deemed correct from the standpoint of one person, an error or a mistaken inference for a second, and vague or indeterminate for a third.

We witnessed the resulting methodological chaos most clearly in the international debate about preventive war or "preemptive self-defense" during the first years of the twenty-first century. One important way to frame the terms of that debate, for example, was to cite the black-letter statutes of international law, treaties, and relevant provisions of the United Nations Charter. This way of arguing about war, the legalist mode of discourse, provided nearly unambiguous support for the view that the war of intervention in Iraq was unjust. International law clearly prohibits the use of military force for any but defensive purposes, even under the most creative interpretations of the concept of "self-defense" or of "collective security" under the provisions of Article 7 of the UN Charter.[11] Even when a case for "anticipatory self-defense" can be made under existing law, there is certainly no provision granting the power to an individual nation-state to act unilaterally in the absence of recognition of an imminent threat by other members of the international community.[12] Instead, the most lenient

gravely misplaced. The more recent experience in Darfur, Sudan (in which the "G-word" has been frequently invoked to utterly no avail) demonstrates the dilemma. In the aftermath of the Rwandan tragedy, a dissident UN faction, the "International Crisis Group," under the leadership of Australian ambassador-at-large Gareth Evans (an unsuccessful candidate for the Secretary-Generalship awarded instead to Kofi Annan), issued a now widely cited report addressing these deficiencies and proposing remedies in law and policy. See Gareth Evans and Mohamed Sahnoun, eds., *The Responsibility to Protect: Report of the International Commission on Intervention and State Sovereignty* (Ottowa: International Development Research Centre, 2001) http://responsibilitytoprotect.org/ICISS% 20Report.pdf. See also the summary of the Commission's findings in Evans and Sahnoun, "The Responsibility to Protect," *Foreign Affairs* 81:6 (2002), 99–110. Interestingly, the prospect of justifiable wars of prevention is raised in the context of this discussion.

[11] Article 2(4) of the UN Charter prohibits the use or threat of force against the territorial integrity or political independence of any state. Article 2(7) extends this prohibition to the collective action of the UN itself, granting full domestic jurisdiction to member states and prohibiting the supranational body from intervening in matters "which are essentially within the domestic jurisdiction of any state," save in the case of collective self-defense as determined through an appropriate deliberative body of the UN (such as the Security Council), as described in Article 51, and Chapter 7. It is as straightforward as such matters can be that none of these conditions pertain to, or were satisfied by, the international deliberations leading up to the most recent war in Iraq.

[12] Thus, despite claims of some international relations scholars that international law governing the resort to force had either broken down or been rewritten in the wake of Rwanda, Bosnia, and Kosovo (e.g., Michael J. Glennon, *Limits of Law, Prerogatives of Power: Interventionism After Kosovo* (London and New York: Palgrave Macmillan, 2001), the preponderance of scholarly opinion seemed to favor the view that states still supported the limitations on the use of force contained in Article 2 (4) of the United Nations Charter, and that "preemptive self defense" is a concept "without legal justification." See Christine Gray, *International Law and the Use of Force* (New York: Oxford University Press, 2000) and Mary Ellen O'Connell, *The Myth of Preemptive Self-Defense* (Washington: American Society of International Law Task Force on Terrorism, August 2002).

characterization one can offer of such practice from the standpoint of law is "vigilantism."[13]

Classical just-war theorists represented in the Western tradition of theology and philosophy, by contrast, have a far more difficult time with the doctrine of preemptive or preventive war. It was certainly not correct to claim, as many critics of the US intervention in Iraq mistakenly did in 2003,[14] that all wars save wars of self-defense are not justified within that canonical just-war tradition, when the historical and textual case, at least, is considerably less clear. What this kind of claim itself preempted was a long-standing debate within that mode of discourse over what constitutes a just cause for war, given that self-defense constitutes the clearest (but not the sole) example of such a just cause. Medieval scholastics and theologians like Aquinas, Vitoria, and Suarez, for example, invoked an important category of justifiable and sometimes even obligatory use of military force that they termed "*bellum offensivum*," or offensive war, fought to resist evil, punish wrongdoers, or redress injustice.[15] Vitoria, whose thought has enjoyed a considerable renaissance during the past two decades on account

---

[13] International vigilantism is the term I first introduced in 2003 as the most accurate characterization of the (proposed) US response to the international community's refusal to act in a number of significant altercations, ranging from Rwanda and Bosnia and Kosovo to the proposed intervention in Iraq. While these were, of course (or turned out to be) very different sorts of altercations, it is important to recall the backdrop of frustration with international inaction that infused the debate at the time. While he does not use the term "vigilantism" specifically, Michael Ignatieff does denounce the weakness, corruption, and anachronism of current statutes and institutions of international law, and calls for their radical reform in the defense and promotion of democracy and human rights in the struggle against the threat of terrorism in his Gifford Lectures, *The Lesser Evil: Political Ethics in an Age of Terror* (London: Penguin Books, 2004). His frustration and contempt for the repeated moral failings of the United Nations and for the moral and intellectual bankruptcy of the concept of "an international community" were forcefully expressed at the NEH institute on "War and Morality" cited above. My own concerns a decade ago for the welfare of these institutions and their need for radical reform reflects more the attitude of "principled internationalism": see G. R. Lucas, "The Role of the International Community in the Just War Tradition: Confronting the Challenges of Humanitarian Intervention and Pre-emptive War," *Journal of Military Ethics* 2:2 (2003), 141–148.

[14] See, for example, the resolution opposing the American-led intervention in Iraq proposed at the time by the American Philosophical Association, which stated: "Both just war theory and international law say that states *may resort to war only in self-defense*" (my emphasis; see www.apa.udel.edu/apa/divisions/eastern for the full text of this resolution). Both James Turner Johnson and Jean Bethke Elshtain refused to include their names among the 100 theologians and teachers of Christian ethics whose collective petition, published in several national newspapers on the eve of the second Iraq war, denounced the proposed preemptive war as "a contradiction of just war teachings." The refusal by both eminent scholars of this tradition to endorse this interpretation of it stemmed from their conviction that this sweeping interpretation was seriously inaccurate as a matter of fact. See Jean Bethke Elshtain, "A Just War?," *Boston Sunday Globe*, October 6, 2002, H1, H4.

[15] See Gregory Reichberg, "Is There a 'Presumption against War' in Aquinas's Ethics?," *The Thomist* 66:3 (2002), 337–367.

of his extended treatment of these issues, even discussed the legitimacy of wars fought for constabulary purposes to defend human rights, and to bring about what we now routinely term "regime change," all within the context of denouncing his own nation's illicit use of force against indigenous peoples during the Spanish Conquest in the sixteenth century.[16]

All that said, the very different structure of justification in this "classical" or "philosophical" mode of discourse about just war quickly comes into play. Not only does this mode of discourse differ methodologically in its approach to justification from the legal discourse cited above, there is, in addition, a disturbing looseness, ambiguity, and *indeterminateness* in the formulation and interpretation of its individual provisions – just cause, legitimate authority, right intention, last resort, and so forth – each of which presumably constitutes a necessary condition for justification of the use of military force. It is not altogether clear how these criteria are to be applied, or in what order. A great deal of latitude is afforded any individual interpreter of the tradition in applying it to specific cases. In an important historical case, Hugo Grotius deliberately elevated the criterion of "just cause" to a position of primacy over "legitimate authority," largely because he could take for granted (as Aquinas and Vitoria could not) what we have come to call the "Westphalian paradigm": namely, that the ruler of a sovereign nation-state explicitly and unilaterally wielded such authority.

By contrast, sovereignty or "legitimate authority" is principally what is at issue in determining whether non-state actors (or their organizations) possess the moral authority to use force, particularly against non-combatants, as well as whether individual nations (like the US) have the right to pursue or punish such acts of aggression without some kind of broader, international approval. All this is to say that the broad consensus, at a high-level abstraction, on the shape of the classical tradition's general

---

[16] See Question 3, Articles 4 and 5, of Vitoria's *De Indis* for a discussion of lawful regime change and wars in defense of human rights, respectively: in Anthony Pagden and Jeremy Lawrance, eds., *Vitoria: Political Writings* (Cambridge University Press, 1992), 287–288. The general discussion of "offensive war" fought for constabulary purposes against "tyrants, thieves, and robbers" is taken up in Question 1, Article 1 of *De Juri Belli*, 296–298. Vitoria writes, for example: "[A fifth just cause for war might arise] either on account of the personal tyranny of the barbarians' masters toward their subjects, or because of their tyrannical and oppressive laws against the innocent, such as human sacrifice practiced on innocent men or the killing of [criminals and prisoners] for the purpose of cannibalism. [The Spanish, even without the Pope's consent, may use military force] *in lawful defence of the innocent from unjust death* [Vitoria's own emphasis].... The barbarians are all our neighbors, and therefore anyone, and especially princes, may defend them from such tyranny and oppression ....War may be declared upon [such tyrannical rulers], and the laws of war enforced upon them; and if there is no other means of putting an end [to such practices], *their masters may be changed and new princes set up* [my emphasis]."

presumption against appeals to force rapidly dissolves when one turns to any sort of substantive debate over the meaning or relative priority of its specific provisions.[17]

This is, in turn, because the classical philosophical tradition is *conceptually incomplete* in at least two important senses. First, just-war theorists in this tradition seldom state the conditions in a uniform or consistent manner. It is impossible to tell whether the number, name, or order of criteria matters. The lists are inconsistent. Thus, not only did Grotius, in the example above, change the order of Aquinas' list to emphasize the moral significance of having a "just cause" for war. Francisco Suarez had also earlier replaced Aquinas' third criterion of "right intention" (itself derived from Ambrose and Augustine's deliberation over war and Christian conscience) with "right means," apparently holding that a "right intention" to seek the restoration of peace through war committed its proponents to fight the war by just means only.

Thus, each entry in the philosophical list of necessary conditions for justified war has a history that affects its proper interpretation, but often those who invoke the list use it as a summary of prior consensus or conclusions, without understanding the origins or anomalous nature of those conclusions. "Public Declaration," for example, does not appear on every list, certainly not those of Aquinas, Vitoria, or Suarez (although Grotius does revive it). It is a criteria, as Grotius notes, that dates back to the writings of Cicero, who is in turn reflecting on ancient practices in Roman law and religion. When these practices are examined in their own right, however, the examinations reveal that this supposedly independent criterion of "public declaration" of war in Roman law was in fact a form of "last resort" to force, a practice that gave an enemy every opportunity for settling a dispute prior to taking up arms.[18]

Second, and as the example of "public declaration" suggests, the meaning of each criterion is far from obvious. Seminal reinterpretations of just-war concepts over the past decade by philosophers Jeff McMahan (proportionality) and David Rodin (with respect to self-defense as a just

---

[17] Henry Shue is especially critical of this feature of the classical or philosophical just-war tradition, complaining about the mechanical manner in which its criteria are invoked, noting that traditions do not attain or deserve moral authority merely by being traditions, and that the medieval contributors cited above countenanced behaviors that any normal moral agent, then or now, would find reprehensible: see his "War," in Hugh LaFollette, ed., *The Oxford Handbook of Practical Ethics* (Oxford University Press, 2003), 734–761; esp. 736–738.

[18] It is also a statement of "legitimate authority," in a religious sense, in that the priests responsible for exercising the procedure were thought, through this exercise, to be securing the consent and blessing of the gods as justification for their nation's military initiatives.

cause for war), reveal that these criteria of just cause and proportionality are far from clear in moral terms.[19] Thus, we do not necessarily agree on the meaning of the individual conditions, let alone on whether, and to what degree, each condition must be satisfied.[20] Specific conclusions, however, depend importantly on the order and the priority of the principles cited, as well as upon what each of these criteria *mean* in their substantive application. The conclusions regarding the moral justification of a specific conflict may also depend upon which specific criteria are included or excluded from various lists, as well as the degree to which each criterion must be satisfied. Hence, it is probably misleading to refer to this classical tradition of moral reflection as a "theory," as many of its practitioners are wont to do. The classical tradition lacks the order, coherence, and precision normally associated with the interlocking elements of a

---

[19] See, for example, Jeff McMahan, "What Makes an Act of War Disproportionate?," Annual Stutt Lecture, US Naval Academy (Annapolis, MD, 2008), www.usna.edu/ethics/Publications/ McMahan.pdf. This problem is discussed at length in the context of unjustifiable wars and "unjust combatants" in Jeff McMahan, *Killing in War* (Oxford: Clarendon Press, 2009). For the problem of self-defense as a justification for use of force, and disanalogies in the individual and international case of justifiable use of force, see David Rodin, *War and Self-Defense* (Oxford University Press, 2001). See also the essays by Rodin and McMahan (and other contributors) on these topics in David Rodin and Henry Shue, eds., *Just and Unjust Warriors: The Moral and Legal Status of Soldiers* (Oxford University Press, 2008).

[20] Noted just-war historian James Turner Johnson lists seven criteria: just cause, right authority, right intention, proportionality of ends, last resort, reasonable hope of success, and concluding with "the aim of peace," in contrast to his earlier and more conventional seventh criterion of "just means" or "proportionality of means." See "The Just War Idea and the Ethics of Intervention," in J. Carl Ficarrotta, ed., *The Leader's Imperative* (West Lafayette, IN: Purdue University Press, 2001), 107–125; 115–116. Martin L. Cook lists eight just-war criteria in *The Moral Warrior* (Albany, NY: State University of New York Press, 2004), 28, adding "Public Declaration" to Johnson's list. In contrast to his earlier work (in which this criterion was omitted) Cook now includes Johnson's final criterion, "the aim of peace," which Johnson argues is greatly stressed in international law, bringing Cook's list of criteria to eight. (The "aim of peace" is central to Augustine's original conception of "right intention," and is thus redundant in a way that Suarez's focus on "just means" is not.) The US Catholic Bishops publish a slightly different list in *The Challenge of Peace* (Washington, DC: US Catholic Conference, 1983), omitting mention either of Johnson's "ends of peace" or Cook's "public declaration," and inserting a criterion of "comparative justice" that includes consideration of whether "sufficient right exists to override the presumptions against war." Interestingly, both the order and description of these seven criteria are different a decade later in the Bishops' revised stance, *The Harvest of Justice is Sown in Peace* (Washington, DC: National Conference of Catholic Bishops, November 1993), specifically substituting a "presumption against *the use of force*" for the earlier description of "comparative justice" as a "presumption against war," presumably to take account of the need for humanitarian military intervention (see http://usccb. org/beliefs-and-teachings/what-we-believe/catholic-social-teaching/the-harvest-of-justice-is-sown-in-peace.cfm). Finally, former US President Jimmy Carter invoked a list of five (rather than seven) criteria in March 2003 to frame the terms of his opposition to military intervention in Iraq, citing, in this order, "last resort," non-combatant immunity, overall proportionality, right authority, and Johnson's "the ends of peace." These are only scattered examples of what might politely be termed "conceptual latitude" in the just-war tradition.

"theory." Properly regarded, it is merely a mode of normative discourse, a philosophical tradition of reflection on the moral constraints of both prudential reasoning and political practice.[21]

The underlying inconsistencies between the normative dimensions of the legal and the philosophical-theological modes of discourse were seldom explored in the context of superpower rivalry and possible nuclear war. The dramatic increase in appeals to military force for the purposes of humanitarian intervention in the wake of the collapse of that superpower rivalry and nuclear threat have forced moral discourse increasingly away from reliance upon the specific provisions of international law, and toward increasing reliance on the underlying moral debate characterized by the classical philosophical tradition. This is an especially noteworthy development when we recognize, with Jeff McMahan, the sharp differences that emerge from discussions of the morality of war, in contrast to the legality of accepted state and military practices in current international law.[22] Preemptive wars of "anticipatory self-defense" that otherwise strain the credulity of our concept of self-defense are, in fact, wars of this very different, constabulary sort that Vitoria first clearly described, for which international law makes no allowance, and classical just-war doctrine admits only with the gravest reluctance.[23]

Thus, the analysis of preventive war throws into clear relief the tension between morality and the law in international relations. Preventive wars are "illegal" in the same sense that preventive self-defense is illegal in domestic law, no matter what the circumstances of perceived future

---

[21] As a well-respected scholar and historian of the just-war tradition, James Turner Johnson describes it metaphorically as a "great river with many tributaries." In a recent work, *Morality and Contemporary Warfare* (New Haven, CT: Yale University Press, 1999), Johnson gives careful attention to recognition of the fact of pluralism in the tradition, and notes the many contributors to the discussion, past and present, including Walzer, to whom he pays a great deal of attention and respect. He notes that "there are differences of content and emphasis and tensions among the various approaches encompassed in just war tradition," but concludes merely that we need to attend carefully to each scholar's particular way of stating and summarizing the tradition, as well as sustaining a dialogue among them (22–26). While evidencing a clear preference in his own work for classical *jus ad bellum* discussions, he does not suggest how or why we might wish to evaluate these different approaches comparatively, or give preference to one versus another in contemporary debate.

[22] See Jeff McMahan, "The Morality of War and the Law of War," in Rodin and Shue, eds., *Just and Unjust Warriors*, 19–43.

[23] See, for example, G. R. Lucas, "The Reluctant Interventionist," in *Perspectives on Humanitarian Military Intervention* (Berkeley, CA: University of California Press/Institute for Intergovernmental Studies, 2001), 1–13. See also Henry Shue, "Let Whatever is Smouldering Erupt? Conditional Sovereignty, Reviewable Intervention, and Rwanda 1994," in A. J. Paolini, A. P. Jarvis, and C. Reus-Smit, eds., *Between Sovereignty and Global Governance: The United Nations, the State, and Civil Society* (London: Macmillan, 1998), 60–84.

(as opposed to "imminent") threat. The legal case rests on what Walzer calls the "domestic analogy," but thereby unintentionally serves to challenge or call into question the adequacy of that analogy itself. The international arena differs sharply from the domestic in this, as in many cases, and it is difficult, upon closer examination to know what inferences are properly to be drawn from such a comparison. Thus, if Rodin has succeeded in showing that there is no clear analogue between the presumed individual right of self-defense and a nation or state's presumed "right" of self-defense, we might similarly observe that what is prohibited to individuals under a situation in which a functioning society properly wields a monopoly on deadly force, does not usefully or meaningfully inform the international context, in which no such monopoly exists, nor are guarantees of security provided. In the domestic instance, there are procedural recourses to perceived threats short of unilateral resort to force. Although there are likewise measures a state might take short of war to ensure its security (or rather, to protect its citizens from threat of harm), there are in the international instance no genuinely efficacious institutional guarantees to secure that protection, short of the threat of war. In this very important respect, domestic and international law are dis-analogous.

The representative selections I cited earlier from early-modern writers debating the legitimacy of preventive war are replete with metaphors designed to capture the moral seriousness of the underlying concerns that might lead to such wars. Vattel's account in particular seems apt caution for those facing the threat of nuclear proliferation today. It is not, he argues, merely the acquisition of, or growth in, power alone that constitutes a preventable threat, but such an expansion of power accompanied by a manifest intent to injure. When, he maintains, "a State has given evidence of injustice, greed, pride, ambition, or a desire of domineering over its neighbors" – or perhaps, more ominously, exterminating them altogether – it may then be legitimately regarded as a threat to be countered by force, if necessary, even before it has grown to the point of being able to carry out its malevolent intentions. In a passage of remarkable clarity and prescience, Vattel concludes: "one is justified in forestalling a danger in direct ratio to the degree of probability attending it, and to the seriousness of the evil with which one is threatened." Those would seem to constitute the beginning of a set of formalizable criteria for the justification of preventive war.[24]

---

[24] Indeed, both Henry Shue and Allen Buchanan subsequently labored to develop both criteria for justification and (in Buchanan's case) a preliminary cosmopolitan outline of institutional procedures for vetting the urgency of resort to force as a preventive measure in international law enforcement.

It is unfortunate that Walzer's otherwise eloquent and compelling work has had the effect of presenting this debate as settled principle, rather than what it seems to constitute in our present era, namely, an *authentic moral dilemma* arising both from the continuing threat of nuclear proliferation, and the proliferation of malevolent non-state actors engaging in acts of terrorism and international criminal conspiracy. How can law-abiding peoples and nations avoid recourse to the destruction of war, while yet responsibly acting to protect themselves against legitimate threats to their security, welfare, and even to the rule of law itself? This question deserves careful scrutiny on its own terms (as the remaining contributors to this volume attest).[25]

For my part, I conclude by noting that one reason that the classical-philosophical approach might be more adept than its rivals at handling these new kinds of problems is that, unlike international law, there is no close connection between the doctrine and any particular form of political organization. International law presupposes the nation-state as the fundamental unit of analysis and also, by convention, as the basic bearer of rights. This is the Westphalian convention mentioned earlier as the backdrop to Grotius' innovations: what Walzer, in his work (as we have also noted), terms the "legalist paradigm." *There is, however, no corresponding political or conceptual structure to which to tie (or, in this case, to bind) the provisions of classical just-war theory.* There is no explicit mention of, or underlying need to presuppose conceptually, entities like nation-states, let alone anything like the modern conception of an "international community" in order to interpret and apply the list of necessary conditions that comprises the classical tradition.

Classical philosophical methodology attains universality of applicability through successive abstractions from any particular arrangements of historical or social circumstances. When such circumstances suddenly and

---

Shue, however, was skeptical of those conditions ever being simultaneously fulfilled in actual practice. See Allen Buchanan, "Justifying Preventive War," and Henry Shue, "What Would a Justified Preventive Military Attack Look Like?," in Henry Shue and David Rodin, eds., *Preemption: Military Action and Moral Justification* (Oxford University Press, 2007), 126–142; 222–246, respectively. In this respect, my earlier work and this essay can be taken to side with Buchanan, and others, like David Luban (both of whose essays are included in the Shue and Rodin volume above) who make cases for the very limited justification of preventive war in defense of international law and human rights. See also Allen Buchanan and Robert O. Keohane, "The Preventive Use of Force: A Cosmopolitan Institutional Proposal," *Ethics and International Affairs* 18:1 (2004), 1–22.

[25] The aforementioned volume on "preemption" ends up giving greater attention to this concern of justifiable prevention, or at least "selective preventive strikes" or what Shue terms, with some skepticism, "early military attacks" (EMAs). Several authors, notably Buchanan and Luban, offer justifications for preventive war in the current context, while others (e.g., Rodin, Crawford, and Shue) think it unlikely or incapable of justification.

dramatically evolve or change (as they have over the past two decades), such occasionally puzzling and frustrating abstractions can provide a decided advantage in offering guidance to the perplexed. We find, for example, in the medieval era in which this classical doctrine was formulated, sovereignty was *distributed* over a number of competing entities: national rulers (kings, emperors), regional authorities to whom these would appeal in order to raise funds and military manpower, national and international church authorities, and "supranational" religious organizations like the Jesuits or Dominicans, or the Papacy itself. Likewise, in what we might term the postmodern, post-nation-state era, we find sovereignty increasingly distributed over national leaders, regional security organizations (like NATO), nongovernmental organizations (still including religious organizations), and supranational entities like NAFTA, the World Trade Organization, the European Union, and of course, the United Nations itself. Thus, we now find ourselves driven back from the well-ordered Westphalian legalist paradigm to a conceptual scheme for evaluating the morality of the use of force that is independent of any particular arrangements regarding sovereignty.[26]

In the past, one was likely to count it among the many weaknesses of the classical philosophical tradition, not only that its provisions were individually somewhat vague and imprecise, but also that the doctrine itself seemed to justify too much, and to place insufficient limitations on the authority of individual rulers to violate the geographical spheres of influence of others. In the wake of destructive religious wars of the Reformation and Counter-reformation, the Westphalian or "legalist paradigm" was proposed as a solution, by legitimating and bounding those spheres of influence and granting them, for the sake of peace, the rights of sovereignty and self-determination within borders secured by a semblance of law.

That compromise was a steep price to pay for peace, even if it seemed a reasonable price to pay at the time. As Henry Shue noted over a decade ago, this convention appears to grant the state unlimited right to do wrong (at least within its own domain) which surely cannot be the intent, and which makes the notion of "right" itself incoherent.[27] The intent of the Westphalian

---

[26] See Maryann Cusimano Love, "Global Problems: Global Solutions," in Love, ed., *Beyond Sovereignty* (2nd edn., Belmont, CA: Wadsworth, 2003), 1–42.

[27] See Henry Shue, "Limiting Sovereignty," in Jennifer Welsh, ed., *Humanitarian Intervention and International Relations* (Oxford University Press, 2004), 11–28; 13–16. Readers will note that, while I have been much instructed by Shue and Rodin, I use the work of both in defense of conclusions at odds with their own in these matters. I believe the arguments of both concerning conditional sovereignty and the primacy of human rights legitimate a doctrine of preventive war, along the lines outlined here and in Buchanan, perhaps more clearly and robustly than in Luban.

paradigm was to grant the state the right to "do wrong," as judged from the perspective of neighboring states, who were nonetheless prohibited from interfering. The "wrong" in question was religious in nature: worshipping the "wrong" god, or worshipping God in the "wrong manner." These "moral errors" (to borrow a phrase of John Rawls) were nonetheless to be tolerated by other states. As Shue again rightly observes, the notion of sovereignty and territorial integrity was *never* intended to permit the state or its agents to abdicate or violate their inherent duties to secure the basic human rights and liberties, and security of person and property, of their own citizens, as routinely occurs today – let alone was it meant to prevent other nations from coming to the aid of the victims of such oppression.

Despite the extraordinary confusion evident during this decade's international debate concerning the moral and legal status of preventive war in Iraq, it turns out that it is only international law, grounded in this Westphalian paradigm, that explicitly and unconditionally prohibits the use of military force preventively. Despite numerous well-intentioned resolutions to the contrary, conventional just-war doctrine simply does *not*. Rather, such questions are posed as *moral dilemmas*, underscoring a tension between competing moral obligations, which it is the responsibility of reasonable moral agents, through the use of practical reason, to adjudicate. John Stuart Mill eloquently captured the nature of this dilemma over a century ago in his analysis of humanitarian military intervention (1859), presciently anticipating the current debates over "the Responsibility to Protect" (R2P).[28] In so doing, he likewise refuted in advance the one-sided claims of those opposed in principle to any use of force preventively (to thwart the international analogue of criminal conspiracies, for example) or for any other purpose beyond self-defense.[29]

---

[28] Evans and Sahnoun, eds., *The Responsibility to Protect*. See also *A More Secure World: Our Shared Responsibility: Report of the Secretary-General's High-level Panel on Threats, Challenges and Change* (New York: United Nations, 2004). See also Alex Bellamy, *Responsibility to Protect: the Global Effort to End Mass Atrocities* (London: Polity Press, 2009).

[29] See John Stuart Mill, "A Few Words on Non-Intervention" [1859], reprinted in *Dissertations and Discussions*, 3 vols. (London: Longmans, Green, Reader, and Dyer, 1867), vol. III, 153–178. There Mill writes: "[*T*]*here assuredly are cases in which it is allowable to go to war, without having been ourselves attacked, or threatened with attack*; and it is very important that nations should make up their minds in time, as to what these cases are. There are few questions which more require to be taken in hand by ethical and political philosophers, with a view to establish some rule or criterion whereby the justifiableness of intervening in the internal affairs of other countries, *and (what is sometimes fully as questionable) the justifiableness of refraining from intervention*, may be brought to a definite and rational test" (153f.; my emphases). Endre Begby analyzes this essay in detail, including Walzer's misreading of Mill's position on intervention, in "Liberty, Statehood, and Sovereignty: Walzer on Mill on Non-Intervention," *Journal of Military Ethics* 2:1 (2003), 46–62.

Evidently there are, or could arise, occasions in which the use of force for purposes other than self-defense would not only be permissible, but even obligatory, if the threat of harm from refusing to act were sufficiently grave. Also, it might turn out to be the case that self-defense, especially in the case of nations that do not respect the most basic rights of their own citizens, is not a right that it would be at all appropriate for them to exercise. Michael Walzer's variation on this tradition proscribes preventive war, but only by arguing for a distinction between preemption and prevention derived from an historical analysis that may, in the end, beg the very question of "imminence" and intent that it purports to solve.[30]

Suffice it to observe at this point that paradigms have histories, and enjoy only finite lifetimes. It is the fate of theoretical models in all disciplines eventually to show their age, and, under the stress of anomalous circumstance, to reveal the fractures and inconsistencies long obscured by compromise and familiarity. It has often been remarked of late that the Westphalian paradigm in international relations is showing its age, and increasingly labors under the stress of irresolvable anomalies. Political and legal discourse has, as a result, been driven back toward reliance on the older, philosophical tradition of just-war discourse in terms of which there is no fundamental and incoherent equivocation between the *conditional or conferred* rights of collectivities like nation-states, and the *unconditional* or inherent rights of the biological individuals that compose them.

The very prospect of arguing for the moral legitimacy, even obligatory nature, of some forms of preventive war finally suggests its own underlying paradigm: that of a community of nations, each and all committed, more or less authentically, and with greater or lesser capacity and competence, toward guaranteeing the most basic rights of their citizens to life, liberty,

---

[30] In *The Spirit of the Laws* (c. 1748), Montesquieu observed: ". . . among societies, the right of natural defense sometimes carries with it a necessity to attack, when one people sees that a longer peace would put another people in a position to destroy it and that an attack at this moment is the only way to *prevent* such destruction" (Book x, Ch. 2, trans. A. M. Cohler, B. C. Miller, and H. S. Stone (Cambridge University Press, 1989), 138–40). The argument there was that it was weaker nations that had the right to fear their destruction at the hands of the stronger, and so it was they who exercised the right of preventive self-defense. Hew Strachan notes that, in the contemporary case, that argument has been turned on its head, with stronger nations like the US claiming a right of preventive self-defense. The difference, he fails to note, is that the "defense" in question is less of sovereignty or national territory, than of the global international order, as a kind of law enforcement. This is the flaw in many recent discussions of prevention, that they still adopt a strictly nation-state-centered approach to supporting or criticizing the prospect, when the issue is more the question of cosmopolitan responsibility to maintain law and order, and to protect the basic rights of vulnerable victims, regardless of their nationality. In any case, the historical treatments by Strachan, and by Marc Tractenburg, suggest the inaccuracy of Walzer's historical broad-brush approach to this problem.

and security under the rule of law. It falls to the members of that international community, then, to exercise the use of force judiciously to protect its members against the vagaries of unscrupulous agents who do not share the community's respect for minimal justice and the most basic rights of its citizens. The substantive procedures that should be put in place to impose restraint and guarantee only the most judicious exercise of such force, while guarding against the inevitable tendency of that community's members toward vigilantism, have yet to be fully formulated. That considerable and formidable task, however, will only be undertaken once we have recognized that the case for preventive war is morally legitimate, and legally and politically incumbent.[31]

---

[31] As noted at the outset, since I initially framed these conclusions in early 2003 and subsequently, both Allen Buchanan and Henry Shue also attempted to address this problem, at least to the point of proposing procedures and institutional arrangements that would accommodate the need for resort to force in defense of the rule of law in the international community: in Shue and Rodin, *Preemption*. These are also the conclusions of a lengthy study nearly two decades ago by Anthony C. Arend and Robert J. Beck, *International Law and the Use of Force: Beyond the United Nations Paradigm* (London: Routledge, 1993), and also Anthony C. Arend, *Legal Rules and International Society* (Oxford University Press, 1999). I basically follow the argument of these works in the account above.

PART II
International law

CHAPTER 5

Does international law make a moral difference? The case of preventive war

Michael Blake

There is more than one moral question to be asked about any complex political issue, and asking the wrong question generally gets us unsatisfying results. What makes a question the right one to ask, I think, depends most frequently upon the context in which it is asked; a question might be fully appropriate in one institutional or argumentative context, but misleading or obfuscating in another. Foundational questions about justice under ideal circumstances might be largely irrelevant for certain applied issues of political practice, for instance; and, similarly, practical issues can sometimes be usefully ignored where we are considering fundamental issues of political justice. Getting the question right, then, is the first step towards getting right answers.

This is relevant, I think, to our understanding of the moral issues surrounding preventive war. We have good reason to ask whether it is ever morally permissible for us to engage in preventive warfare – which I understand, along with most other commentators, as being warfare in the name of self-defense that lacks the "imminent threat" requirement of preemptive warfare as currently defined in international law.[1] We should, however, begin by clarifying which of the several moral questions available to us is the one we are now asking. I think we might distinguish at least two possible questions, here – I suspect we could ask any number, but I will discuss only these.[2] The first is what might be called the *institutional*

---

[1] There are any number of recent analyses of preventive warfare, most of which articulate a similar understanding of what constitutes this category of military action. I have relied for my understanding here upon Michael Doyle, *Striking First: Preemption and Prevention in International Conflict*, ed. Stephen Macedo (Princeton University Press, 2008); David Luban, "Preventive War," *Philosophy and Public Affairs* 32:3 (2004), 207–248; and Allen Buchanan, "Justifying Preventive War," in Henry Shue and David Rodin, eds., *Preemption: Military Action and Moral Justification* (Oxford University Press, 2007), 126–142. There are, of course, subtle disagreements among legal scholars and empirical political scientists about how precisely to understand the category of preventive war, but I believe the brief definition given here is sufficient to begin the discussion.

[2] I will not, for instance, discuss the moral status of soldiers in a preventive war; for an account of this, see Buchanan, "Justifying Preventive War."

question: what form of international laws or norms ought to be developed to constrain preventive warfare? This question begins with the idea that we are collectively deciding, together with whatever other states or international institutions we want to include, on a set of rules to guide our deliberations surrounding appropriate forms of military intervention. This is a question posed in the second-person plural, from the domestic state to the international community: what should *we* – understood as the peoples or states of the world – do together, to guarantee a lasting and legitimate peace?[3] The second question, which might be called the *agency question*, asks a more constrained and local question. If we accept that current international legal norms do not permit preventive warfare, how should we – as a state or a people – respond to that fact? How should we think about the moral constraints on our action created by these legal institutions, which are emphatically not the ones we would have chosen if we had freedom to design them? If this question is asked in the second-person plural, it is asked by domestic citizens from one to the other, in the search for ethically defensible state action.

The two questions are not perfectly separable – what a state does under current legal circumstances may itself alter the character of those legal institutions.[4] They are, however, logically distinct, and it is important for us to decide which of them is our focus in any discussion of preventive warfare. In the present chapter, I want to focus exclusively on the agency question, and ask how a given state ought to think about the morality of preventive war under current legal institutions. This is not meant to impugn the relevance of the institutional question; we have reason to ask about how we ought to reform and alter legal institutions so that they more closely approximate our ideals of justice. I mean only to insist that the more local question of how we ought to think of our current legal institutions is one we ought to ask as well. The question to be asked here is, then, the following: if we accept that preventive warfare is illegal under current legal rules, what difference should that fact make to the relevant moral calculus? If we are speaking as citizens of a state that has (or might

---

[3] Thus, Lee Feinstein and Anne-Marie Slaughter recommend revision of the international legal system to include a right to prevent rogue states from acquiring the means to engage in mass destruction. This is an example of a response to the institutional question. My own interests are in how states ought to act prior to the introduction of such legal innovation. See Lee Feinstein and Anne-Marie Slaughter, "A Duty to Prevent," *Foreign Affairs* 83:1 (January–February 2004), 136–150.

[4] See generally Allen Buchanan, *Justice, Legitimacy, and Self-Determination: Moral Foundations for International Law* (Oxford University Press, 2007). See also Robert Goodin, "Toward an International Rule of Law: Distinguishing International Law-Breakers from Would-Be Law-Makers," *The Journal of Ethics* 9:1 (March 2005), 225–246.

soon) embark on such a course, how should we think about the ethical status of the actions entailed?

Answering this question completely, of course, would likely require a full theory of the authority of international law – a project that is outside the scope of this chapter. I will, in the present context, only offer a few arguments about what such a theory would have to look like, using the issue of preventive warfare as a particularly important case that any such theory will have to be able to handle. I will therefore be happy if the present chapter establishes some modest conclusions about how responsible states ought to understand the moral obligations imposed on them by international law. If we understand the moral difference made by international law in the case of preventive war, we may eventually be able to understand the moral difference made by international law more generally. My present focus, though, will be exclusively on the narrow question: how should a state respond to the fact that international law condemns preventive warfare?

In answering this question, of course, I will have to make some assumptions about the nature of both the state and the international legal system. I will assume, as I have done above, that preventive war is clearly illegal under the Charter of the United Nations.[5] I will also assume that the state proposing to use preventive force is itself a reasonably just state, with a moral right to defend itself; we must here assume that there is some moral value to this state as an ongoing project in the world, such that it is morally possible that violence in defense of this state might be legitimate. I will also assume that the state in question is not making an unreasonable claim about the nature of the threat it faces – where this reasonableness is expressed both as a factual proposition about the severity and likelihood of the threat, and a moral proposition about the proportionality of the military action proposed to the harm to be averted. This rules out, I think, both cases in which the state is clearly wrong about the nature of the threat it faces, or clearly wrong about the morality of risking lives to avert that threat, or both. I will assume, further, that the state in question is possessed

---

[5] Article 2 commits member states of the United Nations to the peaceful resolution of their differences, while Article 51 permits warfare in self-defense against aggression. The tension between these articles is generally accepted as issuing in a permission for preemptive warfare in face of an imminent threat, but a prohibition on preventive warfare. See Christine Gray, *International Law and the Use of Force* (New York: Oxford University Press, 2004). The agreement here is not unanimous, of course, and some scholars have argued that there is room within Article 51 for legitimate preventive warfare. See John Yoo and Robert Delahunty, "The 'Bush Doctrine': Can Preventive War Be Justified?," *Harvard Journal of Law and Public Policy* 32:3 (2009), 843–865.

of a significant amount of military and financial power, sufficient to make good on the threat proposed.[6] I will assume, finally, that the threat in question is one of the newly emerging varieties that is not easily dealt with by classic Westphalian tactics of international diplomacy; the threat in question is not itself a state that can be deterred or reasoned with, but an organization without a defined territory, government, or any interests other than in destruction.[7]

The killing of Osama bin Laden, I think, might help us construct such an example. We might imagine a case in which a state uses military force against a known terrorist or terrorist organization. It uses this force despite the fact that the imminence of the terrorist threat is not known; no one can say with certainty when the terrorist's intentions to cause widespread death might come to fruition. It crosses the border of a state without that state's consent, thereby violating that state's sovereignty, despite being (nominally, at least) an ally of that state.[8] From these materials we might construct a case that is both plausible and plausibly an illegal-but-justifiable case of preventive military action. I do not, I should say, think that the killing of Osama bin Laden is itself such a case – its legal status is controversial, but the past relationship between bin Laden and the United States makes it plausible to understand the killing as a legal act under international law; it is also not clear that the killing of bin Laden is best described as an act of war.[9] Nevertheless, the killing provides us with the raw materials to construct the sort of illegal military action I consider here.[10] Imagine that a responsible state seeks to engage in a military intervention in another country so as to disable a terrorist organization; imagine further that the

---

[6] Indeed, I am thinking here about the morality of the foreign policy of the United States in particular. There are two reasons for this; the first is that I live in the United States and am therefore most familiar with its foreign policy; the second is that the United States has recently undertaken a war it has justified in part as preventive in nature, which has of course given rise to much of the recent reflection on this issue. Nothing in what I say, however, precludes my conclusions from potentially applying to other states as well, although I suspect the arguments I make may lose force as they are applied to states with significantly less power than the United States.

[7] The United States, in the 2002 and 2006 National Security Statements, emphasizes the novel nature of non-state threats as a reason to insist upon a revision of Article 51 as a basis of international agency. See the 2006 NSS at www.strategicstudiesinstitute.army.mil/pdffiles/nss.pdf.

[8] Thus, former president Pervez Musharraf referred to the raid as a violation of Pakistani sovereignty. See M. Giglio's interview with Musharraf in *Newsweek*, May 16, 2011.

[9] As I write this, it is three months after the death of bin Laden, and the scholarly response to the killing has yet to emerge. A good summary of initial responses, though, which tend towards the conclusion that the killing was legal under international humanitarian law, can be found at http://opiniojuris.org/2011/05/04/quick-thoughts-on-ubls-killing-and-a-response-to-lewis/.

[10] The recent military response to Libya, in contrast, is justified through the explicit approval of the United Nations, through Security Council Resolution 1973.

terrorist organization in question poses some threat to the intervening country, but that the precise imminence of the threat is a matter of some (reasonable) disagreement; imagine, finally, that this disagreement is sufficient that the international community refuses to describe the proposed intervention as preemptive war, insisting instead that it be rightly described as preventive in nature. What should the responsible state do, when it is convinced that the intervention in question is morally justified? What difference does the international legal condemnation of the intervention make?

Such a case, of course, is rather specific in its details, and in many real cases they will fail to describe the actual circumstances we face. In these cases, I suspect my conclusions will simply fail to apply, or at any rate will apply with less force. This should not, however, dissuade us from using these assumptions, especially that they seem to describe a situation in which preventive war seems at least potentially justifiable; they eliminate, that is, many of the reasons we would initially have to condemn a preventive military action. Given that the action proposed is a not unreasonable response to the facts on the ground, represents a proportional response to the threat, and can be predictably accomplished by the state in question, we must now ask: what reason could this state have for restraining itself from acting? How should it understand the fact that international law continues, here, to condemn the action proposed as illegal?

In what follows, I will consider three categories of reasons that might be cited to convince the state in question to obey the law. The first looks towards the duties of the state under the law, whether that duty is understood as a duty to other states or to foreign citizens. The second looks towards the consequences of disobedience to law. These reasons, perhaps the most discussed reasons in the literature, focus on the damage done to respect for law and international stability by widespread disobedience to legal norms. The final category looks towards epistemic considerations of multilateralism: here, obedience to law is a proxy for the demand to subject our conclusions to other perspectives, presumably less biased than our own. My conclusions will be largely negative in character: the first two sorts of reason give us very few reasons, in the case of the state described above, to obey the law. The final category, moreover, does not commit us to obedience to law, but rather to intersubjective justification of our conclusions before we use those conclusions in defense of deadly force. This means, in the end, that we may have a reason to obey the law and refrain from unilateral preventive war, but only because we have a reason to avoid acting on biased information and arguments. This reason, finally, will be shown to have only a contingent relationship to international law, given that other forms of intersubjective justification might provide more accurate information. In the end, I will suggest, states may frequently have good reasons to avoid preventive warfare, but the fact that it is illegal will rarely be among them.

DUTY-BASED REASONS FOR OBEDIENCE

I want to begin here by examining reasons for obeying the international prohibition on preventive war that begin with the concept of a duty. There are at least two forms such a duty might take: the first is a duty to other states, which is to be fulfilled derivatively through respect for the international system these states have jointly created. The second is a duty to the inhabitants of these other states, which precludes certain forms of aggressive action against the states they inhabit. There is no bright line between these two forms of duty, given that most people who argue in favor of the rights of states do so in virtue of the rights of their inhabitants. (There is, of course, also no bright line between duty-based reasons and consequentialist reasons, given how few pure non-consequentialists we find writing on international politics.) Nevertheless, we may divide up the categories of reason here based upon the identity of the one who has the legitimate complaint in either case. We will look, first, at those sorts of reasons that imagine that foreign states are the legitimate bearers of rights against preventive war. What sorts of reasons could these be?

We might begin the analysis here by looking at the analogy between the international and domestic systems of law. In either case, we see mutual forbearance understood as potentially justified with reference to some form of social contract; a justificatory contract between citizens, in the domestic case, and between states or peoples in the international case.[11] On this analysis, we might imagine that we have a duty to those who have joined with us in the creation of just or nearly just institutions to ensure the perpetuation of these institutions.[12] If we believe that we have a duty to our fellow citizens to support the law we have made together, so must we believe that states have an obligation to support the legal structures they

---

[11] See, most prominently, John Rawls, *The Law of Peoples* (Cambridge, MA: Harvard University Press, 2001).

[12] Rawls himself insists upon a natural duty to support just institutions to ground these more specific political duties. See John Rawls, *A Theory of Justice* (Cambridge, MA: Harvard University Press, 1971).

have joined together to create. In each case, the logic is the same: respect for those who have agreed to jointly constrain their actions in accordance with law requires that we constrain our own actions even when we have reasons for doing otherwise. In both cases, the legal prohibition on an action provides us with a moral reason for refraining from that action. To refuse to abide by such prohibitions is, in the end, to refuse an obligation that ought to govern our relationship to the other parties with whom we have created a legal relationship.

There are, of course, many things that could be said about such an account by way of criticism. It is not clear, for instance, that we must insist upon an obligation to obey the domestic legal system, even if we regard that legal system as being morally legitimate.[13] More to the point, however, we have a good reason to think that the international legal system differs from the domestic legal system, in such a way that the moral authority of the latter system cannot be simply derived from that of the former. We might examine, here, the divergent sources of law in the two cases. Domestic law, in any just or nearly just legal system, includes provisions for actual participation among the parties whose actions will be coercively constrained by the legal system in question. To a significant extent, we judge the justice of a legal system with reference to its success in providing some opportunity to be heard and to have a voice in the creation of the laws. To the extent that a society fails to provide this opportunity, its moral authority must be understood to diminish accordingly. Law's authority, then, begins with at least some guarantee of equality of standing in the creation of that law.

This procedural justification for authority, however, runs into some striking difficulties in the international case. There is no international legislature or executive, as has been frequently noted. Even the United Nations is not a democratic assembly, nor does it especially pretend to be – especially given the limited number of states seated at any given time on the Security Council.[14] International law, instead, emerges from a variety of distinct sources, many of which should give us pause before we conclude

---

[13] See, for instance, the skeptical challenge of M. B. E. Smith, "Is there a Prima Facie Obligation to Obey the Law?," *Yale Law Journal* 82:5 (1973), 950–976.

[14] Walter Slocombe, Deputy Secretary of Defense in the Clinton administration, noted that requiring United Nations approval for justified military action would preclude any military action not approved of by China or Russia, "no matter how broadly the action is otherwise supported, or how well justified in other international legal or political terms." Walter B. Slocombe, "Force, Pre-emption, and Legitimacy," *Survival* 45:1 (Spring 2003), 117–130, at 122. Quoted in Yoo and Delahunty, "The 'Bush Doctrine'," 847.

that what emerges from them could have moral authority in a manner similar to domestic law:

(a) international conventions, whether general or particular, establishing rules expressly recognized by the contesting states;
(b) international custom, as evidence of a general practice accepted as law;
(c) the general principles of law recognized by civilized nations;
(d) subject to the provisions of Article 59, judicial decisions, and the teachings of the most highly qualified publicists of the various nations, as subsidiary means for the determination of rules of law.[15]

I want, for the moment, to focus on sources (b) through (c). What should emerge from this set of sources, I think, is an idea that there is very little actual opportunity for existing states to propose and make law; indeed, there may be almost no opportunity for subaltern or weak states to do anything but accept the terms of interaction proposed by the more powerful states of the world. If we have reason to think that the moral authority of a social contract fails to the extent that it fails to be responsive to the participatory rights of its members, should we not conclude that the social contract justification for international legal structures is here entirely inappropriate? There is, here, nothing of the democratic, or the participatory; there is, instead, only a reiteration and reframing of the moral power of customs generally accepted as binding by states. I do not mean, in saying this, to denigrate the importance of these customs. Indeed, I accept that doing what these customs require of us is often of great moral importance – although, as I shall discuss, this importance is not derived from their legal status. I mean at present only to assert that the moral duty for this importance cannot be established through analogy with the obligation to obey the domestic law. The sources, and thus the nature, of such law is simply too divergent in the two cases; the authority of one cannot establish the authority of the other.

The most likely source in which we can find a duty to obey international law, of course, is in source (a) – the voluntary acceptance by states of international treaty obligations. This, at least, seems to provide us with a clear way of understanding the obligation to obey those international laws enshrined in conventions and voluntary contractual instruments. If anything can be understood to provide a clear and plausible ground to our moral duties, it is the existence of a voluntary obligation, freely entered

---

[15] Statute of the International Court of Justice, Article 38. Available at www.icj-cij.org/documents/index.php?p1=4&p2=2&p3=0.

into. To refuse to do what we have agreed to do is to violate a moral duty to the object of our promising; whether the object is a natural person or a state makes no difference – in either case, we are obliged in virtue of the fact that we have chosen to become so obliged. Can we not find, here, a clear ground for the obligation to obey international law?

I think we can – but I do not think we can find an obligation sufficient to ground the authority of a norm against preventive war. I accept that states voluntarily entering into contractual relationships create obligations upon themselves to fulfill such obligations.[16] There may be many mysteries surrounding promissory obligation, but its existence does not seem to be one of them. So: can we now assert that a state, in virtue of its acceptance of the Charter of the United Nations, gives up its right to preventive warfare? I cannot see how; the obligation generated by promise simply isn't strong enough to ground this conclusion. There are very few among us who are so non-consequentialist about truth-telling, for example, that we agree with Kant's insistence that we may not lie to the murderer at the doorstep.[17] The reason for this, I suspect, is that most of us look at the obligation to tell the truth – like the obligation to keep promises – as having at most a prima facie moral importance; powerful, but superseded in some cases by the value of maintaining life, especially in face of a violent and unjust threat. If we accept this much, however, it seems we are accepting the proposition that individuals have a right to lie – or to break a promise – when the alternative would be to allow an unjust killing to occur. Once we accept this, however, we are committed to permitting just or nearly just societies to have the right to break their promises when the alternative would be a significant risk of violent destruction at the hands of an unjust enemy. In each case, the power of the promise pales in comparison to the legitimate interest in survival. Individuals and states each seem to maintain the right to defend themselves, even when such a defense might require the use of means or acts otherwise prohibited by voluntary agreement.

There are any number of ways of finding a disanalogy between the two cases here; the state is not a natural person, after all, and we may worry about how significant a danger might be before we can analogize it to the murderer at Kant's imagined doorway. These are, I think, insufficient to

---

[16] I believe that the strength and nature of these obligations may vary depending upon the nature of the political system of the state to which the obligation is owed; this is a complication, however, I do not discuss here.

[17] Indeed, it's not clear that Kantians need agree with Kant here. See Christine Korsgaard, "The Right to Lie: Kant on Dealing With Evil," *Philosophy and Public Affairs* 15:4 (1986), 325–349.

rebut the general worry here, which is simply that promissory obligation does not provide an absolute moral duty, and if anything can defeat a non-absolute moral duty, it is the right to self-preservation against an unjust attack. If the just or nearly just state imagined above is convinced for good reason that it faces such an attack, and that preventive warfare prior to the attack's being "imminent" is the only means to prevent that attack, and that the preventive action is proportional and appropriate to the attack being prepared – can we imagine, in these circumstances, that promissory obligation is sufficient to ground an obligation not to engage in the attack?

I will conclude this section by briefly considering another duty-based reason to avoid preventive warfare – that which emerges from Michael Walzer's "legalist paradigm."[18] This analysis focuses on the rights of states, but derives these rights from the more foundational rights of individuals. The complaint here is properly thought to be held by individuals, whose rights might be thought to be violated by a military action taken in the name of prevention. On Walzer's analysis, we have reason to respect states in virtue of their status as a human achievement; the borders of the state represent the borders of a social world, within which a way of life is practiced in accordance with internally understood values and meanings.[19] On this analysis, which has proven extremely influential, we have reason to refrain from invasions of territorial integrity in virtue of the reasons we have to respect the worlds people have created together. To cross the borders of a state, on this account, is to violate the rights of the people who live there to live by their own values – and, so, it is to do unjust violence to persons, rather than simply to political entities. As such, only aggression can justify warfare; we can only cross the borders of another society when that society has first unjustly crossed our own.[20]

This conception of international relations gives us good reasons to seek peace, and to regard the rights of other states as giving us moral reasons to respect the borders of those states. I do not here want to critique this conception of international society. What I want to do, here, is only to point out how difficult it is, on this account, to get any particular conclusions about the legitimacy of preventive war. The reason for this is

---

[18] David Luban accepts a version of the legalist paradigm, but for reasons unlike those given by Walzer. See Luban, "Preventive War."

[19] This understanding is presented in David Walzer, *Just and Unjust Wars* (New York: Basic Books, 2006) but is extended in interesting ways in his *Arguing about War* (New Haven, CT: Yale University Press, 2004).

[20] This is, of course, something of an oversimplification of Walzer's position, which allows for a limited conception of human rights as a justification for intervention.

that, just as the other society in question has a right to survive as a community, so too does the state facing the unjust threat that might be dealt with by preventive war. We have, here, a situation of rights which must be balanced: the rights of the first state facing a possible terrorist threat to use military force to defend its own territorial integrity and political autonomy, and the rights of the second state – the host of the terrorist entity imagined here – to exactly the same rights to territorial integrity and political autonomy. There can be, here, no general conclusions about the legitimacy of preventive war as a whole – certainly, there can be no wholesale condemnation of preventive military actions, given that such might be the only means by which a given society might be able to survive. We must seek, instead, some more subtle form of balancing of rights, which will sometimes permit the legitimacy of preventive military intervention. Thus, Walzer argues that the six-day war was a valid case of preventive warfare, based on the principle that "states may use military force in the face of threats of war, whenever the failure to do so would seriously risk their territorial integrity or political independence."[21] If the invasion of Iraq did not so count, it was not because preventive war itself was always morally deficient, but because the circumstances in Iraq in 2002 were not akin to those in Egypt in 1967.[22] Walzer is, here, discussing what I have called the institutional question – what rules ought there to be – rather than what I have called the agency question. I do not believe, however, that he can be used to defend a blanket prohibition on preventive warfare, even where such warfare is illegal. Given the central values of the legalist paradigm, and the way in which preventive warfare might be the only means by which such values are protected, it seems that he must sometimes defend the legitimacy of such actions – whether or not our legal instruments regard them as permissible.

CONSEQUENCE-BASED REASONS FOR OBEDIENCE

I think we are unlikely to arrive at a convincing duty-based reason to think that the imagined state above has a good moral reason to avoid preventive war. This is probably not surprising: the majority of our unease with preventive war seems to stem from forward-looking considerations of consequences, rather than from backward-looking considerations of duty. What we seem to fear is a world in which preventive war is widespread,

---

[21] Walzer, *Just and Unjust Wars*, 85.   [22] See Walzer, *Arguing about War*, 147.

and in which states – in particular, states like the United States – presume the right to judge for themselves when a threat is sufficient to ground military action. There are several aspects to this fear, and I think some of them – especially the worry about the epistemic biases that creep into decisions made by unilateral agents – are quite powerful. What I want to do now, however, is look at the more strictly consequentialist arguments that might be invoked to condemn the imagined state. I think these may take several forms: we may worry about other societies following the example of a state willing to engage in preventive war, so that such war becomes the default rather than an aberration. Thus, Henry Kissinger – not generally thought of as an opponent of military action – argues that unilateral forms of preventive war would lead to an unstable and violent world:

> If each nation claimed the right to define its preemptive rights for itself, the absence of any rules would spell international chaos, not order. Some universal, generally accepted principles need to be matched with the machinery of their operation.[23]

Kissinger intends this counsel to argue in favor of a revision of international law, but it could equally well serve as a counsel against the use of preventive war under current international law. Given that such lawbreaking might break down respect for the rule of international law itself, and lead to imitation and widespread use of preventive war across the planet, we have strong consequentialist reason to avoid resorting to preventive war under any circumstances.

This pattern of argument underlies much of our intuitive dislike of preventive war; we fear – and should fear – a world in which the limited security offered by international laws and norms has broken down. I think, however, that the argument as it stands cannot give us solid reason to condemn unilateral preventive war under all circumstances. There are at least three worries that can be cited to show the difficulties in accepting this pattern of argument – at least where this argument is cited to show that all proposed preventive wars, including the form described above, are morally impermissible.

The first of these problems stems from what we might call the mechanism of transmission from the case described above to the imagined parade of malign preventive wars that it is thought to produce. We may, here, shift from the imagined to the particular, and ask how the legitimation of

---

[23] Henry Kissinger, "The Rules on Preventive Force," *Washington Post*, April 9, 2006.

preventive war by the Bush administration has been thought to undermine the international system. I want to do this in the present section only because the recent American military invasion of Iraq has been the starting point of most recent discussions of the consequences of a doctrine of unilateral preventive war, and it will be useful to examine what consequences have been thought to emerge from that military intervention. The complaints about imitation and increased warfare have been a prominent part of these debates. Whether the predictions underlying these complaints are viable, of course, is an empirical question, and requires an empirical answer; but, from the armchair, it isn't clear that we have a solid reason to infer that the witnessing of American preventive military action would encourage other states to engage in such actions themselves. What reasons do we have to think that such imitation would occur? Imagine a state which wants very much to engage in preventive warfare against its closest neighbor; imagine next that this same state witnesses the United States engaging in some action of preventive warfare. What, exactly, has changed in the second step of this story? The primary change, I suspect, is that the United States has lost a great deal of its moral authority, and the other states of the world will look with a certain amount of skepticism at any general condemnation of preventive warfare issued by the United States. But what reason do we have to think that it is this perception of moral authority that is the primary reason for the imitating state to engage in preventive warfare? It seems odd for us to think that it is only the moral coherence of the United States that is standing in the way of this flood of preventive warfare. Indeed, I suspect that most nations of the world would be at least mildly hostile to the idea that the United States has a great deal of moral authority to begin with; it seems a bit of a stretch to imagine that it is this authority that has kept the tide of preventive wars in check.

I should be careful here to note that I do not take any of the preceding as a reason to engage in preventive warfare – or, still worse, as praise of hypocrisy or the squandering of whatever moral authority the United States might have. There are independent moral reasons to condemn hypocritical and self-serving actions. I will try to establish later that unilateral preventive war does not always entail such actions, but it should be clear that many real cases of preventive war might seem to involve them. All I want to do here is express the more modest point that the perception of hypocrisy cannot be reliably used as a predictor for any particular political consequence. The loss of moral authority entailed when other states regard a given state as hypocritical is not tied to state action in a sufficiently robust way that we can make any strong predictions here about outcomes. Simply put, we cannot infer from the fact that a strong nation engages in preventive war that weaker nations will increasingly follow their lead.

I would argue, indeed, that it is entirely possible that the opposite result might occur. Examine, for a moment, the so-called Ledeen doctrine, taken by some as emblematic of the limit case of neoconservative political thought:

> Every ten years or so, the United States needs to pick up some small crappy little country and throw it against the wall, just to show the world we mean business.[24]

As a piece of normative political philosophy, this is noxious; whatever may or may not count as just military actions, the use of deadly force simply to assert global primacy would seem to be ruled out. (Indeed, the Ledeen doctrine seems simply to do away with the idea of justice entirely.) I do not want to defend this doctrine as a piece of guidance for state actors. I would note only that the causal story it imagines – that military adventurism by a superpower might reduce military adventurism by weaker powers – is not obviously implausible. The arguments against preventive war discussed above have tended to assume that the usual response to preventive war by the United States would be an increase in the number of preventive wars generally. It is possible, though, that we could face an opposite reaction; a demonstration by a superpower that it is willing to use force in its interests might reduce military actions undertaken by others, simply by increasing the perception that the United States is not unwilling to throw its weight around. I want to emphasize, again, that I am not *advocating* for this position. We have good – indeed, overwhelming – moral reason to refrain from military actions under all but the most rare and well-defined circumstances. I am only arguing that the causal story we frequently use to condemn the use of preventive war by the Bush administration is not the only story we might tell. In the end, it must remain an empirical question as to what global consequences would emerge from the use of preventive war by a powerful state such as the United States.

The most plausible consequentialist story, I think, begins with the idea that disrespect for law might emerge in a more gradual and nuanced way. If the United States argues that it has the right to engage in preventive warfare, even in face of a legal condemnation from the United Nations – and is able to act on that presumed right, without fear of significant

---

[24] Jonah Goldberg has attributed this remark to Michael Ledeen, who is popularly thought of as its author. See Jonah Goldberg, "Baghdad Delenda Est, Part Two," *National Review*, April 23, 2002.

negative consequences – then it seems that the United States is able to ignore law without fear of reprisal; this, surely, makes international law less law-like, insofar as its reach is no longer universal. It will surely reduce respect for law when weaker states see the United States able to flout unwelcome restrictions at will. In the long run, this inequality under the law will make the law itself less useful as a tool for reform, given that its character is no longer that which we might have thought necessary for law to exist *as* law. In this way, over time, we erode one of the few sources of international deliberation and reform available in the international arena.

I think this story has much in it that is correct. There are, however, two things that must be noted prior to accepting the conclusions that are here thought to follow from the story. The first is the simple one that law may be able to take more disobedience than we might be assuming here.[25] It simply isn't clear that individual acts of lawbreaking have any significant effects upon the actual attitudes of agents towards that law. I am speaking, here, not of whether or not the disobedience is justified; I am speaking only of how the witnesses to disobedience will react. Other states may regard the United States as having violated the law in unilateral preventive war; it does not follow that these states will, of necessity, regard the law as now less law-like – they are, I think, likely instead to think that the law persists, and that the United States is morally wrong for having broken it. Since my project here involves trying to articulate when powerful states may justly break such laws, I have to say that not all the stories such states will tell about the injustice of lawbreaking will be accurate. I can accept, however, that many of them will be; the United States in practice is rarely the imagined ideal state I have discussed above. My present point is only that United States disobedience might lead to a reduction in respect for the United States – rather than respect for the law that has been broken.

The second thing I want to note, though, is that it is possible to rephrase this argument so that the conclusion becomes much more plausible. The idea is that we can predictably expect states to reason in the following way: the United States has taken for itself the right to be a judge in its own case. It would be *unfair* for us to be denied the same privilege. Therefore, to the extent that the law prohibits such actions, we have good reason now to regard the law as irrelevant – or, at the very least, premised upon an inequality sufficient to undermine its authority. This pattern of reasoning, I think, is what many of us imagine when we worry about the consequences of the United States accepting the legitimacy of preventive war.

[25] See the arguments of M. B. E. Smith on this.

The argument is that this pattern of reasoning is sufficiently powerful that we can expect widespread disrespect for the status of the legal norms against preventive war. This is a consequentialist argument, I think, because what we are worried about are the consequences that would emerge from widespread acceptance of a certain pattern of argumentation.

The proper response to this argument, I think, is getting clear on what – exactly – would justify preventive warfare in the first place. We may now return from the real case of the United States, to the hypothetical case of the ideally justified state imagined above. What could such a state say in response to those who might argue that they are entitled to similar rights?

The first response would be to simply say yes – you are indeed entitled to similar rights. Where the conditions discussed are met, all states have the right to engage in unilateral preventive war. But the key here is to see that the justification does not cover all cases in which you might want to engage in warfare, with preventive warfare as a useful justifying story. Unilateral preventive war is available to all, when the situation is as we have described. Imagine once more the following: the state is reasonable and reasonably just; the threat is significant, and cannot be dealt with by other means; the military action proposed is proportionate to the threat, and likely to succeed. If what I have said is correct, *any* state with these circumstances and attributes has the right to use military force under such circumstances. They do not have a right to use military force for their own purposes, and then cite preventive war later. Thus, a stronger state might say to a weaker state: we are, indeed, being treated as equals – we have equivalent rights to break the law, where these highly specific circumstances are met. The principle that permits this is indeed a principle we can regard as universally available. You are justified in acting against the law when such lawbreaking is, in fact, justifiable; so are we. There is not inequality here worth worrying about.

The weaker states of the world would not be satisfied with this argument, I think. Their response would be to note the different abilities to *act* on one's judgment, which follows from the different strengths held by different states. The stronger states have the ability to rely on their own judgment; where they believe that the preventive war is morally justified, they may act accordingly, even in the face of legal disapproval. Their strength immunizes them to a strong degree from legal repercussions or sanctions. The weaker states are much less able to withstand the consequences of legal condemnation. When they are convinced that the case is just, they are not as easily able to ignore the law as the more powerful states. The worry here is not about an inequality of right, but an inequality of power leading to an inequality in ability to make *use* of that right. The weaker countries of the world can justly regard themselves as being under a burden not faced by their stronger neighbors.

All this is entirely true. My concern, however, is what follows from it. Recall that we are asking the agency question from the standpoint of a more powerful state. The fact that weaker states do not enjoy the same abilities as powerful states should give us moral pause. It should make us seek institutional change – an issue I have refused to consider in the present context. What it should not do, I think, is tell us that the powerful states should not *now* make use of the abilities they have to defend their rights. The above story was originally intended to show these stronger states why they should refrain from preventive warfare. We imagined that they might be told to refrain from engaging in such action, because the inability of other countries to similarly break the law with impunity would lead to widespread disrespect for law. I do not think the story has entirely succeeded. It is possible for a stronger state to say: we have this moral right to break the law, and we have the ability to act on that right. It is likely unfair that you do not have a similar ability, and we ought to work together to reform the world so that you do. But – under present circumstances – we should not refrain from using our rights simply because you are not able to do so. The right to preventive war – *where* the highly specific circumstances described above are met – is a right held by all states, or at least all reasonably just states. We cannot ignore this right under present circumstances simply because those circumstances do not effectively guarantee this right to all.

I think this discussion has given us some reason to distrust arguments that ground the prohibition on preventive war on consequentialist grounds. It may have done more than this, though. The last exchange above has shown that the real issue in preventive war might not be the justifiability of preventive war itself; where certain highly specific facts hold true, pursuing preventive war even in violation of the law may be morally justified. The real key, however, seems to be the epistemic credibility of those who are allowed to make the judgment that these highly specific facts do, in fact, obtain. We may now proceed to the final justification we will consider, which begins with this issue.

EPISTEMIC REASONS FOR OBEDIENCE

The defense I have offered above has assumed a conditional form: *if* the circumstances in which the decision is made resemble those discussed in our idealized case, *then* there may be good moral reason to engage in preventive warfare even in face of a legal ban. I have simply stipulated that the idealized case I have described meets these conditions. In the world of political practice, of course, things are not always so easily categorized. We have reason to worry about our ability to get an accurate picture of how great a given threat truly is, how effective we might be at neutralizing that threat, or how close that threat is to being mobilized. These issues are difficult in the abstract, but even more difficult when seen in the light of the pressures of political conflict and democratic debate. Clarity of information is required for the justification I have imagined, and in this context perfect clarity seems impossible.[26]

These facts seem to suggest that we have a strong duty to get our facts straight before we engage in military adventurism in the name of prevention. This, in turn, suggests to me that the strongest reason for a reasonable state to obey the law is because the law surrounding preventive war seems to provide a forum within which the case for war might be made public. I think we can begin to make the case by noting the porous border between preemptive war and preventive war. The line between the two is understood as resting primarily on the concept of the imminence of the threat; the concept of imminence, however, is not an empirical one – there is no quantity of time that can be shown scientifically to be the line between imminence and its opposite. Imminence, rather, is a term requiring judgment and thought; it is a term inviting moral analysis and argument. The prohibition on preventive war, then, might properly be thought of as a demand that those who seek war in response to a yet-unrealized threat have an obligation to convince the rest of the world's states that the threat is, indeed, sufficiently grave that it ought to fall on the line of preemption, rather than prevention. (It is interesting to note, here, that the National Security Strategy describes the United States as engaging in preemption, rather than prevention, even though the concrete recommendations it makes are better described as the latter.) Status as a preemptive attack is the conclusion of a process of mutual discourse, in which states are instructed to seek the assent of other states – in particular, their assent to the proposition that the moral calculus underlying the decision to invade is correct. I will understand the line between preemption and prevention, from this point on, as reflecting a conclusion about the legitimacy of the action, rather than an independent description of its empirical attributes.

---

[26] This argument is taken by Arthur Schlesinger, Jr., as a dispositive reason to condemn all preventive war. Arthur Schlesinger, Jr., "Unilateral Preventive War: Illegitimate and Immoral," *Los Angeles Times*, August 21, 2002.

In this, I think we can reinterpret the unhappiness of other nations at the unilateral adventurism of the United States as a concern not about preventive war, but about the refusal of the United States to accept any judgment other than its own. The chief complaint here is not, on this account, the unfairness involved in that the United States gets to use such policy tools where they are prohibited to weaker states. It is, instead, that the United States, in virtue of its greater military power, presumes the right to be judged in its own case, with the predictable biases in judgment that result.

This may lead us back to a proper understanding of why the state involved may have an obligation to obey the law against preventive war. This reason is epistemic in nature, and rests upon the obligation to seek correction against predictable errors in judgment by means of reasoned discourse and the giving of evidence. The prohibition on preventive war is, in reality, a prohibition on anticipatory wars that could not be justified to other states as sufficiently urgent to merit the term "preemptive." If we understand the legal doctrine in this way, we can reinterpret it as a demand for the giving of evidence sufficient to legitimate the use of military force. If this account is correct, then even the idealized state I have described above has an obligation to obey the law, where this law is understood as mandating the seeking of intersubjective agreement on the nature of the threats involved prior to military attack. The obligation here does not emerge directly from the fact that preventive war is illegal. The obligation emerges, instead, from the fact that the international community's prohibition on preventive war creates an opportunity to provide that community with reasons justifying that anticipatory war, and a state proposing to engage in such warfare has an obligation to make use of this opportunity.

I will not fully explore this epistemic account of obligation here, except to note that it seems to me the only plausible reason to think that the state above has any moral reason to obey the law against preventive warfare. I will close, however, by noting an implication of the account I have offered here: namely, that the present legal system is, at best, a poor proxy for the imagined discourse I here described. We might well seek to develop a better set of international legal instruments, sufficient to effectively adjudicate which military actions are morally legitimate.[27] In the absence of such instruments, though, a powerful state might regard itself as morally

---

[27] Allen Buchanan and Robert Keohane have done excellent work in imagining what such a set of institutions might be. See Buchanan and Keohane, "The Preventive Use of Force: A Cosmopolitan Institutional Approach," *Ethics and International Affairs* 18:1 (2004), 1–22. See also Feinstein and Slaughter, "A Duty to Prevent."

obligated to maintain those few instruments which do seek to provide a forum for the giving and evaluating of evidence. Our obligation is, in a way, to do no harm to those few legal instruments that actually provide us with a forum for such discussions. But we should not think that it is only the information provided by such states that has relevance for our deliberations. Seeking the approval of the international community involves seeking the assent and approval of many diverse international agents, all of which have their own biases and political pressures. Gaining the assent of these entities provides some evidence for the legitimacy of the imagined warfare, but it does not provide any dispositive proof. Indeed, it may well be that a responsible state would have an obligation to seek correction and discourse with any number of non-state agents, including NGOs set up to provide accurate analyses of international relations. The obligation of the state, on this epistemic account, is not limited to an obligation to other states to obey the law; it is to seek whatever sources of information and discourse exist that might reliably correct biased and self-interested decisions. We might, indeed, regard the assent of Human Rights Watch to a given plan of military action as providing more evidence for the legitimacy of that plan than the assent of the government of Uganda – even though the latter is currently a member of the Security Council of the United Nations.[28] The obligation to obey the law, here, is really only part of a larger obligation – to justify our plans to those who might usefully challenge them, and in so doing seek to correct those biases found in cases of unilateral action. Law is part of this obligation, but it is by no means its only focus.

To be more precise: it might be the case that an action of intervention is considered as illegitimate by the requisite institutions of international law, and yet legitimately undertaken by the state in question. The institutions of international law might describe the action as preventive war, given the current rules and standards of international law; what this means is that the intervening state has failed to convince the other members of the international legal community that the threat in question does in fact rise to the level required to describe it as preemptive, rather than preventive, war. This does not require the other states of the world to be mistaken about the law; indeed, what these states of the world are willing to sign on to is, itself, what determines the legal status of the proposed intervention. We

---

[28] This is not intended as a slight against Uganda; it calls to attention only that the assent of a highly abusive regime such as the Ugandan government might provide little, if any, evidence for the accuracy of our moral judgments.

cannot therefore say that the international legal community is getting the law wrong in describing the action as preventive, rather than preemptive. What I want to insist upon here is that this legal status does not determine the moral value of the proposed intervention. A state might be morally justified in engaging in an act that is legitimately described as preventive war under international law, as this law now stands. The state has an epistemic obligation to listen to the case against the proposed military action, and the institutions and norms of law provide a site within which this process of intersubjective justification might be undertaken; the dissenting states, presumably, have reasons for their dissent. In the end, however, the possibility exists that the institutions of international law may be legitimately ignored. The intervening state has a moral duty to listen to the reasons provided; this does not entail a duty to regard these reasons as superior to its own. If a responsible state seeks to engage in preventive warfare, but is unsuccessful in convincing other governments that the warfare is justifiable, and is roundly condemned by NGOs as illegitimate, then the state in question has a good prima facie reason to regard its own calculations as flawed. In the end, though, the state must regard all these things as merely things to be factored into the moral calculus underlying its own actions. It is, after all, always possible that the one is right, and the many are wrong.[29]

This means, in the end, that judgment is inescapable, and the obligation to obey the law I have asserted here is ultimately rather weak in character. It is an obligation, properly understood, only to seek the most appropriate sources of information, and to engage in the justificatory project of arguing for the appropriateness of the action proposed. It is not, therefore, an obligation to obey the law *because it is the law*, but rather an obligation to listen to the arguments and reasons of others about the moral status of the intervention in question; law simply provides a space within which this exchange of reasons might occur.[30] When that dialogue ends, the fact that others are not convinced is good evidence that the action proposed is

---

[29] Deen Chatterjee has urged me to consider the possibility that international law might provide a forum for ex post facto evaluation of military actions; this seems appropriate, given that actions undertaken against perceived imminent threats are frequently undertaken prior to the obtaining of permission from international legal institutions. I cannot adequately consider this possibility here, but I think it is likely true that the conclusions I derive here would apply with equal force to such ex post facto evaluations; it may still be true that the international community's judgment about whether or not a given threat was truly imminent enough to count as preemptive is a judgment that can legitimately be disputed by the intervening state. Again, the state has the responsibility to listen to the other states of the world, but no obligation to defer to their judgment.

[30] I am grateful to Deen Chatterjee for urging me to be more precise on this point.

illegitimate – but it is not dispositive. In the end, the state cannot avoid acting on its own judgment in such matters.

If all this is true, then the best source we can find for the obligation to avoid preventive war does not, in the end, truly give us an obligation to avoid preventive war. It gives us, instead, a prima facie duty to show that the proposed action is legitimate, and therefore is not really preventive war at all. What a responsible state may do in the name of self-defense is ultimately a decision that the state must make for itself. International law provides us with a tool by which that decision might be made better; but, to answer the question of this paper, we must conclude that the legal facts here do not ultimately change the moral facts. A responsible state must seek dialogue with others, but in the end it may – and must – rely upon its own moral judgment.

CHAPTER 6

Threat diplomacy in world politics: legal, moral, political, and civilizational challenges

Richard Falk

FRAMING THE INQUIRY

A deepening global crisis centers on efforts of Western countries led by the United States and spearheaded by Israel to thwart Iran's alleged efforts to acquire nuclear weaponry. On the one side is Iran's insistence that its nuclear program is devoted to exercising its rights under international law to develop and acquire the means to produce nuclear energy, coupled with assurances that it has no intention to develop nuclear weapons. On the other side are most influential governments, backed by United Nations sanctions and International Atomic Energy Agency suspicions, that contend that steps must be taken to dissuade Iran from acquiring nuclear weapons by all necessary means and with a sense of urgency. Israel quite openly announces its intention and capabilities to mount an attack on Iran's nuclear facilities in the event that Iran does not provide convincing reassurance of the non-military character of its nuclear program. Israel's threat is made against the background of its 1981 attack on the Iraqi reactor at Osirak that supposedly succeeded in derailing Saddam Hussein's plans to become a nuclear weapons state. The United States has used a more subtle language than Israel, but with a similar resonance, leading the effort to stiffen sanctions, repeatedly indicating its refusal "to take the military option off the table," and backing up its warning with threatening naval deployments. It is intriguing and revealing that all of the international discussion so far has been focused on how to meet this emerging Iranian threat, and almost no attention has been given to the legality and propriety of the military threats directed at Iran, a sovereign state that is a member of the United Nations and entitled to the protection of international law.

Such issues take on an added resonance when the earlier rationale put forward to justify an attack upon Iraq in 2003 is taken into account. It will be recalled that the United States government sought unsuccessfully (and deceptively) at the time to convince the UN Security Council that force should be authorized because Iraq's possession of chemical and biological weaponry and program to develop nuclear weapons constituted unacceptable threats, which also violated the terms of the cease-fire negotiated to end the Gulf war in 1991 and inscribed in a series of UN Security Council resolutions. As we now know, no weapons of mass destruction were found in Iraq, the alleged danger was non-existent or so remote as to be not capable of any show of reality, and the war of aggression launched against Iraq in 2003 produced widespread death, displacement, and destruction along with the desired regime change in Baghdad. But what has still not been widely discussed is the extent to which Iraq was not only the victim of an unlawful use of force by the United States and its "coalition of the willing," but that Iraq was never protected from unlawful threats issued by the United States in the period preceding the March 21, 2003 invasion. The Security Council has been properly praised because it resisted intense American pressure to legitimate the invasion by giving its formal blessings, but this main UN organ has rarely been criticized for failing to exercise its responsibility to protect Iraq from unlawful threats directed at its political independence and sovereign integrity that preceded the invasion. It is a characteristic of the prevailing discourses in world politics that the concerns of dominant states shape the public debate often occluding the perspectives of international law and morality, as well as the vital security interests of outlier states such as Iran.

In effect, the geopolitical dominance of the global diplomatic discourse has distorted our perception of the rights of secondary sovereign states. In effect, these latter states, if perceived as hostile and dangerous by the United States and its principal allies, are subject to dire threats to their survival in a manner that is inconsistent with international law and morality as written into the UN Charter with great deliberation after the Second World War. The main intention of this constitutional framework for world order was to outlaw all uses of force, including threats, except those uses of force and wars that could be justified to the Security Council by satisfying a restrictively specified right of self-defense. What is particularly relevant for this inquiry is that this war prevention goal was expressed in a manner that did not distinguish between threats and uses of international force. Thus Article 2(4) of the United Nations Charter was formulated in a deliberately unconditional language that intended to be unambiguous: "All Members shall refrain in their international relations from the threat or use of force against the territorial integrity of any state, or in any manner inconsistent with the Purposes of the United Nations."

This prohibition is reinforced by Article 2(3), which obliges members of the UN to "settle their disputes by peaceful means." Article 51 does confirm "the inherent right of individual and collective self-defense if an armed attack occurs," but even that grant is made contingent on the primary obligation of the Security Council to uphold international peace and security. It must be admitted that throughout the existence of the UN questions have been raised by governments and academic commentators to challenge this narrow understanding of self-defense, as well as to insist that this Charter conception on the use of force must be read in conjuction with the provisions designed to put in place an operational system of collective security. This line of reasoning argued that the restrictive ideas about the use of force were interrelated with the collective security mechanism, and without the latter, then states needed to fill the vacuum with a wider ambit of discretion as to threats and uses of force. Whether this effort to rewrite the Charter should be given legal weight remains a matter of acute controversy among legal experts.

There are several pressing world order issues that arise against this background: (1) to what extent has this Charter approach to the use of force been rendered obsolete by contemporary circumstances, especially large-scale transnational terrorism and preoccupations with further proliferation of nuclear weaponry? The Charter appears to restrict valid claims to use force to *reactive* forms of self-defense while the new realism alleges the necessity of *anticipatory* forms; (2) is it realistic and desirable to prohibit all *threats* to use force?; (3) can certain threats maintain peace and security or contribute to the injunction to seek peaceful settlement contained in Article 2(3) by inducing recourse to diplomacy?

From a geostrategic perspective reliance on threats as a cornerstone of world order has taken two different principal forms since the end of the Second World War, and in both instances this threat diplomacy was principally articulated with respect to American foreign policy. The first cycle can be identified with the core reliance on nuclear weapons to implement policies of deterrence and containment during the period of the Cold War, and leading to an imitation of this reliance by the Soviet Union as soon as it acquired comparable weaponry in 1952. The second cycle can be associated mainly with the American response to the 9/11 attacks, and particularly with the sense that certain countries must be prevented from acquiring nuclear weaponry, and possibly other weapons of mass destruction, providing the main rationale for the invasion of Iraq in 2003 and the ongoing effort to threaten Iran with military attack to the extent that it is perceived as possessing, or even nearly possessing, nuclear weapons. In both instances, the threat merges with a use that if undertaken violates fundamental rules of international law and morality. Yet ambiguity is inherently present. The threat may be intended primarily or partially as an inducement to negotiate diplomatically, and as a preferred alternative to carrying out the military threat. It has been so phrased by the Obama presidency, abandoning the more inflammatory rhetoric of "the axis of evil" that had been so prominently relied upon by the Bush presidency in the aftermath of 9/11.

These issues address some fundamental aspects of sustainable global governance in the early twenty-first century. Their examination in this inquiry will consider the evolution of the global setting so far as security threats and responses are concerned, and cautiously advance some recommendations about how to address this series of sensitive, contested, and underlying difficulties, balancing a concern with the overall conditions of world order against a more specific focus on the ongoing confrontation with Iran. To simplify this inquiry five overlapping dimensions will be discussed with a dual attention to evolving circumstances and the identification of useful conceptual perspectives.

FIVE DIMENSIONS OF THREAT DIPLOMACY: EVOLVING CONCERNS AND CONCEPTUAL PERSPECTIVES

(1) International law

The Charter norms as expressive of international law have been summarized in the introductory section. The International Court of Justice in the Nicaragua Judgment of 1986 authoritatively affirmed the validity of these norms in contemporary international law. Particularly important was the confirmation of the narrowly circumscribed character of the right of self-defense under customary international law, that is, independent of the UN Charter. The most relevant conclusion was that it was unacceptable for a state to claim the right to use force against a foreign state on the basis of self-defense unless it could demonstrate convincingly that it was responding to "a prior armed attack."

What has received almost no attention is the status of a *threat* to use force, which is prohibited equally to force by the language of the UN Charter, and reflects the view that a credible threat endangers peace both by leading a weaker state to give in to demands that are inconsistent with its sovereign rights to political independence and territorial integrity, and by tempting a threatened state to strike first out of fear or to gain some advantage in wartime. Whether the UN Security Council needs to give its approval to such a claim of "defensive" force in a situation not involving a prior armed attack, but only a threat, is an unresolved issue. It is much discussed in light of the so-called "Bush doctrine" and more generally, in the shifting security atmosphere after the 9/11 attacks, which was highlighted by a shift from reactive to anticipatory tactics. This shift in practice, most clearly articulated and evident in the practice of the United States, particularly its attack on Iraq and justification for escalated warfare in Afghanistan in 2009, had been causing uncertainty among international law specialists as to whether the Charter/Nicaragua framework should continue to be treated as an authoritative statement of international law at the present time. The more realist strain of thinking in international law has always assessed uses of force by reference to whether the claimed usage was "reasonable" given the context, which in some formulations included whether the values being served were in accord with political democracy and human rights. The new realism definitely endorses the reasonableness of anticipatory uses of force in defensive modes to support counter-terrorist campaigns.

The essential policy and ethical dilemma here is whether to endorse a rule-centric approach to the use of force that tries to limit the domain of discretion as much as possible to avoid self-serving justifications for the use of force or to go along with a more hegemonic approach that acknowledges the role of power and practice in shaping the contours of acceptable behavior by states. The hegemonic realists are more in accord with the existential character of world order while the legalists are far more sensitive to the establishment of desirable normative limits on the discretion of states to act violently in world politics. To the extent that aggressive war-making, including reliance on threats, is perceived as generally dysfunctional in the current global setting, the legalist framework may gain influence. There is much evidence supporting the view that had American foreign policy been guided by international law with respect to the use of force ever since the Vietnam war and up through the Iraq war, its national economic and international political standing would be higher and its global leadership position more widely accepted. In other words, the realist orientation that frees policy-makers from the constraints of international law has not served the national interests of the United States (and other aggressive states) well since the end of the Second World War, whereas in earlier periods of international relations aggressive uses of force, which were not legally prohibited until 1928, seemed often to contribute to national power, territorial scope, and material wealth.

(2) Deterrence

The idea of deterrence is to dissuade an opponent from doing something undesirable by threatening such a strong retaliatory response as to make it irrational to perform the act. It became centrally important during the Cold War with respect to reliance by the West on nuclear weapons to contain the Soviet Union without provoking a Third World War. The central feature of deterrence were threats to devastate in their totality the cities of an enemy without any deference to customary international law limitations on the use of force even in situations of legitimate self-defense, which only authorize attacks directed at distinct military targets. Deterrence theory and practice carried the legal logic of *reactive* security to genocidal extremes. It was appropriately labeled the "balance of terror," and more technically known as "mutual assured destruction," which gave rise to the suggestive acronym, "MAD." In the realist school, there are prominent writers such as John Mearsheimer who give deterrence much credit for keeping the peace during the Cold War.[1] Others are far less sure, pointing to accidents and miscalculations, as well as to the good luck that it was the Soviet Union that was willing "to lose face" and back down during the Cuban missile crisis of 1962 in an encounter that could have easily crossed the nuclear threshold.[2]

From the perspective of international law, the World Court 1996 Advisory Opinion on *The Legality of the Threat or Use of Nuclear Weapons* is highly relevant to a consideration of threats.[3] The majority opinion discusses the idea of threat in general terms as it is used in Article 2(4) of the UN Charter. The position taken there is that "[i]f the envisaged use of force is itself unlawful, the stated readiness to use it would be a threat prohibited" under Article 2(4). In effect, "[t]he notions of 'threat' and 'use' of force ... stand together ... In short, if it is to be lawful, the declared readiness of a State to use force must be a use of force that is in conformity with the Charter." The Advisory Opinion, supported only by an 8–7 vote, and that made possible by the President of the Court breaking a 7–7 tie with a second casting vote (although three of the seven judges dissented because they believed the majority did not go far enough in prohibiting nuclear weaponry), concluded that

---

[1] John Mearsheimer, "Why We Will Soon Miss the Cold War," *The Atlantic Monthly* 266:2 (1990), 35–50.

[2] See R. Falk and D. Krieger, *The Path to Zero: Dialogue on Nuclear Dangers* (Boulder, CO: Paradigm Publishers, 2012); D. Krieger, *The Doves Flew High* (Santa Barbara, CA: Artamo Press, 2007).

[3] *Legality of the Threat or Use of Nuclear Weapons: Advisory Opinion* (ICJ Reports, 1996), 226.

a use of nuclear weapons could not categorically be declared unlawful if plausibly used for the purpose of the survival of a state. As significantly, the Court does acknowledge that deterrence does require a credible intention to use nuclear weapons under certain circumstances, and yet declines "to pronounce upon the practice known as the 'policy of deterrence,'" arguing that there continues to be a strong adherence to deterrence among states such that it is impossible to conclude that threats to use nuclear weapons are intrinsically unlawful." Judge Weeramantry strongly disagrees, and since he devotes his long dissent to a comprehensive demonstration of the unlawfulness of *any* use of nuclear weaponry, he views deterrence as containing a definite threat to use, and hence unlawful by reference to the Charter. In his words, deterrence "leaves the world of make-believe and enters the field of seriously intended military threats."[4] His broader argument views reliance on nuclear weaponry, because of the tendency to be indiscriminate and disproportional in the extreme, as well as violate the neutrality of non-belligerent states, to amount to recourse to "terror" as distinct from war as legally understood.

Deterrence has been criticized sharply on moral and legal grounds, and yet it continues to be a prime feature of the security posture of the nuclear weapons states, and remains a preferred security option for nuclear weapons states over attempts to achieve negotiated disarmament despite the periodic calls, ever since the bombings of Hiroshima and Nagasaki, for a world without nuclear weaponry.

Perhaps the most relevant line of criticism of nuclearism as an omnicidal and criminal *threat* system in the Cold War was formulated in a celebrated essay by E. P. Thompson, the notable British historian and social activist.[5] The essence of Thompson's argument was the idea that the embrace of a security posture that threatens military outcomes that "must be the extermination of multitudes" represents a willingness to commit a human atrocity of apocalyptic proportions. Thompson also quotes C. Wright Mills' famous line, implicating threats as inseparable from the actions threatened: "the immediate cause of World War III is the preparation of it." Such an indictment of nuclear weaponry goes well beyond the allegations of illegality, insisting that disposition to rely on such threats is a

---

[4] *Legality of the Threat or Use of Nuclear Weapons: Dissenting Opinion of Judge Weeramantry* (ICJ Reports, 1996), 540.
[5] E. P. Thompson, "Notes on Exterminism: The Last Stage of Civilization," in Thompson et al., *Exterminism and Cold War* (London: Verso, 1982), 1–3.

denial of the most fundamental civilizational commitment to show respect
for the dignity and survival of humanity, deemed morally far more decisive
than the survival of this or that state.

This willingness over the course of decades to persist in threatening
the use of nuclear weaponry, not even willing to limit the option of use
to a response to nuclear attack, suggests an absolutist political consciousness that privileges the state and its interests over the well-being
of humanity as a whole and devotion to the sacredness of human life.
Such a militarist consciousness was prefigured by the tactics used to
prevail in the Second World War, which included the massive indiscriminate bombing of German and Japanese cities, as well as the atomic
bombing of Hiroshima and Nagasaki without even prior warnings to
the known presence of tens of thousands of civilian inhabitants. It
suggests that preparations and threats, as well as actual uses, help define
the normative identity of a political actor, and that the American
reliance on such a security posture is both dangerous and inconsistent
with the most minimal commitment to the rule of law, appropriate
adherence to the just-war tradition, and some commitment to the ethos
of human solidarity.

(3) The long war

The 9/11 attacks on the United States produced a response based on
launching a war against the shadowy network of Islamic extremists
associated with the Al-Qaeda network led by Osama bin Laden. There
remain serious doubts as to whether this general understanding of 9/11
and its aftermath reflects the true reality, and assessing these doubts bears
on what seems reasonable to do to uphold security. Immediately
following the attacks the Bush presidency mobilized the country for war
based on its presentation of the enemy and the acute security threats that
it contended existed at the time. What is most relevant for our purposes
was the realization by the US government that neither former counter-
terrorist tactics based on law enforcement nor traditional war fighting and
retaliatory approaches could succeed against an enemy that had no
territorial base and was willing and able to mount suicidal attacks against
major targets. Two basic approaches were adopted: first, initiate wars
against those states that gave direct or indirect aid and comfort to such
terrorist groups; second, threaten other states with possible intervention
or attack if they did not join the counter-terrorist war being waged by the
United States.

The wars against Afghanistan and Iraq were both rationalized on this basis, although the emphasis in relation to Iraq was partly based on its alleged links to the 9/11 attacks (later refuted) and its supposed arsenal of hidden weapons of mass destruction that might fall into Al-Qaeda hands (no such weapons were found). The Iraq war seemed motivated, as well, by undisclosed strategic goals of the United States in the Middle East, and did not fit convincingly into the long war template. This distinction was relied upon by President Obama in his campaign for the presidency and during his time in office to justify and seek a rapid exit from Iraq and, in contrast, an escalated presence in Afghanistan to meet the supposed threat to American security that was claimed to result from a Taliban victory followed by a presumed Al-Qaeda re-establishment of a base area in the country from which to conduct future transnational terrorist operations.

If Afghanistan is put to one side, as there exists a plausible basis for a military response based on a claim of self-defense arising from the imminence of the continuing threat, the overall American response to 9/11 completely disregarded the Charter and international law frameworks of restraint governing the use of force. President Bush announced an intention in the future to attack preemptively, even preventively (that is, without the claim or evidence of an imminent danger), and it even threatened states with force if they failed to join the counter-terrorist war, thereby denying sovereign states the international law option of neutrality, that is, the right of a state under customary international law to opt out of a war.

Even though there has been a change of presidency there is no substantial discontinuity in the assessment of the post-9/11 scope of permissible use of force, and certainly no abandonment of the logic and practice of the long war. Afghanistan in the present phase of this extended war is a counterinsurgency struggle with a preventive rationale – to prevent the return to power of the Taliban, with the presumed consequence of a renewed Al-Qaeda capacity to pose imminent threats of massive transnational terrorism. Such counterinsurgency modes of preemption and prevention rest on extremely conjectural factual assumptions about future threats and intentions, and represent a war fighting alternative to the threat diplomacy being relied upon, to date, to dissuade Iran from developing nuclear weapons. The essential difference is this: with deterrence there is an assumed shared rationality, while in relation to terrorism there is an assumed willingness of the adversary to engage in highly self-destructive undertakings, and therefore not being dissuadable by relying on even highly credible retaliatory threats.

(4) Countering nuclear proliferation

As mentioned in the introductory section, threat diplomacy has been relied upon by the United States and Israel as a means of discouraging Iran from acquiring nuclear weapons. Such an approach is indirectly explicated and rationalized in the important official document of the US government, *Nuclear Posture Review 2010* (NPR).[6] Preventing nuclear terrorism and proliferation of nuclear weapons are treated as the highest priorities in this post-Cold War and post-Bush formulation, which seeks to combine continuity of policy with a more visionary commitment to reduce, and ultimately eliminate nuclear weapons in accord with President Obama's Prague Speech of 2009.[7] The dangers associated with proliferation are explicitly associated with North Korea and Iran, countries accused of having violated "non-proliferation obligations, defied directives of the United Nations Security Council, pursued missile delivery systems, and resisted international efforts to resolve through diplomatic means the crises they have created." This policy document makes it evident that the main proliferation goal is "reversing the nuclear ambitions of North Korea and Iran." It proposes doing this by "[C]reating consequences for non-compliance ... states that violate their obligations must not be able to escape the consequences of their non-compliance by withdrawing from the NPT."

Such a doctrinal approach seems geopolitically driven rather than seeking a world order based on the rule of law. First of all, if freedom from proliferation were the priority, especially in the conflict zone that the Middle East has become, it would be impossible not to stress the problems (and untested opportunities) posed by Israel's undeclared status as a nuclear weapons state that has flown beneath the non-proliferation radar without arousing critical scrutiny by the self-appointed guardians of the non-proliferation regime. If proliferation were the priority, would it not make the effort far more persuasive if the emphasis was placed on making the entire region free from nuclear weapons rather than leaving Israel as the only state possessing nuclear weapons? Given Israel's history of belligerency in the region, as well as its military primacy in conventional warfare, would it not be reasonable for states in the Middle East to pursue their own policy of deterrence? The disingenuousness of the American current

---

[6] *Nuclear Posture Review Report*. US Department of Defense, 2010.
[7] Remarks by President Barack Obama. Hradcany Square, Prague, Czech Republic, April 5, 2009.

position is accentuated by its view that Iran has somehow forfeited its legal right to withdraw under Article 10 of the NPT that allows a party to withdraw "if it [the government] decides that extraordinary events . . . have jeopardized the supreme interests of its country." Despite the language of the treaty clearly allowing the government of a state to decide on its own whether to withdraw, the United States overrides this fundamental sovereign right by insisting on the primacy of its geopolitical assessment. In effect, double standards and a geopolitical approach to the implementation of the NPT produce inevitably a policy toward non-proliferation based on coercion and unlawful threats.

Such an inference is not merely a matter of speculation. As mentioned, the US government refuses to remove the military option from the diplomatic table, and it refrains from any criticism of Israel's frequent overt threats and moves toward launching an attack on Iranian military facilities and any mention of Israel's formidable arsenal of nuclear weapons. Furthermore, in the NPR the United States actually calls attention to its expansion of "negative security assurances" (that is, the commitment to refrain from using nuclear weapons against a non-nuclear state), but with a notable exception framed to expose Iran and North Korea to a conceivable nuclear attack: "The United States will not use or threaten to use nuclear weapons against non-nuclear states that are party to the NPT and in compliance with their nuclear non-proliferation obligations." Such a sentence when read together with the previously quoted warning to these states that non-compliance will have adverse consequences is the sort of scary threat that could encourage the acquisition of the weaponry as a deterrent. In the eyes of many, Iraq was invaded not because it had these weapons, but because it didn't possess them. Similarly, the more cautious approach to North Korea, unlike Iran, has generally refrained from relying on military threats precisely because it is believed that North Korea already possesses several nuclear warheads and their means of delivery, and could if provoked sufficiently, inflict catastrophic damage on its neighbors.

(5) Nuclear terrorism

President George W. Bush identified "the gravest danger" after 9/11 as lying "at the crossroads of radicalism and technology" enabling "even weak states and small groups" to acquire "a catastrophic power to strike great nations. . . . Our enemies have declared this very intention, and have been caught seeking these terrible weapons. They want the capability to blackmail us, or to harm us, or to harm our friends – and we will oppose them with all our power."[8]

This position has been endorsed on numerous occasions by President Obama, and most authoritatively set forth in the NPR in the following language: "The most immediate and extreme threat today is nuclear terrorism. Al-Qaeda and their extremist allies are seeking nuclear weapons. We must assume that they would use such weapons if they managed to obtain them." In this respect, the threat posed by nuclear terrorism combines concerns about transnational terrorism with those associated with proliferation to states presumed to be hostile. Manifestly, nuclear terrorism does pose a dire threat to humanity, but it does not resolve the problem of choosing the most appropriate response.

As suggested, to date the response has been to adhere to a non-proliferation approach (that is, a two-tier world) reinforced by increased coercive efforts to prevent proliferation to specified countries, with a threat of military attack kept as an option, not even excluding reliance on nuclear weapons. Is not this an embrace of a diplomacy of "blackmail" that former President Bush initiated but President Obama now has evidently codified? The Bush presidency had claimed a right of preemption and started the war against Iraq on this basis without even clearance from the UN Security Council or the presence of a threat from Iraq that could be credibly described as imminent. The Obama presidency avoids such doctrinal claims although its threats against Iran and its enlarged intervention in Afghanistan can be interpreted as equivalent to preemptive/preventive reliance on force or the threat of force in settings where the right of self-defense as set forth in the UN Charter does not provide a justification and where no UN mandate to use force for the sake of peace and security has been sought or given.

This critique of the response to nuclear terrorism proceeds on two levels: first, it presupposes the legitimacy and viability of a world order in which some political actors are authorized to retain and even use nuclear weapons while others are forbidden, and may be subject to aggressive uses of force if they seek to join the nuclear weapons club; the non-proliferation regime has always proceeded on the questionable assumption or geopolitical mind game that the primary danger to world order comes from the countries that seek the weapons rather than from those that possess them. And second, it chooses threat diplomacy and double standards as the means to

---

[8] George W. Bush, Graduation Speech, United States Military Academy, West Point, New York, 2002.

prevent nuclear terrorism rather than seeking to establish nuclear-free zones and nuclear disarmament that present seemingly feasible options and desirable alternatives.

CONCLUDING REMARKS

There is no doubt that the nature of the twenty-first-century security environment does push governments away from a willingness to rely solely on reactive forms of self-defense. In that respect, there is a greater international recognition of the reasonableness of relying on anticipatory initiatives, but there is also the realization that if this is left to the discretion of major states, the result would be to return the world to the pre-Charter domain of discretionary warfare that the 1928 Pact of Paris and the 1945 Nuremberg Judgment tried to counteract in dramatic fashion.

The United States as the self-described "preeminent" military power in the world has insisted so far on the unilateral and non-accountable authority to use military force as it deems necessary to uphold its security and those of its allies. The current reliance on threat diplomacy in dealing with Iran expresses this orientation clearly, as well as its disregard for UN procedures and international constraints on the use of force. Admittedly, if threats bring Iran to accept a diplomatic solution or bring it to the negotiating table, then it could be argued that threats served the cause of peace, as without such threats, there might well have been a military attack generating a range of serious negative consequences. Some doubt is thrown on whether this role of threats can be taken seriously in view of the American refusal to forego a fourth round of UN sanctions after Brazil and Turkey had succeeded in reaching a tentative agreement in 2010 by which Iran would allow most of its low enriched uranium to be enriched outside its territory, thereby minimizing risks of diversion to possible military uses. More recently, Israeli leaders have continued to threaten Iran with attack should it persist with its nuclear program, especially the enrichment of uranium, which certainly appears to constitute unlawful diplomacy about which the United States and the UN do nothing to counteract or condemn.

The argument here is that American reliance on coercive diplomacy and engagement in the long war has so far seemed both imprudent and dysfunctional. Better and more acceptable policy options exist. Part of the difficulty arises from the blind spot relating to Israel's possession of nuclear weapons, and the related spillover of Washington's one-sided and unconditional support of Israeli behavior. A further difficulty stems from the deeply entrenched nuclear weapons establishment in the United States, and in other nuclear weapons states, that makes the non-proliferation approach nullify efforts to achieve nuclear disarmament, which seems like the most reliable way to address the very genuine dangers posed by both the imperfections of deterrence and of nuclear terrorism. These constraints on the adoption of policies more in accord with international law, international morality, and regional/global peace and stability lead to an unacceptable and likely ineffectual dependence on threat diplomacy and military intervention as the primary modes of geopolitical management. Neither is likely to achieve desired results at acceptable costs, as developments relating to nuclear proliferation in relation to Iran and counter-terrorism with respect to Afghanistan both confirm.

CHAPTER 7

Preventive war and trials of aggression

Larry May

Aggression should count as a crime against peace when there are serious violations of human rights involved in non-self-defensive war, not merely when borders are crossed. This opens the door for seeing preventive war as a form of aggression. Indeed, for hundreds of years, preventive war has been seen as a form of aggressive war that may trigger justified response in terms of armed conflict. Today preventive war may also be seen as a form of aggression that could trigger trials of those who are responsible for the initiation of such wars. But before that happens, preventive war needs to be distinguished from preemptive and anticipatory wars. Quite a bit can be learned from the just-war tradition in this respect.

Practically, one question to ask is what should be the mechanism for deciding when a war is aggressive, especially in those hard cases of preventive war. In international law, this issue is called the question of the "trigger." Should a court make this determination or should a non-judicial body like the United Nations Security Council? And what criteria should be used to make such a determination as the first step in the prosecution of individual political and military leaders for the crime of aggression? This is an especially pressing issue in international criminal law as the International Criminal Court (ICC) has just been granted authority to begin prosecuting cases of the crime of aggression along with the other three crimes under the ICC's jurisdiction, namely, crimes against humanity, genocide, and war crimes. If aggression is to be prosecuted internationally, should preventive war be one of the forms of aggression that is so prosecuted?

One of the most difficult aspects of the question of the "trigger" concerns transitional justice. Once a determination is made that one state has engaged in aggressive war against another, and the aggressor state has been branded as a criminal state, the members of that state will find themselves the subject of hostility, and are likely to experience reciprocal hostility toward their accusers. Such a situation is likely to make reconciliation considerably harder. So, as we think about the triggering mechanism for establishing that a state is an aggressor we should do so apprehensive of the fact that the decision-maker needs to be as uncontroversial and unbiased as possible given the nearly inevitable reaction on the part of the state that has been determined to be an aggressor.

In this chapter I will examine the complex issues centering around the process used to determine whether or not a state is an aggressor. In the first section I examine some of the historical debates on the nature of aggressive war. In the second section I will review the contemporary debates in international law about aggression, especially about what counts as preventive war. In the third section, I will explain the current controversy about the "trigger" and indicate why this is of such pressing concern. I will examine the two most common proposals for an appropriate institution to make the "trigger" decision, a non-court such as the United Nations Security Council and an international court such as the International Criminal Court. In the fourth section I will explore the issue of determining aggression from the context of transitional justice, especially concerning the goal of reconciliation. And finally, I will draw some conclusions about the idea of state aggression in light of the problematic case of preventive war.

TRADITIONAL JUST-WAR ADHERENTS AND THE JUSTIFICATION OF PREVENTIVE WAR

Two of the leading figures at the end of the sixteenth and beginning of the seventeenth centuries in effect debated the issues I will address in this chapter.[1] Their views are often clearer and more cogent than those presented today, although often not presented with as much subtlety. Gentili and Grotius disagree about most things, beginning with whether it matters that one is engaging in a defensive or offensive war. Both agree that defensive wars can, and should, be seen as justified wars. But they clash over the justifiability of offensive wars, and their disagreement is insightful for debates today about how best to understand first strikes and last resorts as well as anticipatory self-defense and preventive war generally. In this first section I will deal with Gentili's arguments as well as the strikingly different arguments of Grotius.

Alberico Gentili wrote at the end of the sixteenth century. He was a trained lawyer who became one of the most prominent members of the

---

[1] For a good historical discussion of the views of those who came before and those who came after Gentili and Grotius, see Gregory M. Reichberg, "Preventive War in Classical Just War Theory," *Journal of the History of International Law* 9:1 (2007), 3–33.

faculty at Oxford University at his time. Gentili's views, as we will see, are quite non-standard, even as they seem to arise out of engagement with the just-war tradition. His views can best be seen, I believe, as embodying a kind of common-sense approach that clearly resonated with his students and readers. He was not the theoretician or historian that Grotius was, but his views have held up surprisingly well over the centuries and to my ear have a distinctly contemporary ring. Indeed, Gentili could have been one of the advisers in US President George W. Bush's cabinet when the decision was made to attack Iraq because of a fear that it had weapons of mass destruction that could be used against the United States.

Gentili said that wars can be divided into offensive and defensive ones. Defensive wars are waged for either self-defense or defense of others. And the best argument in support of defensive wars is derived from necessity, that is, "when one is driven to arms as a last resort."[2] But it also turns out, in Gentili's view, that even "an offensive war may be waged justly . . . there is always a defensive aspect, if they are just."[3] Gentili supports this claim by the following argument:

we have discoursed at length of the law pertaining to every kind of defense. . . . As a matter of fact, offensive warfare has the same motives, arising from necessity, expediency, or honor. Necessity, however, we understand in the sense that we cannot maintain our existence without making war. . . . A second variety of this necessary warfare will be found in the case of those who, because they have been driven from their own country or are compelled to leave it through some emergency and to seek another home, from necessity make war upon others. . . . the destruction of their cities has driven them into the lands of others.[4]

As we will see, Gentili goes on to argue that many forms of offensive war, not just those waged by exiles trying to support their own livelihood, can be justified. If offensive wars can be waged for necessity, then there is a sense in which offensive wars can be waged as a last resort and can be justified. This curious position requires explanation.

Concerning the case of exiles who must fight a war to preserve themselves from destruction, Gentili says:

Or do we think it right for men to have no pity for their kind, and allow nothing but death for these exiles, who have been driven from their fatherland? Yet care must be taken lest those wanderers grow discontented with the humble means which of course they can acquire for themselves without war.[5]

---

[2] Alberico Gentili, *De Jure Belli* (On the Law of War) (1598), trans. John C. Rolfe (Oxford: Clarendon Press, 1933), 15.
[3] Ibid., 30.   [4] Ibid., 79.   [5] Ibid., 80.

Underlying Gentili's general position here is the idea that people should not be forced to do what is opposed to their sense of honor and dignity. In a very curious passage, Gentili says:

> Suppose that someone desires to issue a scurrilous book against you, and that there are no available magistrates to whom you may appeal. I maintain that it is your right to protect yourself from insult by force of arms.[6]

Apparently, Gentili thinks that generally one should not have to flee rather than use violent force to defend what is valuable to you.

By taking the position that he does, Gentili disputes the age-old idea that those who strike first are prima facie in the wrong, even as he supports the idea that last resort is of key, although not of completely overriding, importance for determining when offensive war might be justified. Gentili maintains that "to kill in self-defense is just, even though the one who kills may flee without danger to himself"[7] for "every method of securing safety is honorable"[8] and that it is almost always dishonorable to be forced to flee rather than to stay and defend one's rights.[9] Indeed, Gentili defends the idea that wars can be fought in anticipation of "dangers already meditated and prepared" but not yet launched.[10]

Concerning this latter doctrine, Gentili is justly famous for providing two key analogies to explain why first strike as anticipatory defense is justifiable. First, he argues that:

> we ought not to wait for violence to be offered us, if it is safer to meet it half way ... one may at once strike at the root of the growing plant and check the attempts of the adversary who is meditating evil.[11]

And employing another metaphor he says:

> That is an excellent saying of Philo's, that we kill a snake as soon as we see one, even though it has not injured us and will perhaps not harm us. For thus we protect ourselves before it attacks us.[12]

These two powerful images, of stopping the growing plant before it is a major problem for us to weed out, and killing a snake that has not yet shown any signs of harming us but might eventually do so, play into deep seated intuitions of many people. Indeed, Gentili drives this point home when he says: "No one ought to expose himself to danger. No one ought to wait to be struck unless he is a fool."[13] It is only reasonable that precautions of various types be taken, "even though there is no great and

---

[6] Ibid., 84.   [7] Ibid., 58–59.   [8] Ibid., 59.   [9] Ibid., 83.   [10] Ibid., 66.   [11] Ibid., 61.
[12] Ibid.   [13] Ibid., 62.

clear cause for fear, and even if there really is no danger, but only a legitimate cause for fear."[14] Gentili adds further support by saying that it is also reasonable that "while your enemy is weak, slay him." And he then concludes this discussion by saying that "a defense is just which anticipates dangers that are already meditated and prepared, and also those which are not meditated, but are probable and possible."[15]

Gentili does his best to blur the line between regular self-defense and anticipatory self-defense by urging us to think about long-term issues, not merely the short term. He also tries to undermine the distinction between dangers that are impending and those that are probable or even only possible. In some ways, Gentili then sets the stage for the Bush doctrine of seeing war as a legitimate means of self-defense even if there is only little evidence that a danger is impending. Gentili accomplishes these tasks by relying on evocative and intuitively plausible examples. He thus makes significant inroads into the traditional doctrine of seeing first strike and last resort as the key factors to consider in determining if war was justifiably initiated.

Hugo Grotius wrote at the very beginning of the seventeenth century and is today considered to be the founder of international law. While not a trained lawyer, Grotius lectured extensively in law and religion, and held an important professorship at Leiden in the Netherlands. Like Gentili, Grotius also represented various states in international disputes, most famously defending the Dutch for seizing pirate ships that contained vast fortunes that had been stolen from other European countries, and not returning the stolen goods to those countries. His book, *De Jure Belli ac Pacis* is still one of the most often cited texts in all of international law, both in legal scholarship and court opinions.

With Gentili's arguments clearly in mind, Grotius argues that it is very difficult to justify offensive wars, even in anticipation, or fear, of attack. Grotius maintains that "those who accept fear of any sort as justifying anticipatory slaying are themselves greatly deceived."[16] For, as he says, "there are certain causes which present a false appearance of justice" and that "such a cause is the fear of something uncertain." Grotius develops an example here that is also quite telling:

Wherefore we can in no wise approve the view of those who declare that it is a just cause of war when a neighbor who is restrained by no agreement builds a fortress

---

[14] Ibid., 62–63.   [15] Ibid., 65.
[16] Hugo Grotius, *De Jure Belli ac Pacis* (On the Law of War and Peace) (1625), trans. Francis W. Kelsey (Oxford: Clarendon Press, 1925), 173.

on his own soil, or some other fortification which may some day cause us harm. Against the fears which arise from such actions we must resort to counter fortifications on our own land and other similar remedies, but not to force of arms.[17]

This example, perhaps not as powerful as those of Gentili, clearly seeks to counter the intuitive support that Gentili's own examples had received. Fear may justly motivate to do something but not necessarily justly motivate to go to war when less lethal means are available.

Another example that is directed specifically at first strikes, Grotius takes from Gellius, a second-century Roman author.

When a gladiator is equipped for fighting, the alternatives offered by combat are these, either to kill, if he shall have made the first decisive stroke, or to fall, if he shall have failed. But the life of men generally is not hedged about by a necessity so unfair and so relentless that you are obliged to strike the first blow, and may suffer if you shall have failed to be first to strike.[18]

Grotius then adds this gloss on our theme: "while it is permissible to kill him who is making ready to kill, yet the man is more worthy of praise who prefers to be killed rather than to kill."[19]

When Grotius talks of those who are most worthy of praise, he often engages in this discussion in terms of honor and virtue rather than in terms of the dictates of justice. Honor is a key component in war for Grotius because when soldiers do not act from honor they are nothing but simple killers. Acting in a severely restrained way, even as one does kill, makes one more than a simple killer who strikes for greed or hatred. Killing only in certain situations when one is required to do so raises the act of the soldier onto a higher plane for Grotius. Gentili also speaks of honor, but is primarily concerned with not shaming oneself by allowing oneself to be pushed into a corner. Grotius employs a broader notion of honor that is connected to the restraints of mercy that display one's true virtue.

At another point in his seminal work on the laws of war and peace, Grotius argues:

that the possibility of being attacked confers the right to attack is abhorrent to every principle of equity. Human life exists under such conditions that complete security is never guaranteed to us. For protection against uncertain fears we must rely on Divine Providence, and on a wariness free from reproach, not on force.[20]

---

[17] Ibid., 549.   [18] Ibid., 174.
[19] Ibid., 176. This passage should remind us that Grotius seems to adopt a non-standard form of pacifism that I have elsewhere called contingent pacifism.
[20] Ibid., 184.

Equity here is that gap-filler which gives us a fair and reasonable way to act when there do not seem to be rules that prevent violent conduct. Grotius then puts his position in stark contrast to that of Gentili when he says: "I maintain that he cannot lawfully be killed either if the danger can in any other way be avoided, or if it is not altogether certain that the danger cannot be otherwise avoided."[21] And Grotius provides us with the simple formula that is still the doctrine in international law today: "The danger, again, must be immediate and imminent in point of time."[22] To establish this condition, evidence of planning that is virtually completed needs to be shown.

One of the main reasons why Grotius argues against the position that Gentili had defended is that Grotius believes that it is too easy to speak of fear as a mere "pretext" for clearly unacceptable grounds for going to war.[23] Pretexts are the publicly declared reasons for going to war, but behind them lurk other reasons that are hidden and would be considered unjustifiable grounds for going to war if exposed to the public light of reason. Grotius argues that it is important not to confuse "the terms 'cause' and 'pretext'," for example, "the 'pretext' of the Second Punic War was the dispute over Saguntum, but the cause was the anger of the Carthaginians at the agreements that the Romans had extorted from them in times of adversity."[24] The difficulty of distinguishing "pretext" from "cause" makes Grotius much more cautious than Gentili, especially in respect to anticipatory attacks.

For example, some have said that the Iraq war of 2003 was started on a pretext, namely the fear of attack by Saddam Hussein's use of weapons of mass destruction, but that the hidden cause was merely to gain control over Iraq's extensive oil reserves by the United States.[25] We should think of the having, or apparently having, of long-range missiles that allow almost any state to say that another state presents a threat to it, as thereby undercutting any restraint on what would count as a just cause for anticipatory attack. Weapons of mass destruction (WMDs) ratchet up the concern about long-range missiles, since WMDs are as the name implies, meant to be even scarier than regular weapons launched from one state into another unsuspecting state.

One possible way to bring Gentili and Grotius together would be to have two different standards for the principle of first strike or priority. We could follow Grotius when we are asking when a state should be condemned and sanctioned for acts of aggression, and follow Gentili when we

---

[21] Ibid., 175.   [22] Ibid., 173.   [23] Ibid., 169.   [24] Ibid., 546.
[25] Seymour Hersch, among many others, has defended this view. See his series of articles in *The New Yorker*, as well as his book, *Chain of Command* (New York: HarperCollins, 2004).

are asking when the state aggression element of the crime of aggression is satisfied and individuals can be prosecuted and punished. The reason for such a bifurcation is that there are two quite different reasons to appeal to the first strike or priority principle, one having to do with states and another having to do with individuals. I would argue that we should be more cautious in the case of individuals than in the case of states.

THE PRIORITY PRINCIPLE IN INTERNATIONAL LAW

In contemporary politics and international law there is a debate about the very same issues that vexed Gentili and Grotius. In this section I wish to give the flavor of that debate. Let us begin this section by turning to Ian Brownlie, one of the most respected theorists of international law. He says:

In all probability the question which should be posed is not when is anticipatory action justified but, when has an attack occurred? This is a question which is not solved by reference to the "priority principle." . . . Thus if an unexplained force of warships or aircraft approached a state via the high seas and the superjacent airspace, this will constitute a threat to the peace but, it is submitted, does not itself justify forcible measures of self-defense since there is no resort to force by the putative aggressor and there is no unequivocal intention to attack.[26]

This is the standard "Grotian" approach taken by contemporary international law scholars, at least until quite recently.

The Grotian approach was to recognize that there is a right of self-defense for states, but to see such a right as severely limited by certain temporal and spatial considerations, that is, following Grotius' injunction that "the danger, again, must be immediate and imminent in point of time."[27] Yoram Dinstein talks of this principle as the "immediacy condition," which he finds articulated most recently in the International Court of Justice's Nicaragua case.

Immediacy signifies that there must not be an undue time-lag between the armed attack and the exercise of self-defense. However this condition is construed "broadly." Lapse of time is almost unavoidable when – in a desire to fulfill letter and spirit of the condition of necessity – a tedious process of diplomatic negotiations evolves, with a view to resolving the matter amicably.[28]

---

[26] Ian Brownlie, *International Law and the Use of Force by States* (Oxford: Clarendon Press, 1963), 367.
[27] Grotius, *De Jure Belli ac Pacis*, 173.
[28] Yoram Dinstein, *War, Aggression, and Self-Defense* (3rd edn., Cambridge University Press, 2001), 184.

Immediacy has to do with how close in time an attack *has occurred* in order for the state attacked to claim that it can engage in a reprisal war as a means of self-defense.

Imminence is responding to an attack that is seemingly *about to occur.* There is a lively debate in international legal circles about whether the doctrine of imminence countenances anticipatory self-defensive acts. Yoram Dinstein, like Brownlie, argues that threats of attack, even if imminent, only allow counter-threats not anticipatory attacks. But he does allow for a category he calls interceptive self-defense.

Interceptive, unlike anticipatory, self-defense takes place after the other side has committed itself to an armed attack in an ostensibly irrevocable way. Whereas a preventive strike anticipates an armed attack that is merely "foreseeable" (or even just "conceivable"), an interceptive strike counters an armed attack which is "imminent" and practically "unavoidable." It is the opinion of the present writer that interceptive, as distinct from anticipatory, self-defense is legitimate even under Article 51 of the Charter [of the United Nations].[29]

Dinstein joins the majority of contemporary international law scholars in thinking that imminence must be read very narrowly. The example that he gives is telling: if the United States had figured out that the Japanese carrier striking force was on its way to Pearl Harbor and the US Navy destroyed it while still en route, this would be justified as a form of interceptive rather than anticipatory self-defense. Notice that the United States would have to know that the Japanese had irrevocably begun their attack.

Another excellent example, written about by both Dinstein and Michael Walzer, is Israel's six-day war in 1967. Dinstein agrees that the first strike by Israel was justified as interception of Egypt's forces massing on the border, even as Dinstein recognizes that this case is somewhat different from the Pearl Harbor case.

True, no single Egyptian step, evaluated alone, may have qualified as an armed attack. But when all of the measures taken by Egypt (especially the peremptory ejection of the United Nations Emergency Force from the Gaza Strip and the Sinai Peninsula; the closure of the Straits of Tiran; the unprecedented build-up of Egyptian forces along Israel's borders; and constant saber-rattling statements about the impending fighting) were assessed in the aggregate it seemed to be

---

[29] Ibid., 172. The first part of Article 51 of the United Nations Charter says: "Nothing in the present Charter shall impair the inherent right of individual or collective self-defense if an armed attack occurs against a Member of the United Nations until the Security Council has taken measures necessary to maintain international peace and security."

crystal clear that Egypt was bent on an armed attack, and the sole question was not whether war would materialize but when.[30]

By contrast, in the hypothetical Pearl Harbor case, there was no question of when the attack would occur. Similarly, Walzer uses Israel's six-day war to illustrate what he calls "just fear" because the massing of Egypt's forces at Israel's border "served no other more limited goal."[31]

Walzer differs from Dinstein, though, in recognizing that his conclusion about the justifiability of Israel's six-day war requires a "major revision" of the just war doctrine, as it is understood today.

For it means that aggression can be made out not only in the absence of a military attack but in the (probable) absence of immediate intention to launch such an attack or invasion. The general formula must be something like this: states may use military force in the face of threats of war, whenever the failure to do so would seriously risk their territorial integrity or political independence.[32]

Walzer is thus not clearly still working within the Grotian tradition, perhaps moving closer to Gentili, although still keeping to the spirit of Grotius' concerns about limiting self-defense nonetheless.

Recently, a clearer shift away from the Grotian tradition occurred when the United States declared a new doctrine, largely in response to the September 11, 2001 terrorist attacks on its shores. Here is the key provision of the so-called "Bush doctrine":

Nations need not suffer an attack before they can lawfully take action to defend themselves against forces that present an imminent danger of attack.[33]

This statement might not have been all that different from Grotius' own view, especially given the reference to "imminence." But the Bush doctrine also includes a claim that "uncertainty and lack of evidence should not preclude preemptive action where a serious threat to America's security is deemed to exist."[34] With the addition of this dimension, the Bush doctrine looks much more like something that Gentili could have penned, allowing for preventive attacks, not merely those that were interceptive or even anticipatory.

The Bush doctrine is also clearly different from the Grotian tradition in that it calls for war to be used as an instrument of United States foreign

---

[30] Ibid., 173.   [31] Michael Walzer, *Just and Unjust Wars* (Boston: Basic Books, 1977), 84.
[32] Ibid., 85.   [33] National Security Council, The National Security of the United States (2002).
[34] Amy E. Eckert and Manooher Mofidi, "Doctrine or Doctrinaire – The First Strike Doctrine and Preemptive Self-Defense Under International Law," *Tulane Journal of International and Comparative Law* 12:1 (Spring 2004), 117–151;122.

policy. The Grotian tradition sees war as a last resort, not as a part of normal policy. War can only be justified, in the Grotian view, when diplomatic efforts have been extensively tried and come up wanting. So, regardless of how we understand the priority principle, the use of this principle will be at odds with the Bush doctrine and any other attempt to expand the domain of self-defense to include anticipatory or preventive attack.

THE CONTROVERSY OVER THE "TRIGGER"

The discussion about which institution should make the determination of whether or not a state has engaged in aggressive war has so far been largely political and practical. In this section I wish to expand the debate to include core normative and conceptual considerations as well. I will focus especially on concerns about fairness and authority. In the global arena, issues of authority come to the fore whenever the actions of a state are subjected to scrutiny from outside that state. Who has authority to make such determinations turns first on the question of how to understand authority in a context where there is no recognized institution that regularly assesses state behavior and issues binding declarations or norms. Authority can be initially understood as Hobbes first described it, namely, as a relationship between two people where one person has the right to speak for the other person and to bind the other person by these words.[35] Normally, in political matters a person has the right to speak for others because of an express or tacit grant by the person for whom he or she speaks. In the global arena, no state or other institution has the prima facie right to speak for, and bind, any other state. In many respects, the only authority comes from mutual consent on the part of states especially in the form of multilateral treaties.

The two most obvious institutions that would have a claim to some kind of authority to decide when a state is an aggressor are the United Nations or one of the international courts. In both cases, the initial source of authority comes from the large multilateral treaties that established these institutions. The United Nations is generally regarded to have the most authority over international matters of war and peace by virtue of its founding Charter ratified by nearly all states, and continuously reaffirmed by the behavior of states, even those that did not ratify the Charter, over the last sixty years. And a very large body of customary law has developed that confirms the authoritative status of the United Nations, especially the

---

[35] See Thomas Hobbes, *Leviathan* (1651), ed. Richard Tuck (Cambridge University Press, 1996), chapter 16.

Security Council. Of course, there is considerable debate about the extent of this authority and this is no more evident than in the determination of whether a state has engaged in aggression. But I will start with this solution to the most pressing part of the "trigger" issue since it is the least controversial in many respects.

The main advantage of having the United Nations make aggression determinations is that as it was originally established, the United Nations was to be the institution that put an end to aggressive war. The Preamble of the Charter of the United Nations says: "We the people of the United Nations [are] determined to save succeeding generations from the scourge of war." And one of the chief means of accomplishing this goal is "to ensure ... that armed force shall not be used, save in the common interest." And while the Preamble is meant to be hortatory rather than strictly binding on states, one quickly gets the idea that all that follows in the rest of the Charter is in service of the larger goal of greatly limiting if not eliminating altogether the use of armed force by one state against another. So, if the United Nations was set up to be the institution that put an end to aggressive war, there is strong plausibility to the view that if any institution has the authority to make determinations of which states act aggressively, it is the United Nations.

There is though still dispute about which part of the United Nations should make this determination of aggression. Here there are at least three strong contenders: the Security Council, the General Assembly, and the Secretary General. In each case there are serious drawbacks and hence there is collectively a problem with having the United Nations be the forum for decisions about the trigger. The Security Council is unrepresentative of the states that have ratified the Charter, and this has been a constant source of criticism of the Security Council since its inception. The General Assembly, while representative of the states of the world, since each state gets a vote, gives much greater representation to smaller and less wealthy states than those states that contain the bulk of the world's population or the bulk of the world's wealth. The Secretary General of the UN is perhaps the best bet, since he or she is put into office by the concurrence of both large and small states. But, over the last fifty years many of the Secretaries General have not been held in very high esteem, and the making of decisions about aggression would not necessarily be seen as having the weight of authority of the United Nations because as just one person, typically selected as a compromise between competing factions, he or she may not be thought to be completely trustworthy for such momentous decisions.

There is a very serious question, though, about whether any proposed test for what constitutes state aggression should be administered by a court or by some more explicitly political body. One strategy is to take out of the hands of the Prosecutor of the International Criminal Court any case concerning the crime of aggression that has not been referred by the Security Council of the United Nations. Article 13 of the Rome Statute lists three ways that a case can come to the Court: (a) referral from a state party, (b) referral from the Security Council, and (c) direct initiation from the Prosecutor of the ICC. It might make sense to restrict jurisdiction of the Court concerning crimes of aggression only to (b) as a way of shielding the Court from getting involved in making decisions that will be at least seen as highly political.

The drawback is that the Court is then, at least concerning this matter, subordinate to the Security Council, not independent of it. And given the history of the Security Council, there are very good reasons to think that it will become embroiled in political controversy about whether a member state has engaged in aggression. Indeed, even in otherwise clear-cut cases, it may be that a state that has a veto on the Security Council will stop a referral to the ICC. The Security Council is not like normal legislatures since it gives more power, many would say too much power, to certain states that may have vested interests in blocking prosecutions that come from certain parts of the world where those states also reside.

My view is that it will be better, although far from problem-free, mostly to let the ICC decide whether state aggression has occurred rather than to let the Security Council make this determination. The ICC will be somewhat tainted by making these political decisions, but at least it will retain its independence from the Security Council, which would be likely either not to issue many referrals or to issue them for the wrong reasons. Independent judges are, in my view, better able to make these often highly politically charged decisions than is the Security Council. Of course, if there were major changes to the Security Council in the future, or if a true international legislature were to arise that had the power of referral, I might change this assessment.

PROBLEMS OF TRANSITIONAL JUSTICE

One of the neglected issues concerning preventive war is the effect that this doctrine has on *jus post bellum* considerations. Reconciliation is made much harder after a preventive war because of the fact that such a war is not clearly defensive. And on different grounds, when there is a trial of the leaders who brought on a preventive war there is even more difficulty in reaching reconciliation after war's end. These trials, when they take place, will highlight differences in how various states see their responsibility to their people. If it is determined by an international body that aggression has occurred, even though it appears to the people of a given state that it was justified as prevention, anger and animosity will be fueled rather than dampened.

Jus post bellum principles are different from *jus ad bellum* principles. Justice may demand that wars be condemned and even that those who lead a state to war also be prosecuted. But in *jus post bellum* terms, such condemnations may not be what justice requires. Indeed, there is a conflict between two quite disparate goals, or branches, of justice. We might characterize this difference as one between the justice of retribution versus the justice of peace, where the latter is forward rather than backward looking and calls for measures that will bring people together rather than merely placate those who feel, and actually are entitled to feel, aggrieved. *Jus post bellum* principles urge that retribution be softened so that a lasting peace can be formed after war's end. Trials for the leaders of a state that pursued a preventive war will often exacerbate rather than soften the animosity that people feel at the end of a war.

I have previously defended the view that one of the main *jus post bellum* principles is:

It is a universal human obligation to engage in actions to support a "just" peace, where minimally this involves reasonable compensation to individuals for rights violations.[36]

As I pointed out, it is not always possible to provide compensation commensurate with the rights violations. Aggressive war is one such occasion. But this does not mean that trials for aggression are unproblematic especially in light of their effects on the maintenance and continuation of a just peace. The justice of peace is a serious matter that is at least as important as retributive justice. Even if a war is waged that is clearly aggressive, it may be that the justice of peace tells against prosecuting a political or military leader for initiating that aggressive war.

So, there are several competing considerations concerning trials for aggression after a preventive war. On the one hand, there are considerations of deterrence and retribution. These are the standard considerations in favor of holding trials in the aftermath of crimes, especially mass crimes.

---

[36] See Larry May, *After War Ends: A Philosophical Perspective* (Cambridge University Press, 2012).

On the other hand, there are considerations of reconciliation and of fairness. Here are considerations that are often not in play when one is discussing garden-variety trials, but that come into play when we are discussing international trials for the waging of aggressive war. In the remainder of this section I will explore these considerations in more detail and indicate a partial adjudication among these considerations in the end.

So, on the one hand we should think of deterrence. Given the worries expressed in earlier parts of the chapter about the waging of preventive war, one of the main reasons to have trials of the leaders of such wars is to deter future leaders from following in their footsteps. While preventive war may sometimes be justified, it is generally so problematic morally that political and military leaders should be discouraged from waging this type of war. There are some who think that international trials do not clearly have deterrent effects.[37] But this is clearly the minority view, and in any event there haven't been enough international trials to draw firm conclusions about their deterrent effects.[38]

And in addition, retribution is the most commonly cited reason for holding international trials for leaders who wage aggressive, including preventive, war. The Nuremberg model was to prosecute the Nazi leadership for waging aggressive war against Germany's neighbors. Especially in the majority of cases where preventive war is unjustified as being aggressive, wrongs have been done and those who are most responsible for these wrongs should be held responsible. Retributive responsibility and punishment are meted out against individuals, and the political and military leaders of a state that commits aggression by waging a preventive war are those who are most liable for such punishment.

On the other hand, considerations of reconciliation weigh heavily against conducting trials in the aftermath of preventive wars. Reconciliation is the cornerstone of *jus post bellum*. When war comes to an end, what people most seek is to achieve peace, as long as the peace is a just peace. And achieving a just peace requires that hostilities between and among people in the war-torn society must come to an end.[39] Trials, though, often have the effect of increasing rather than decreasing hostilities between previously warring factions in a society. The adversarial nature of

---

[37] See Mark Drumbl, *Punishment, Atrocity, and International Criminal Law* (New York: Cambridge University Press, 2007).

[38] See my response to Drumbl in the final chapter of my book, Larry May, *Aggression and Crimes Against Peace* (Cambridge University Press, 2008).

[39] See Erin Daly and Jeremy Sarkin, *Reconciliation in Divided Societies: Finding Common Ground* (Philadelphia: University of Pennsylvania Press, 2007).

at least Anglo-American criminal trials intensifies the sense that one party is in the wrong and the other party in the right, with very little room in the middle for accommodation. Given such considerations, trials are difficult, although not impossible, to hold in the midst of attempts at reconciliation.

Finally, fairness considerations loom large in prosecuting state leaders for initiating or waging preventive war. Preventive war is generally something that is engaged in for all of the best reasons and motives, calling into question the fairness of prosecuting these well-meaning political and military leaders. It is very rare that an individual, even a political or military leader of a state, should be prosecuted for initiating and waging preventive wars regardless of the fact that at least some of these wars could be characterized as aggressive. We should only prosecute individuals for clear-cut cases of aggressive war, and from what we have seen in this chapter, preventive war is anything but clear-cut. While we might want to condemn and even sanction states for waging preventive wars, it is rarely justified to prosecute even the state's top leaders for any form of the crime of aggression.

CONCLUSION

In contemporary international criminal law there are at least three elements of the crime of aggression. First, the prosecution must show that there is state aggression. This is often highly contentious, especially when considering wars waged for preventive reasons. State aggression is an element of the crime of aggression where that means that in order to convict an individual for the crime of participating in an aggressive war one must first prove that the war in question was indeed a war that a state was waging aggressively. This is why the "trigger" issue is so important. Second, there is the matter of *actus reus*, and normally this means that one had a fairly high level of participation in the waging of a war of aggression. Third, one must also prove that the individual in question had *mens rea*, that is, that he or she intended to participate in a war of aggression. And while any individual human person could be prosecuted for such a crime, the ICC has made it clear that only state leaders will be so prosecuted, if anyone is.

One of the main reasons to think that prosecutions even for state leaders for waging preventive war are not likely to be successful comes from considerations of *mens rea*. For most wars this is the stumbling block for individual prosecutions in any event. State leaders are often doing what they think is in the best interest of their country, or are doing their patriotic duty, or merely following orders by those who are even higher up the chain of command. These intentions and motives make it hard to show that state leaders had a guilty mind when they participated in initiating or waging aggressive war. And this is especially true since it is often hard for state leaders to figure out whether a given war is indeed a war of aggression, and hence difficult to tell whether these leaders meant to be participating in an aggressive war.

The general idea behind *jus post bellum* normative principles is that an international system of justice has at least two components: the promotion of human rights, that is, the rights of those who are members of the world community, and the fairness and non-arbitrariness that comes from rule by law rather than by the whim of "men." In moving toward an international system of justice, one of these components should not be sacrificed for the other. We may countenance some loss in one for some gain in the other, but we should prefer solutions that do not diminish either.

In *jus post bellum* situations, care must be taken so that criminal trials in the aftermath of war preserve rather than retard the general protection of human rights in the global society. Force may be used to bring leaders to justice for crimes committed during war when human rights are not risked and when such trials promote the rule of law.[40]

---

[40] This paper incorporates, and expands, ideas originally presented in various chapters of my book *Aggression and Crimes Against Peace*.

PART III

Critiques of preventive war

CHAPTER 8

The conditions of liability to preventive attack
Jeff McMahan

The objection to preventive war that is perhaps the most compelling is also, unsurprisingly, the most common. It is that to the extent that the prevention of future aggression is accepted as a just cause for war, the constraint against the initiation of war will be correspondingly eroded. For the claim that another state will, unless prevented, engage in aggression at some point in the future can be cynically exploited as a pretext or public rationale for virtually any unjust war of aggression. To the extent that states would avail themselves of this pretext for the resort to war, they would also become more fearful of becoming the target of an allegedly preventive war. Given the strategic advantages of striking first, each state in an adversarial relation with another would then have an increased incentive to strike first just to avoid being the victim of a first strike.[1] Wars for which the public justification is that they are preventive thus tend to decrease security everywhere.

The reason this objection is so compelling is that it suggests that the acceptance of a doctrine of preventive war could have dreadful consequences, particularly in areas plagued by settled animosities, such as those between India and Pakistan, North and South Korea, and Israel and most or all of its neighbors. This objection, in other words, gives us reasons, as individuals, to *fear* any tendency to recognize preventive war as a form of just war.

In this essay, I will focus on a different concern about preventive war, one that is less a matter of prudence, or practical concern, and more a matter of moral principle. It is a concern that I have explored in two previous essays, so my aim here will be to try to take the discussion deeper

---

[1] See David Luban, "Preventive War," *Philosophy and Public Affairs* 32:3 (2004), 207–248. The logic of this objection to preventive war parallels that of the main objection in the literature on nuclear strategy to the development of a "counterforce capability."

than I was able to in that earlier work.[2] The question I will address is this: if preventive war can be justified at all, what *form* might the justification take? Because preventive war, like other forms of war, involves intentionally killing people, a moral justification for preventive war must be a moral justification for intentionally killing people. While there is, I will suggest, a form of justification that explains the permissibility of killing in at least some wars of national self-defense against an actual attack, there are reasons to doubt whether this form of justification can be applied to preventive wars.

There are at least four possible forms of justification for intentionally killing a person. Retributivists believe that it can be permissible – or, as Kant thought, morally required – to kill a person who *deserves* to be killed. If a person deserves to be killed, assuming that is possible, he must have acted in a way that not only stripped him of his right not to be killed but also gave others, though perhaps only those with proper authority, a moral reason to kill him that is not instrumental in character. That is, the reason is not that the killing is a means to a further end. According to one interpretation, what this means is that, while the killing is bad *for* the person who deserves it, it is nevertheless intrinsically or impersonally good.

Another possible justification for killing a person is that the person has freely consented to be killed, or waived her right not to be killed. Normally, a person's free and informed consent to be killed is on its own insufficient for the permissibility of killing her. There must also be an independent and substantial reason to kill her. The most common such reason is that it would be objectively better for her to die than to continue to live. Thus many people, myself included, believe that it can be permissible to kill a person if it would be bad *for her* to continue to live *and* if she freely consents (or better yet, forcefully pleads) to be killed.

I will assume that no extended defense is necessary for the claim that preventive war cannot be justified on the ground that those who are its targets either deserve to be killed or have consented to be killed. Because preventive war is not, by hypothesis, a response to a wrongful harm that has been inflicted but is instead based on the anticipation of future harms, it verges on incoherence to suppose that it could be justified as a form of retribution. And even if, as some have argued, combatants consent to

[2] Jeff McMahan, "Preventive War and the Killing of the Innocent," in Richard Sorabji and David Rodin and, eds., *The Ethics of War: Shared Problems in Different Traditions* (Aldershot: Ashgate Publishing, 2006), 169–190; and "Comment," in Michael Doyle, *Striking First: Preemption and Prevention in International Conflict*, ed. Stephen Macedo (Princeton University Press, 2008), 129–147.

become legitimate targets once war has begun, no one, to my knowledge, has argued that when people adopt the role of a soldier, they thereby consent to become legitimate targets of attack when no war is in progress and they threaten no one but are instead engaged in peacetime activities on their home bases.[3]

The two other forms of justification are more promising. One of these provides what I think is the best explanation of the permissibility of killing in self-defense and in defense of others. When people act in certain ways, they can lose their right not to be attacked if attacking them is instrumentally necessary to achieve a certain end and the attack is proportionate in relation to that end. When this is true, these people are, as I will say, *liable* to be attacked. Because they lack a right not to be attacked in certain ways and for certain reasons, they have no justified complaint and are not wronged if they are attacked in such a way. If, for example, a person culpably poses a serious threat to another's life, he thereby makes himself liable to be killed if that is a necessary and proportionate means of averting the threat. Although desert of harm and liability to be harmed both entail the loss of one's right not to be harmed, a liability-based justification for the infliction of harm requires that the infliction of the harm be an effective means (or, in some cases, an unavoidable side effect) of the achievement of an end. By contrast, the infliction of deserved harm is, arguably, an end in itself. Traditional just-war theory can be understood as offering a liability-based justification for intentional killing in war: all combatants are liable to attack because they pose a threat to the lives or basic liberties of others and attacking them is necessary to avert the threat and proportionate in relation to the seriousness of the threat.

Traditional just-war theory offers quite a different justification for at least some of the *unintended* killing of people who are not liable to attack that inevitably occurs in war. Non-combatants are, on the traditional view, not liable to attack because they are not active participants in the war and thus do not pose a threat to their state's adversaries. Yet they are often foreseeably harmed or killed as a side effect of attacks on military targets. Just-war theory must have a justification for this, for if it is never permissible to harm or kill non-combatants in this way, the correct theory of the morality of war is contingent pacifism, not the theory of the just war. The

---

[3] Among those who have argued that combatants consent to be legitimate targets of attack in war are Thomas Hurka, "Liability and Just Cause," *Ethics and International Affairs* 21:2 (2007), 199–218, and Yitzhak Benbaji, "A Defense of the Traditional War Convention," *Ethics* 118:3 (2008), 464–495. If either of their arguments is to support traditional just-war theory, it must, it seems, assert that soldiers consent to be targets of a surprise attack that initiates a preventive war or a war of aggression.

justification that just-war theory offers is one of *necessity*. The killing of non-liable people as a side effect can be justified as necessary for the prevention of a greater evil, usually the killing of a greater number of non-liable people by one's adversary. That a necessity justification presupposes that the number of non-liable people who are prevented from being killed must exceed the number who are killed reflects an underlying moral asymmetry between killing and letting die.

A person who neither deserves nor is liable to be attacked or killed retains his right not to be attacked or killed. If the killing of such a person can nevertheless be justified on grounds of necessity, we say that his rights are overridden, or that they are justifiably infringed in the service of averting a greater evil. When the justification for attacking or killing a person is one of necessity, the person attacked or killed is *wronged*, albeit justifiably, and is entitled to compensation for what has been done to him (though that is of course difficult, though not necessarily impossible, if he is dead).

A justification of necessity is a weaker form of justification than a liability-based justification. Suppose that the lives of certain people are threatened by other people who are, because of the threat they pose, liable to be killed in defense of their potential victims. It may be permissible to kill these latter people on grounds of liability even if they significantly outnumber their potential victims. But suppose, alternatively, that the only way to prevent the original people from being killed will not kill any of the threatening people who are liable to be killed but will kill as a side effect some other people who are not liable. If this act is to be justified on grounds of necessity, those saved must, as I noted, outnumber those who would be killed. Justifications of necessity are, moreover, sensitive to the intentions with which agents act. If, for example, the only way to prevent the original people from being killed is to kill some non-liable people *as an intended means*, those saved must *substantially* outnumber those killed.

Defensive war can normally have a liability-based justification. According to traditional just-war theory, those who initiate a war pose a threat to others, thereby making themselves liable to defensive counterattack. Yet the theory of the morality of war that has most explicitly defended a liability-based account of permissible killing in war is a revisionist account according to which the basis of liability to attack in war is responsibility for a threat of wrongful harm that is serious enough to make a violent, potentially lethal attack a proportionate response. On this view, those who initiate an unjust war of aggression are responsible for a serious threat of wrongful harm and thus make themselves liable to defensive attack. This is, however, not true in the case of all defensive wars. Those who initiate a *just* war – for example, a war of humanitarian intervention – do not pose a threat of *wrongful* harm, at least not to those whom they intentionally attack, who have made themselves liable to attack. The initiators of the just war may, of course, pose a threat of wrongful harm *as a side effect*, but if they have a necessity justification for this, that seems sufficient to exempt them from liability to defensive attack.[4]

But while both the traditional and revisionist accounts of the just war can thus give a liability-based justification for most defensive wars, it is less clear that either can give such a justification for preventive war. The reason for doubting whether this form of justification is available for preventive war seems obvious. Preventive war is not a response to an attack that has occurred, is occurring, or has been initiated even if no military engagement has yet occurred. It aims instead to prevent a threat from arising in the future. Yet liability derives from what a person has done or is doing; therefore there seems to be no basis for liability to preventive attack.

If there is no liability-based moral justification for preventive war, it seems that the only possible justification is a necessity justification. But preventive war involves intentional killing and for there to be a necessity justification for the intentional killing of people who are not liable, the harm that would be averted must substantially exceed that caused by the killing itself. Given that the harms that might be averted by preventive war are speculative, they must be discounted for uncertainty when weighed against the virtually certain harms that would be inflicted by preventive war. But only harms that would be near-apocalyptic in magnitude would, even after being discounted for uncertainty, *substantially* outweigh the extensive and certain harms that would be caused by a preventive war. If, therefore, preventive war requires a necessity justification, it seems likely that preventive war will in practice be seldom if ever justified.

The problem in trying to find a liability-based justification for preventive war is not that no one can be liable now to defensive action against a threat that he *will* otherwise pose later. For often those who will, unless prevented, pose a threat in the future have even now acted in ways, such as planning and preparing for a future wrongful attack, that make them liable to preventive action now. Even the mere formation of an intention to kill a person next week, or when the opportunity arises, can make a person liable to be killed. For the formation of that intention alters the objective

---

[4] See Jeff McMahan, *Killing in War* (Oxford: Clarendon Press, 2009), 41–44; and Jeff McMahan, "Self-Defense Against Justified Threateners," in Helen Frowe and Gerald Lang, eds., *How We Fight: Issues in Jus in Bello* (Oxford University Press, forthcoming).

probabilities. It significantly increases the potential victim's objective risk of being killed. If the intended killing would be wrong and the only way to prevent it is to kill the potential murderer *now*, that person is liable to be killed and would not be wronged by being killed. Subjective and objective conditions sufficient for liability are both present: a blameworthy intention and an increase in the objective probability of a person's being wrongly killed. One might argue that killing the potential murderer in advance of his actually acting on the intention he has formed would be to fail to respect him as an autonomous person by denying him the opportunity to change his mind. But it is highly doubtful that an innocent person ought to bear a significantly increased risk of being murdered in order to enable a person who wrongfully intends to commit a murder to have the chance to abandon his intention. By forming that intention, the potential murderer has wrongfully created a situation in which, by hypothesis, either he must be killed or his potential victim must be exposed to a high risk of being murdered. Justice requires that the one who is morally responsible for this situation bear the cost.

The same is true even when a potential murderer has not formed an intention to kill but is seriously considering whether to murder someone. Even to deliberate about whether to commit a murder is blameworthy and increases the objective risk that the potential victim will be murdered. Suppose that before the potential murderer conceived the idea, the objective probability that the potential victim would be murdered was near zero. But while the potential murderer deliberates, the objective probability rises to 10 percent. If the *only* opportunity for intervention is *now*, why should a wholly innocent person have to bear a 10 percent risk of being murdered in order that the person who has wrongfully created that risk should be spared?

In practice, of course, these reflections are idle, since an intention alone without any external manifestation cannot be detected and even if somehow the intention becomes known, there are usually ways, which I excluded in the example by mere stipulation, of preventing a future murder other than killing the potential murderer well in advance. The point is only that it is in principle possible for a person to be liable to attack now to prevent him from doing that he would otherwise do only much later.

This may not, however, provide a secure foundation for a liability-based justification for preventive war. For those who are culpably responsible in advance for an increased risk of future aggression are the political leaders who conceive of, deliberate about, intend, and plan and prepare for such a war. For a variety of reasons, such people generally are not and cannot be the targets of preventive war. The targets must instead be those who would later carry out the orders from the political leaders to fight a war of aggression – namely, soldiers who at the time are engaged in peacetime activities and may be entirely unaware of the intentions of their leaders.

Many proponents of traditional just-war theory can be expected to resist the suggestion that the theory can offer only a necessity justification for preventive war and thus effectively rules out the prevention of future aggression as a just cause for war. They can point out that the traditional theory makes the principles of *jus in bello* wholly independent of the principles of *jus ad bellum*, so that what it is permissible for combatants to do in war is independent of whether the war itself is just or unjust. But if this is so, it seems that the theory implies that unjust combatants do no wrong merely by fighting, even in an unjust war of aggression, provided they confine their attacks to military targets, do not mistreat prisoners of war, ensure that their attacks are proportionate to their military objectives, and do not exceed the degree of force necessary to achieve those objectives. This is true, these theorists might point out, even when unjust combatants initiate an unjust war of aggression with a surprise attack against unmobi-lized soldiers on their bases. For a military base is a military target. If unjust combatants do no wrong in attacking a military base during the course of a war, they also do no wrong if they initiate a war with such an attack. No traditional just-war theorist has, to my knowledge, held that *individual combatants* are guilty of wrongdoing if they initiate a war with a surprise attack on unmobilized soldiers, though all of course claim that the political leaders who order a surprise attack to initiate an unjust war of aggression are guilty of a heinous moral wrong. No one, in other words, suggests that a surprise attack that initiates a war is the sole exception to the independ-ence of *jus in bello* from *jus ad bellum* – the sole instance in which an attack that harms only soldiers who have been neither injured nor captured constitutes a moral wrong or, morally speaking, a war crime.

It therefore seems that traditional just-war theory should be able to find a justification for at least some instances of preventive war that is not a necessity justification. For if it can be permissible for combatants to attack unmobilized soldiers in initiating an unjust war of aggression, surely it can also be permissible for them to attack unmobilized soldiers as the first act of a preventive war that may actually prevent unjust aggression in the future. Yet the assumption that it is open to traditional just-war theorists to advance this argument is an indication not so much of the range of the traditional theory's resources as it is of the theory's possible incoherence. For it is doubtful that the theory can consistently concede that it is morally permissible for combatants to initiate an unjust war – or indeed a just war – by conducting a surprise attack on unmobilized soldiers.

Recall that I noted earlier that traditional just-war theory asserts that all combatants are legitimate targets in war because they are liable to defensive attack, and they are liable because they actively pose a threat to others. This idea is presupposed by the pervasive use of "innocent" to refer to those who are *not* legitimate targets, together with the explicit identification, in many documents in the just-war tradition written after the early "classical" period, of the *innocent* with those who are *unthreatening* – an identification licensed by the etymology of the term. But if liability is a function of posing a threat and unmobilized soldiers on their home bases pose no threat, they cannot be liable to attack even if they are "military" and thus constitute a military target.[5]

Traditional just-war theory therefore faces a dilemma. Either unmobilized soldiers are liable to attack and thus are legitimate targets or they are not. If combatants are legitimate targets in war only because they pose a threat to others, and if unmobilized soldiers in peacetime do not pose a threat to others and are thus not combatants in the relevant sense, then unmobilized soldiers are not legitimate targets. There is much to be said for this claim. Unmobilized soldiers in peacetime would seem to be *hors de combat* in the relevant sense, for there is no combat in which they are participants. But in that case, individual combatants act wrongly if they participate in the initiation of either an aggressive war or, in the absence of a necessity justification, a preventive war that requires an attack on unmobilized soldiers. While it may seem plausible to suppose that it is wrong to participate in an attack that initiates an unjust war of aggression, this supposition is incompatible with the traditional theory's claim that it is not impermissible to fight in an unjust war provided one fights in accordance with the rules. If just-war theory were to concede that it can be wrong to participate in an attack against unmobilized soldiers that initiates an unjust war, that would, as I noted above, be tantamount to its accepting that there is one exception to the independence of *jus in bello* from *jus ad bellum*.

If, by contrast, unmobilized soldiers engaged in unthreatening activities on their bases in peacetime are nevertheless legitimate targets of attack, just-war theory cannot continue to claim that the sole basis of liability to

---

[5] I pressed this challenge some years ago in McMahan, "Innocence, Self-Defense, and Killing in War," *Journal of Political Philosophy* 2:3 (1994), 193–221; 196–198, but to my knowledge it has never been discussed in the just-war literature.

attack is posing a threat to others. "Innocent" cannot mean "unthreatening," and the categories "innocent" and "noncombatant" cannot be assumed to coincide. If people can be liable to attack in war for reasons other than that they pose a threat, it may then be possible to justify preventive war without appealing to a necessity justification. But if traditional just-war theorists wish to adopt this option while retaining the essential elements of their view, they must identify a criterion of liability to attack that implies that while unmobilized soldiers and combatants in war are both legitimate targets, non-combatants are not.

Since just-war theory has tended to assert that combatants act permissibly if they confine their attacks to military targets, the obvious candidate for the criterion of liability to attack in war is membership in the military. But that has the implausible implication that if one were to go onto a military base in peacetime and attack someone in uniform, one would not have wronged that person, who would have no justified complaint about what one had done. Perhaps the appropriate response to this is to claim that the liability of military personnel is not liability to attack *by anyone* but liability to attack only by enemy combatants. But this is still not right, since it implies that if a soldier of one state, acting on orders, were to go onto a military base in another state during peacetime and attack someone in uniform, the person attacked would not be wronged. To avoid this counter-example, the alternative criterion of liability needs to be qualified so that it applies only in wartime, or while war is in progress. This yields an understanding of liability that should satisfy the demands of traditional just-war theory – namely, that a person who is a member of the military is liable to attack by enemy combatants acting under orders during wartime.

There are, however, various objections to this account of liability to attack. They can be divided into two broad challenges: (1) that the account implies that much that is morally significant depends on whether the act occurs *during wartime*, and (2) that the account makes liability a matter of membership rather than action. I will consider these objections in turn.

If membership in the military makes a person liable to attack only when his state is *at war*, then in order to know whether a person is liable to attack at a particular time, one must have a criterion for determining whether a conflict is a *war* or some lesser form of conflict, as well as a criterion for determining precisely when wars begin and when they end. It may seem obvious that if unmobilized soldiers on their base are killed in a surprise attack by combatants of a state with which their state has not been at war, they cannot have been liable to attack. For they were attacked when their state was not at war – that is, at a time when no war was in progress.

Yet the just-war theorist who wishes to argue that preventive war can be justified without an appeal to necessity might claim that the surprise attack itself constitutes the first act in a war, so that the unmobilized soldiers were in fact killed *in war*, though admittedly very early in the war, and so were liable to attack.

There are at least two strong objections to this suggestion. First, it presupposes that the political leaders on the side that initiates a war have remarkable powers of moral alchemy. By declaring that the surprise attack is an act of *war*, they seem to be able to strip unmobilized soldiers of their right against enemy soldiers not to attack them, making them liable to attack without their having done anything to change their moral status. Suppose, for example, that the leaders and their agents who launched the attack were spectacularly obtuse and intended it not as an act of war but only as a test of their missiles. In that case, the soldiers killed might not have been liable, since they would have been killed as a side effect of a missile test rather than in a war. Of course, the leaders of the state whose soldiers were the victims of the attack might not care what the other leaders' intentions were. They might go to war in retaliation even if they accept that the other leaders simply acted callously without intending to start a war. Or they might not. This is the second objection: that whether or not the surprise attack is the opening act of a war may depend on how the state that is the victim of the attack decides to respond. Suppose that the state that has been attacked refrains from retaliating and instead pursues diplomatic activity that is later rightly credited with having averted a war. In that case the surprise attack was not an act in a war but an attack that might have but did not precipitate a war, so that the victims of the attack were not liable according to the criterion of liability that seemed so promising for traditional just-war theory. That criterion thus implies that the victims of a surprise attack also have powers of moral alchemy: they can determine, by their response to an attack, whether those killed were liable to be killed or whether, instead, the killings were murders.

The second broad objection to the claim that members of the military are liable to attack only by enemy combatants and only in war is that it is ad hoc and devoid of moral significance. Although it is a mistake to suppose that posing a threat to others is a sufficient condition of liability to attack, one can at least see how that criterion has prima facie moral significance. But what is the significance of membership in the military in a time of war, given that many members of the military pose no threat in war and bear no responsibility for the acts of their fellow members who do? This criterion makes liability a matter of membership rather than of action.

Or perhaps the claim that members of the military are legitimate targets for opposing combatants in war is not a claim about liability at all. It might be more plausibly regarded as a claim about the instrumental value of identifying certain sharply defined categories ("soldier" and "civilian") that are widely *perceived* to have moral significance, and assigning the members of the different categories different moral, conventional, or legal statuses. This is in fact one way in which certain prominent just-war theorists have sought to defend the claim that all soldiers in war are liable to attack (though they sometimes run this instrumental justification in tandem with the claim that soldiers are legitimate targets because they threaten people they have been trained to harm).[6] This is a form of justification for killing people – that it is morally permissible to kill certain people if it would be better for people generally if they were to agree to act on the assumption that it is permissible to kill these people – that I will not consider here, other than by making two points: first, that it is a form of justification I do not accept, in part because it makes our moral status contingent on extrinsic circumstances, and, second, because even if it were true, I doubt that it would support the idea that all soldiers, but no civilians, are legitimate targets in war. But these are topics too large to be addressed here.

The conclusion I draw from this discussion of the traditional theory of the just war is that it seems unlikely that that theory has the resources to support a liability-based justification for preventive war, at least when preventive war would involve attacks on unmobilized soldiers, who have not been involved in the planning and preparation for the aggression that the war would be intended to prevent. Traditional just-war theory must either condemn preventive war or appeal to one or the other of two different forms of justification: a necessity justification or a justification that claims that it is instrumentally valuable to treat unmobilized soldiers as legitimate targets.

Earlier I noted that there is a revisionist account of the just war according to which the criterion of liability to defensive attack is responsibility for a threat of wrongful harm that is sufficiently serious to make killing a proportionate response. This account, I suggested, can give a liability-based justification for at least some instances of preventive attack against those who intend, plan, and prepare for an unjust attack. But can it supply a liability-based justification for preventive attacks against

---

[6] For a recent example, see Avishai Margalit and Michael Walzer, "Israel: Civilians and Combatants: An Exchange," *The New York Review of Books* 56:8, May 14, 2009, 21–22. For an able defense of a related view, see Benbaji, "A Defense of the Traditional War Convention."

unmobilized soldiers, particularly if they are non-culpably ignorant of their government's plans for aggression? Because this revisionist account makes liability a matter of action rather than membership, it implies that some members of the military who make no contribution to an unjust war may not be liable to attack even when the war is well underway. It may therefore seem unlikely that it could recognize unmobilized soldiers as liable to preventive attack. Yet in the earlier work to which I referred at the beginning of this essay, I argued that unmobilized soldiers can be liable to preventive attack if two conditions are satisfied: (1) that they chose to become members of the military, even if they did so under a certain degree of compulsion, and (2) that there is a substantial probability that they will obey an order to fight if it is given.

On its own, the fact that there is a high risk that a person will pose a threat of wrongful harm in the future – supposing this fact were knowable – seems insufficient for liability to preventive attack. But if, in addition to this, the person has made a choice that had as a foreseeable risk that he would later pose a threat of wrongful harm, he may then be liable to preventive attack *provided* that the likelihood of his becoming a threat is traceable to his having risked becoming one. His choice to risk becoming a threat may not be a basis of liability if the reason he is likely to become a threat is independent of that choice. But in actual cases, the reason why unmobilized soldiers contribute to the risk that their leaders' plotting imposes on others derives from their being the ones who will later implement their leaders' plans. That they might later be in this position, even without knowing it at the time, was foreseeable when they chose to become members of the military.

One reason why there is normally a substantial probability that soldiers will fight if ordered to do so is that in most cases, they precommit their wills to obedience when they join the military. They know that this is expected of them and in most cases there is even a formal precommitment at induction in the form of an oath of obedience, which tends to strengthen their sense that they have a moral duty of obedience. The precommitment of the will is then reinforced by the knowledge that virtually all of those who join have that there are severe penalties for disobedience. For these and other reasons, the act of joining the military tends to create a high probability that the soldier will fight if ordered to do so, even if the war in which he is ordered to fight is unjust, and even if he recognizes this.

When it is true that a soldier is strongly predisposed to fight if ordered to do so, and when his leaders are in fact planning to order him to fight in an unjust war, his presence in the military increases the objective risk faced by the potential victims of this potential unjust war. If he has chosen to join when these conditions were among the foreseeable possible outcomes of his joining, that seems to provide a basis of liability to preventive attack, as a means of reducing the risk to which his action has contributed.

An initial objection to this explanation of how unmobilized soldiers can be liable to preventive attack is that many members of the military do not become members by choice, so that in their case the first of the two conditions of liability is not met. But in fact almost all members of the military are members by choice, even if the choice is made under duress. It is, of course, possible that a person's government has the authority to induct him into the army against his will, assign him a rank, and lock him in a military prison if he resists. In that case he could be a member without any choice on his part. Anyone who has become a member of the military in this way, without any element of choice on his part, cannot be liable to preventive attack on the basis of his membership. But soldiers rarely become members of the military in this way. Usually they enter the military by choice, even if their choice is made under considerable pressure. People who make choices under duress may be exempt from *culpability* for their choice, but that is not the same as being exempt from *responsibility*. Provided they could have chosen differently, they may be responsible for the consequences of their choice even if, in the same circumstances, most people of reasonable firmness would not have chosen differently. And responsibility can be a basis of liability, even in the absence of culpability. This is most obvious in the case of liability to pay compensation for having caused harm. A person who chooses under duress to harm an innocent person, and lacks a justification of necessity for the harm caused, may clearly be liable to compensate his victim, even if the duress made his choice non-culpable.

While liability to compensate a victim for a harm caused does not entail liability to defensive action *ex ante*, there are examples that suggest that responsibility can also be a basis of liability to defensive action even in the absence of culpability. Here is one I have used in previous work to illustrate this point.

The Conscientious Driver: A person who keeps her car well maintained and drives carefully and alertly decides to drive to the cinema. On the way, a freak event that she could not have anticipated occurs that causes her car to veer out of control in the direction of a pedestrian.[7]

---

[7] McMahan, *Killing in War*, 165.

Suppose the pedestrian can defend himself, but only by killing the driver. Given that it is unavoidable that one of them will be killed, it seems that the driver's having chosen to engage in an activity that is known to involve a small risk of killing an innocent person makes it just for the pedestrian to kill her, provided there are no other considerations that weigh heavily against the pedestrian's acting in self-defense. The driver's earlier voluntary choice to impose the risk on others provides the basis of her liability to defensive action.

Not everyone, of course, agrees with this judgment. And there are several morally significant differences between the driver in this case and unmobilized soldiers whose government is secretly planning an unjust war of aggression. One such difference suggests that the grounds for attributing liability to preventive attack to unmobilized soldiers are actually stronger than those for attributing liability to defensive attack to the conscientious driver. This is that what the soldiers risk doing is more seriously wrong than what the driver risks doing. Whereas the driver risks killing innocent people accidentally, the unmobilized soldiers risk being in a situation in which they will *intentionally* kill people – soldiers who seek to defend their country against unjust aggression – who are innocent in the sense identified as relevant by the revisionist account of the just war. They risk being in a position in which they will kill such people either because they will mistakenly believe that the victims are not innocent or because they will lack the strength of will to refrain from killing them despite being aware that they are innocent.

There are, however, other differences between the cases that suggest that the grounds for attributing liability to the conscientious driver are stronger. One is that while the conscientious driver freely chose to drive for reasons of self-interest, many unmobilized soldiers may have joined the military only under duress. In those cases, the duress makes a difference to the degree of the soldiers' responsibility for their contribution to the threat of unjust war, thereby diminishing the degree of preventive harm to which they are liable.

But not all unmobilized soldiers join the military under duress. Many enlist voluntarily, for a variety of reasons. Some are culpable for enlisting – for example, if their government has a history of flagrantly and egregiously immoral action which makes it reasonable to expect that it is likely to use its military to wage unjust war. In such cases, it is not difficult to find grounds for attributing liability, even to preventive attack, to those who have willingly converted themselves into instruments of violence in the service of notorious wrongdoers.

Others who enlist voluntarily do so for admirable and even noble reasons. They may join, for example, knowing that doing so puts them at considerable personal risk, but in the *reasonable* expectation that they will be ordered to fight only in wars that are just. They may, in other words, expose themselves to substantial risk in order to help defend innocent people against wrongful attack. It is hard to see how they could thereby make themselves liable to attack. As I noted earlier, it seems that action done with moral justification – that is, action that is permissible and that there is a positive moral reason to do – is not a basis of liability to defensive harm. If so, unmobilized soldiers who were morally justified in joining the military cannot be liable to preventive attack simply by virtue of having joined. In this respect they contrast with the conscientious driver, whose driving is morally permissible but not morally justified, in that there is no positive moral reason for her to drive to the cinema. This may explain why we might think that she is liable to defensive attack while unmobilized soldiers who had a positive moral reason to join the military are not. Mere permissibility, without positive moral justification, seems insufficient to exempt a person from liability.

Yet given that their government is in fact planning and preparing for an unjust war of aggression, it seems that their joining the military, or remaining in it, was not justified in what Parfit calls the "fact-relative" sense – that is, justified in relation to the facts. At best their action was justified in the "evidence-relative" sense – that is, in relation to the evidence available to them.[8] While they may have acted in good faith on the basis of beliefs they were epistemically justified in having, some of the beliefs they had that were relevant to the justifiability of their action were false, so that their action turned out to be unjustified in the fact-relative sense. It is only justification in the fact-relative sense that excludes liability. While evidence-relative justification is sufficient to exempt unmobilized soldiers from culpability for having joined, it is insufficient to exempt them from liability to preventive attack.

Some philosophers believe that mere evidence-relative justification does exempt an agent from liability to defensive harm. But many of these same philosophers reject my claim that fact-relative justification excludes such liability. They argue, for example, that a pilot who has a fact-relative lesser evil justification for dropping a bomb on a military target when that will foreseeably cause unavoidable but proportionate harm to innocent civilians

---

[8] Derek Parfit, *On What Matters*, vol. 1 (Oxford University Press, 2011), chapter 7, section 21.

can be liable to defensive attack.[9] While I think this particular claim is false, I concede that there are cases in which justification does not exclude all forms of liability. Suppose, for example, that through no fault of his own, a person has gone into a diabetic coma and will soon die unless he is administered an injection of insulin. One has no insulin oneself but one can steal the necessary amount from someone else who has an ample supply. It seems clear that one would be morally justified in stealing the necessary amount of insulin but that one would then be liable to compensate the original owner for having stolen his property. It might be fairer, all things considered, if the owner of the insulin were to waive his right to compensation, or if the diabetic who benefited from one's intervention were to compensate him instead. But if neither of these people volunteers to bear the cost, it seems that one is liable to compensate the person from whom one has stolen, despite the fact that one acted with moral justification.

It seems, therefore, that my earlier claim that justification excludes liability was, at a minimum, overstated. Justification does not always exempt one from liability to compensate innocent people harmed by one's action. Yet even if a moral justification for acting is compatible with liability to compensate innocent victims of the action, the justification may still exclude liability to *defensive* harm. It seems to be true, for example, that in justifiably stealing the insulin, one would not be liable to defensive action, even though one would be liable to compensate the owner. So it may be that justification always excludes liability to defensive action, even if it does not always exclude liability to compensate innocent victims. (The explanation of why one would not be liable to defensive action in the insulin case might be that the circumstances had deprived the owner of his liberty-right to keep the insulin, so that one would be forcing him to do what he ought to do. But he might still retain a claim-right to keep the insulin – an instance of a right to do wrong. The theft is justified because that claim-right is overridden, yet the overriding of that right may be what gives the owner a claim to compensation.)

Even if, as the insulin case suggests, fact-relative justification (either a liability justification or a lesser evil justification) exempts an agent from liability to defensive attack, it is, I suggested, considerably less plausible to suppose that mere evidence-relative justification does so. But unmobilized soldiers whose government is secretly preparing for an unjust war of

---

[9] See, for example, Uwe Steinhoff, "Jeff McMahan on the Moral Inequality of Combatants," *Journal of Political Philosophy* 16:2 (2008), 220–226; and Adam Hosein, "Are Justified Aggressors a Threat to the Rights Theory of Self-Defense?," forthcoming in Frowe and Lang, *How We Fight*.

aggression seem to have had only an evidence-relative justification for joining the military, no matter how admirable their motives may have been. Their having joined has placed them now in a position in which there is a very high probability that they will participate in an unjust war of aggression unless they are forcibly prevented from doing so. Since this was a foreseeable possible result of their joining – for everyone knows that soldiers often fight in unjust wars and that very few ever refuse an order to do so – their having joined seems to constitute a basis of liability to preventive attack.

Some people's intuitions will rebel at this suggestion. Suppose that at the time they joined the military, a group of unmobilized soldiers were epistemically justified in believing that their government would fight only in wars that would be just. Yet now, contrary to reasonable expectation and unbeknown to them, their government will soon order them to fight in an unjust war of aggression. In all that they have actually chosen and done, they may be morally indistinguishable from unmobilized soldiers on the other side who may soon be ordered to conduct an attack against them to prevent them from later engaging in unjust aggression. It therefore seems as if the account of liability I have defended implies that they have become liable to attack by bad luck alone. That seems an arbitrary basis for the attribution of liability.

Indeed, it *is* an insufficient basis for the attribution of liability, *on its own*. But recall that my claim is that there are *two* conditions that must be met for unmobilized soldiers to be liable to preventive attack. One is that they chose to join the military when there was a foreseeable risk that that would result in their fighting in an unjust war; the other is that they would in fact obey the order to fight in an unjust war that they will receive unless they are preventively attacked. While their prior choice to join the military may be a necessary condition of their being liable to preventive attack (and thus distinguishes them from civilians who will soon receive notification of conscription and thus will also pose a threat of unjust harm in the future), it is not sufficient. There is a further condition – what they would do if ordered – that is also necessary for liability. For unlike the conscientious driver, the unmobilized soldiers would have to make a further choice in the future before they would actually pose an unjust threat. They would have to choose to fight when ordered to do so.

They have not, ex hypothesi, made that choice; not yet. And those who would not make it – that is, those who would not be ordered to fight or would refuse to obey the order – are not now liable to preventive attack. For they fail to satisfy the second of the two conditions of liability. This second condition is essential, as it distinguishes those who would later pose a threat from those who would not. And the first condition is essential as well, as it distinguishes soldiers from high school students in a country with universal conscription, of whom it may be true that they later will pose a threat but who as yet have made no choice that explains why they may become a threat.

Even though unmobilized soldiers have not as yet chosen to fight, it is statistically certain in advance that virtually all of them will fight if they receive the order. This is what virtually all soldiers have always done. And we understand the reasons why they have done so and will continue to do so unless the relevant conditions change. They obey when ordered to fight because they have precommitted their wills to obedience, because they have been conditioned to obey, and because they believe, however mistakenly, that their war is just. *Or*, even if they recognize that it is unjust, they will nevertheless obey because they would be harshly punished and ostracized if they do not, because patriotism and a sense of professional and contractual obligation impels them to obey, and so on. I knew a full colonel in the US army who told me, when the war in Iraq had been in progress for a couple of years, that he believed with great conviction that the war was unjust and that he despised the Bush administration for having started it, but that he would fight to the best of his ability if he were deployed to Iraq. His view was unusual among the army officers I knew at the time only in being volunteered without prompting or hesitation.

It seems, therefore, that when unmobilized soldiers will otherwise receive an order to fight in an unjust war of aggression, most of them are liable to attack if that is the only way, or even just the best way, to prevent them from engaging in an unjust attack. This claim is not, moreover, restricted to soldiers who will be ordered to engage in external aggression. It applies equally to soldiers who will be ordered to engage in domestic repression. As I am making final revisions to this chapter, soldiers in the Syrian army are attacking and killing protesters against the government in various cities throughout that country. Suppose that in the evening one were to learn that President Assad had just sent an order that a particular unit of the army would receive the next morning to attack certain neighborhoods in Hama. And suppose that although one would be unable to attack the members of that unit once they had begun their assault, one could attack them preventively during the night. The account I have defended implies that they would be liable to that attack.

In many cases of preventive attack, however, there may be a proportion of those attacked who are not liable because they would not later pose a threat of unjust attack. Some would have left the military by the time the order was given; others would already be assigned to tasks unrelated to the war that would occupy them for its duration; some would be ill or otherwise incapacitated; and some might refuse on moral grounds to fight in an unjust war of aggression. These soldiers would be innocent in the relevant sense, yet a preventive attack on them would appear to involve killing them intentionally. Could that be morally justified, and if so on what grounds?

Although this may seem to be an issue of discrimination, it is actually an issue of proportionality. The requirement of discrimination is a moral constraint on the intentional killing of innocent people. In intentionally attacking a group of unmobilized soldiers, some of whom one knows to be innocent in the relevant sense, one might seem to be intentionally killing at least some people one knows to be innocent, so that one would be in violation of the requirement of discrimination. But this is a mischaracterization of what one would be doing – or at least of what one *might* be doing.

Traditional just-war theorists concede that it can be permissible to kill innocent civilians as a foreseen side effect of intentionally attacking a military target, provided that the killings are not disproportionate in relation to the importance of destroying the target. Suppose, for example, that a pilot fighting in a just war sees a large concentration of enemy ground forces in the center of a large open area. There are hundreds of them, all en route to his nation's capital to participate in a vicious siege and all currently vulnerable to attack. He also sees, however, that they are holding a few civilian hostages; but he correctly concludes that bombing the unjust combatants is sufficiently important to make the unintended killing of the innocent hostages a proportionate side effect. It may seem, of course, that bombing this group that includes both a great many people who are liable to be killed and a few who are not is relevantly different from bombing a group of unmobilized soldiers that also includes some who are liable and others who are not. For the pilot in the former case can identify the individual civilian hostages and exclude them from among those he intends to kill, whereas a pilot attacking the unmobilized soldiers cannot tell which of them are not liable to attack and so must intend to kill them all, including those who are in fact innocent, or not liable.

But suppose that the first pilot, having surveyed the concentration of enemy forces, now circles back to drop his bombs, only to discover that the civilian hostages have been hastily dressed in combatants' uniforms in the hope that the pilot will believe that he can no longer conduct a discriminate attack, since he will now have to intend to kill all of the people in uniform, knowing that a few of them are innocent. But the enemy forces have underestimated the pilot's philosophical intelligence. He knows that his intentions have not changed. He can still drop his bombs without intending to kill innocent people. It is only that he is now unable to identify those whose deaths he does not intend. It does not matter whether his inability to identify them results from their being hidden inside a building or their being hidden inside a uniform.[10]

For both pilots, the only relevant issue is one of proportionality. Each recognizes that he has no reason to kill those who are not liable, for neither the civilian hostages nor the unmobilized soldiers who would not fight if their country were later to initiate an unjust war of aggression constitute a threat; hence killing them would serve no purpose. What each pilot needs to know to determine whether it would be permissible to attack is just roughly how many innocent people he would kill, and perhaps the rough proportion among the people he would kill who would be liable to be killed. This is a question about whether his attack would be proportionate, not about whether it would involve the intentional killing of the innocent.

There is a further issue that is relevant to the moral status of unmobilized soldiers who, for whatever reason, would not later fight in the unjust war for which their government is currently preparing. This is that in having chosen to join the military, they are to some degree responsible for having engendered a reasonable expectation among their potential adversaries that they will fight if ordered to do so. They are therefore responsible in some measure for *appearing* to pose a threat of unjust harm when those who are the potential victims of their government's planned war of aggression discover the plan.

There are at least three ways in which this fact might be morally significant. One is that this fact is sufficient to make these unmobilized soldiers liable to preventive attack along with the others who *would* fight. Consider a case involving only two individuals that is analogous except that it involves apparent defense rather than apparent prevention. Suppose the friends of a person who is known to relish the terrified excitement he experiences while watching trashy horror movies decide to organize a treat for him. They arrange to pay a particularly large and powerfully built actor to dress up in the usual regalia of the Hollywood killer (leather mask, etc.) and to pretend, as realistically as possible, to be intent on sadistically killing their friend. The plan is that just as this terrifying figure appears to be

---

[10] The arguments in these paragraphs are drawn from McMahan, "Innocence, Self-Defense, and Killing in War," 215–221, and *Killing in War*, 229–230.

preparing to strike the fatal blow, the friends will emerge from their hiding places to reveal that it was all just a special treat. But the best-laid schemes, this one among them, gang aft agley. When the pretended killer appears, the horror movie fan, reasonably believing he is about to be murdered, fires the derringer he has unexpectedly concealed in his pocket, killing the actor before he has even had the chance to utter a fiendish taunt. The question is whether the actor had actually made himself liable to be killed by deliberately creating conditions that were indistinguishable, from the point of view of the fan, from a situation in which he was actually about to be murdered. One might argue in the following way that he had. Suppose that an armed and fully informed third party improbably arrives on the scene just as the fan is about to kill the actor. This person knows both that the actor poses no threat and that the fan has a gun and is about to fire it in what he believes to be justified self-defense. In these circumstances, a killing is unavoidable. The third party must choose between killing the fan in defense of the actor and allowing the fan to kill the actor. One might initially think that because the fan has chosen to kill someone but has made a mistake about the justification for that choice, he bears responsibility for the situation in which a killing is inevitable and on this basis is liable to be the one who is killed. But on reflection it seems that the actor's responsibility for the situation is greater, for he has knowingly produced the fan's mistaken belief. Given that it is unavoidable that one of them will be killed, the third party ought to act to ensure that it is the actor rather than the fan, on the ground that the actor bears greater responsibility for its being inevitable that one of them will be killed. This has the appearance of a liability-based justification for non-intervention by the third party.

It is hard to believe, however, that the actor could make himself morally liable to be *killed* simply by trying to frighten someone, however reckless or imprudent the attempt may have been, given that he does not in fact pose a threat. To the extent that it is credible to suppose that he could be liable, it is because his action was culpable.[11] But unmobilized soldiers who were justified in the evidence-relative sense in joining the military and would not later fight are neither culpable nor threatening. It is thus even harder to believe that they could have made themselves liable to be preventively

---

[11] My thinking here is indebted to Kai Draper's criticism of some of my earlier work in his paper, "Defense," *Philosophical Studies* 145:1 (2009), 69–88, esp. 74 and 86–87. In McMahan "Self-Defense and Culpability," *Law and Philosophy* 24:6 (2005), 751–774, I offer intuitive grounds for the claim that culpability alone can be a basis of liability to be killed in defense of another, even if one poses no threat oneself. My argument there may support the view that the actor is liable to be killed.

killed simply by having knowingly made it reasonable for their potential adversaries to believe that they would fight if ordered to do so.

But even if their responsibility for appearing to pose a threat of unjust harm is insufficient to make them liable to preventive attack, it might be relevant in a second way. Assuming that they are not liable to attack, they would be wronged by being attacked. But because they have chosen to be in the military, thereby knowingly making it reasonable for others to suppose that they will fight if ordered to do so, they lack a right to kill in self-defense if others attack them on the basis of the reasonable and epistemically fully justified belief that they will soon receive an order to fight in an unjust war of aggression and will respond with obedience. Because they are themselves responsible for their attackers' mistaken belief, they must accept the unavoidable cost of having made that belief reasonable, rather than imposing the cost on the same innocent people on whom they imposed the belief.

The third possible implication of the unmobilized soldiers' responsibility for appearing to pose a threat is that it diminishes the extent to which they are wronged by being preventively attacked when the reason they are attacked is precisely that they present that appearance, thereby giving their attackers an evidence-relative justification for attacking them. Even if they are not liable to attack, they may have little ground for complaint about being attacked if they have knowingly chosen to make it reasonable for their attackers to believe that they may justifiably be attacked. If this is so, it seems it must be at least relevant to the weight their deaths should have in determining whether a preventive attack would be proportionate.

Having identified three ways in which the responsibility of unmobilized and unthreatening soldiers for appearing to pose a threat might be morally significant, I should concede that whether this responsibility actually makes them liable, whether it actually deprives them of the right of self-defense, and whether and to what extent it actually diminishes the extent to which they are wronged by being preventively attacked may depend on the *degree* of their responsibility for the appearance they present, which in turn depends on the degree to which their joining and remaining in the military have been voluntary. If they entered and have remained in the military only under great duress, that mitigates their responsibility for appearing to pose a threat when in fact they do not and will not.

Even when their entry into the military was fully voluntary, the fact that soldiers who will not fight are nevertheless responsible for appearing as if they will is at best a weak basis of liability to preventive attack. The principal conditions of liability to prevent attack, according to the revisionist account of the just war, are the following. First, soldiers have chosen to be in the military, thereby granting their government the authority to order them to fight and usually precommitting their wills to fight if ordered to do so. Second, they would in fact fight if ordered to do so – a condition that it is reasonable to expect to be met in most cases, for the various reasons I gave earlier. Third, their government will soon, unless prevented, order them to fight in an unjust war of aggression. When these three conditions obtain, unmobilized soldiers can be liable to preventive attack. There may always be some who fail to satisfy the first or second conditions – for example, those who have been forcibly dragooned into the military, or who will no longer be in the military when the order to fight is given, or who will receive that order but conscientiously refuse to obey it. Unless these soldiers can be liable to preventive attack merely on the ground that they are responsible for appearing to pose a threat, there can be no liability-based justification for killing them. It does not follow, however, that preventive attack cannot be justified. For the foreseen killing of unmobilized soldiers who are not liable to attack may be justifiable in the same way that the foreseen killing of innocent civilians as a side effect of military action can sometimes be justified in the course of just warfare. In other words, the killing of unmobilized soldiers who are not liable may be justifiable provided that it is not intended as a means to victory, is unavoidable in the circumstances, and is proportionate in relation to the moral importance of the military goal. This is a necessity justification, which supplements the liability-based justification for killing those soldiers who satisfy the three conditions of liability. According to the revisionist account of the just war, then, the primary justification for preventive attack – the justification for the killings that are intended – can be liability-based, though this justification must often be supplemented by a necessity justification for the unavoidable killing as a side effect of people, including some soldiers, who are not liable to attack. As in the case of most justified military action in modern war, considerations of liability justify the harms that are intentionally inflicted, while considerations of necessity or lesser evil justify those that are unintended.

Of the three conditions of liability, two require knowledge of one's adversary that it is difficult to have – namely, that the government is planning an unjust war and will at some point order its soldiers to fight, and that those soldiers will obey the order when they receive it. But the relevant knowledge is not impossible to obtain. Knowledge of a government's secret plans may be obtained by espionage and knowledge of what soldiers will do is given by history and psychology. Conditions would be quite different, however, if there were no reasonable expectation that virtually all soldiers will obey an order to fight in an unjust war of aggression. If people's understanding of the morality of war were to shift away from the traditional just-war doctrine, which holds that soldiers do no wrong in fighting in an unjust war, provided they obey the rules governing the conduct of war, so that people came to believe instead that it is seriously wrong for soldiers to kill people in pursuit of unjust aims, then soldiers might become reluctant to fight in wars they believe to be unjust. If the consensus about the morality of war were to shift in this way, and if this change were to lead to the adoption by civilized peoples of more generous legal provisions for conscientious refusal to fight, it might become much more difficult for the revisionist account of the just war to provide a liability-based justification for preventive war.

CHAPTER 9

Are preventive wars always wrong?

Stephen Nathanson

Because the legitimacy of preventive war was embraced and promoted by leading figures in the administration of President George W. Bush, it was easy at the time to identify the preventive war option with the reckless attitudes and actions of President Bush and others who embraced the aggressive neoconservative, foreign policy agenda. Even now, it might be tempting to think of preventive war as an aberration from former policies that has only limited support. This would be a serious mistake for two reasons. First, the Bush administration's embrace of preventive war did not radically depart from past United States policy. Second, arguments in favor of preventive war are rooted in widely shared moral and political beliefs. If preventive war is to be rejected, its opponents must show why it is wrong and must work to make the reasons for rejecting preventive war part of public understanding so that the general public will resist the arguments of preventive war's advocates.

My main aim in this paper is to show that traditional just-war theory provides useful criteria for reining in the tendency to engage in preventive war. Had these criteria been better understood and taken more seriously, the Bush administration's case for the 2003 war attack on Iraq might have been rejected. After discussing the just-war criteria and their application to the 2003 Iraq war, I will show why the traditional, multi-criterion version of just-war theory provides a better basis for rejecting preventive war than the abbreviated version supported by Michael Walzer in *Just and Unjust Wars*.[1] I will then argue that both the traditional just-war criteria and the prohibition of preventive war can be strongly supported by rule-utilitarian arguments.

---

[1] Michael Walzer, *Just and Unjust Wars* (New York: Basic Books, 1977).

PREVENTIVE WAR IN US POLICY

In its 2002 National Security Strategy (NSS), the Bush administration claimed that "the United States has long maintained the option of preemptive actions to counter a sufficient threat to our national security." Critics charged that this embrace of preventive war was a radical departure from past policies of containment and deterrence.[2] William Galston, for example, called it "a new doctrine for US security policy" that rejects the "successful strategies of the Cold War era."[3]

On this historical point, I believe that the Bush administration was correct. Although the United States never directly attacked the Soviet Union during the Cold War, the strategy of containment committed the US to resist any expansion of Soviet power and led to major wars in Korea and Vietnam and lesser interventions elsewhere. While neither Korea nor Vietnam were threats to the United States, successive US administrations invoked the "domino theory" to show that unless we fought communism in far-off places, we would someday have to fight it at our own borders. This view dominated US policy for four decades. George Schulz, Secretary of State in the Reagan administration, invoked it when he stated that the US did not have to wait until a "threat is at our doorstep" but could justifiably use force to "prevent the threat from growing."[4]

This same reasoning led to the Cuban missile crisis. The US saw the placing of missiles in Cuba as a threatening, unacceptable increase in Soviet power. Both the joint chiefs of staff and leading members of Congress favored a military strike against these missiles. While an attack on the missiles alone would not have been a full-scale war, President John F. Kennedy saw that it could escalate into a nuclear war. Kennedy's attempts to avoid a military strike were so out of step with popular opinion that his negotiated swap of US missiles in Turkey for Soviet missiles in Cuba was kept secret.[5] The key fact about the missile crisis, which is still

---

[2] The National Security Strategy does not distinguish preemptive from preventive attacks. I discuss this distinction below.

[3] William Galston, "The Perils of Preemptive War," *Philosophy and Public Policy Quarterly* 22:4 (Fall 2002), 2–6.

[4] Quoted in Hew Strachan, "Preemption and Prevention in Historical Perspective," in Henry Shue and David Rodin, eds., *Preemption: Military Action and Moral Justification* (Oxford University Press, 2007), 38.

[5] On the secrecy of the missile swap, see McGeorge Bundy, *Danger and Survival: Choices About the Bomb in the First Fifty Years* (New York: Vintage Books, 1990), 432–433. I discuss the missile crisis in S. Nathanson, "Kennedy and the Cuban Missile Crisis: On the Role of Moral Reasons in Explaining and Evaluating Political Decision-Making," *Journal of Social Philosophy* 22:2 (1991), 94–108.

seen as the closest case of an almost nuclear war, is that the US was responding neither to an actual nor an imminent threat of attack. The Soviet action was quite comparable to the earlier placement by the US of similar missiles near the Soviet border with Turkey.

These events from the Cold War era make clear that the logic of striking first before a threat worsens is not a new idea in American policy.[6]

PREVENTION, THE RIGHT TO LIFE, AND COMMON-SENSE MORALITY

A second reason for taking preventive war seriously is that its legitimacy is apparently supported by widespread moral views about self-defense and the right to life. The right to life is generally understood to include both a negative right of immunity to attack and a positive right to defend oneself. Individuals who are attacked have a right to fight back and, if the harm threatened is great enough, to kill the attacker. Analogous rights play a central role in the ethics of war. Countries have a negative right not to be attacked by others. When such attacks occur, they are called aggression and are generally condemned. Countries also have a positive right to defend themselves, and defensive wars are generally seen as morally justified.[7]

Difficulties emerge in ambiguous circumstances. At the individual level, these difficulties are illustrated by the case of Bernhard Goetz. In December 1984, Goetz shot four young men on a New York subway. Although he apparently feared that they were going to attack him, none of the men he shot had actually attacked him. While Goetz did not kill any of the four, one man was left paralyzed for life. Assuming that Goetz believed that his life was in danger, the question emerges whether he had a right to shoot.

The case is difficult because there is a conflict between the four men's negative right of immunity to attack and Goetz's positive right to defend himself. Had Goetz waited to be attacked, his chances of successfully defending himself might have been weakened. Yet, by acting preventively, he may have violated the rights of people who had no intention to harm

---

[6] For more on preventive war thinking in American policy, see the essays by Hew Strachan, "Preemption and Prevention," Marc Trachtenberg, "Preventive War and US Foreign Policy," and Neta Crawford, "The False Promise of Preventive War," in Shue and Rodin, eds., *Preemption*.

[7] See David Rodin, *War and Self-Defense* (Oxford University Press, 2001) for an analysis of the right of self-defense. Rodin denies that individual rights of self-defense can be extended to justify war by states.

him. Because the incident occurred at a time of high crime rates, public opinion was very sympathetic to Goetz.[8]

The tension in our thinking about rights of immunity versus rights of self-defense is at the heart of the preventive war debate. Opponents of preventive war fear mistaken, unnecessary wars while advocates fear costly wars or defeats that could have been avoided by taking action sooner. The case for preventive war resonates very strongly with many people. It currently remains a serious option in order to prevent Iran from becoming a nuclear weapons power.

TRADITIONAL JUST-WAR THEORY

I want to approach the preventive war question from the perspective of just-war theory, which is central to philosophical discussions of warfare and which plays some role in public discussions of going to war.[9] I believe that a more prominent role for just-war theory could improve public deliberation about war and should be supported for this reason.

As is well known, just-war theory contains two parts: the *jus ad bellum* provides criteria for justifiably going to war while the *jus in bello* provides criteria for evaluating the means by which wars are fought. The problem of preventive war concerns going to war and is thus a *jus ad bellum* issue.

According to just-war theory, there are multiple criteria, all of which must be satisfied for entry into war to be morally justified.

Just cause: To be morally justified, a country or other group must go to war for a certain kind of reason. Not any cause will do. For example, neither economic advantage nor the acquisition of valuable territory is a just cause. Defense against an aggressive attack is currently the paradigm case of a just cause.

Right intention: If there is a just cause for a country to go to war, this cause must be the real motivation for the war. Going to war for different reasons would be wrong.

Legitimate authority: The group going to war must have the authority to do so. Usually governments are assumed to have this authority while private

---

[8] For description and analysis of this case, see George Fletcher, *A Crime of Self-Defense: Bernhard Goetz and The Law on Trial* (New York: The Free Press, 1988). For an account of the conflicts between components of the right to life, see S. Nathanson, *Terrorism and the Ethics of War* (Cambridge University Press, 2010), chapter 12.

[9] Michael Walzer describes an increased public use of just-war language in "The Triumph of Just War Theory (and the Dangers of Success)," in Walzer, *Arguing About War* (New Haven: Yale University Press, 2004), 3–22.

groups do not. In some cases, however, non-governmental groups can acquire legitimate authority.[10]

Probability of success: Although fighting against great odds may seem admirable, just-war theory discourages wars that have little chance of success. Because war inevitably results in serious damage both to individuals and their social environment, these harms should not be risked when prospects for success are low.

Proportionality: Since war typically causes serious damage to human life, the reasons for a war must be sufficiently serious to justify this extreme measure. In addition, the expectable negative results should not be excessively large in relation to the war's expected benefits.

Last resort: War should not be initiated if there are reasonable, alternative options that have not yet been tried.[11]

These criteria reflect a morally serious attitude toward war. While they accept the possibility of justified wars, they show a strong aversion to war and do not treat it as an ordinary policy option.

APPLYING JUST-WAR THEORY TO THE 2003 US WAR ON IRAQ

The just-war criteria place a strong burden of proof on advocates of preventive war. Had public debate about the Iraq war been framed by these criteria, the result might have been different. To see why, consider Colin Powell's speech at the United Nations on February 6, 2003. Powell's main argument for a US attack on Iraq was that Iraq possessed "weapons of mass destruction."[12] Since this allegation was the focus of his speech, most of the discussion afterward assumed that the central issue was the factual question: did Iraq possess nuclear, chemical, or biological weapons?

Had just-war theory provided the framework for deliberation, the central question would have been: even if Iraq possesses weapons of mass destruction, does this justify going to war? And this question would have generated further questions about whether going to war for this reason was a just cause, whether the United States had legitimate authority to go to war, whether success was probable, whether this was a last resort, etc.

---

[10] On the possibility of non-governmental groups having legitimate authority, see Bruno Coppieters, "Legitimate Authority," in B. Coppieters and N. Fotion, eds., *Moral Constraints on War* (Lanham, MD: Lexington Books, 2002), 41–58.

[11] For presentations and discussions of these criteria, see National Conference of Catholic Bishops, *The Challenge of Peace* (Washington, DC: US Catholic Conference, 1983), 28–31; James Turner Johnson, *Morality and Contemporary Warfare* (New Haven: Yale University Press, 1999), 27–35; and A. J. Coates, *The Ethics of War* (Manchester University Press, 1997).

[12] Owen R. Cote criticizes the use of the term "weapons of mass destruction" in "Weapons of Mass Confusion," *Boston Review* 28:2 (April–May 2003), 26–27.

These issues were ignored both by Powell's speech and by many who discussed it afterward.

We can get a sense of the usefulness of the just-war perspective by considering how the discussion might have gone if the case for the war had been considered from the perspective of traditional just-war theory. How would the war be assessed by someone using its criteria? In answering this question, I will not contest several assumptions that favor the pro-war position. I will assume (1) that depriving Iraq of dangerous weapons was a *just cause* because the aim was defensive rather than aggressive; (2) that the US government was acting with *right intention*, i.e., that its proclaimed defensive aim was its real reason for the war; and (3) that the US government had *legitimate authority* to go to war against Iraq. Even if the war met these criteria, we cannot know that it was justified without considering the criteria of probability of success, proportionality, and last resort.

Probability of success

President Bush and other officials thought that US military superiority over Iraq was so great that the US could easily defeat Iraq and destroy its weapons. The probability of success was seen as nearly certain.

This judgment is plausible only if success is defined narrowly as defeating the Iraqi army. The actual requirements for success, however, were more demanding because the US goal was to replace Saddam Hussein's government with a democratic regime that would be friendly to the United States. The goal of regime change made success much more difficult to achieve. It required the US to occupy and govern Iraq and to complete a nation-building project that would create an effective, pro-American government. As critics warned, there was less reason for optimism about achieving these ambitious goals. In the fall of 2002, William Galston, drawing on publicly available information, warned that the "goal of 'regime change' would probably require 150,000–200,000 US troops" and that the US would have to "assume total responsibility for Iraq's basic territorial integrity, for the security and basic needs of the population, and for the reconstruction of its system of governance and political culture."[13] The fact that many people predicted these difficulties shows that they were not unforeseeable and thus that the probability of success was lower than US leaders expected.

---

[13] Galston, "The Perils of Preemptive War," 2. Thomas Ricks describes the Bush administration's poor planning for the post-war period in *Fiasco: The American Military Adventure in Iraq* (New York: Penguin Press, 2006).

Proportionality

The proportionality criterion requires that the cause for which a country goes to war must be sufficiently serious to justify a war. Of course, if we imagine the destruction that an Iraqi nuclear attack on the United States would have caused, that prospect is sufficiently dreadful to make war a proportionate response. The issue becomes cloudier, however, when we consider that such an attack was far from certain. Like Bernhard Goetz on the New York subway, the United States faced a possible rather than an actual attack. US officials did not know that an attack would ever occur. While a war that protects a country from a devastating nuclear attack could satisfy the proportionality criterion, a war against a non-existent threat of such an attack clearly fails to meet this requirement.

Last resort

Even if the US attack on Iraq had satisfied all the other criteria, it would have been unjustified if there were other ways to diminish or eliminate the alleged nuclear threat. The most obvious question that should have been raised after Powell's speech was whether there were other ways to prevent Iraq from using nuclear weapons against the United States. And, of course, there were. Most obvious was the option of allowing inspections to continue so as to determine whether Iraq actually possessed a nuclear arsenal. The criterion of last resort failed to be met.

My point in reviewing the debate about the US war on Iraq is to illustrate the usefulness of the just-war criteria. In the welter of confusing, frightening things that are said in debates about going to war, it is helpful to have a checklist of widely recognized, relevant criteria to guide public judgment. The traditional *jus ad bellum* criteria would have enabled people in the United States to assess more effectively the arguments that were made for a preventive war against Iraq.

WALZER ON JUST-WAR THEORY AND PREVENTIVE WAR

To further clarify the virtues of traditional just-war reasoning on preventive war, I want to compare it with the views of Michael Walzer, who is often cited as a prominent just-war theorist and is also a critic of preventive war. I will show how Walzer's views differ from traditional just-war theory and why these differences weaken his criticisms of preventive war. This will further strengthen the case for traditional just-war theory.

Although Walzer's view of the traditional just-war criteria is not always clear, my view is that he rejects all of the traditional *jus ad bellum* requirements except for just cause. The resulting view is simple: aggression is always wrong, and resistance to aggression is always justified. "All aggressive acts," he writes, "have one thing in common: they justify forceful resistance."[14] Because the just cause of resisting aggression is sufficient, none of the other criteria need to be satisfied for war to be justified.

Although Walzer rejects both proportionality and probability of success, I will focus on his treatment of the last resort criterion because it is central to the rejection of preventive war.[15] Walzer sometimes appears to affirm last resort. Discussing Israel's decision to strike first in the 1967 war, he writes, "One always wants to see diplomacy tried . . . [so] that we are sure that war is the last resort." He then adds, however, that "it would be difficult in this case to make an argument for its [i.e., the "resort" to diplomacy's] necessity."[16]

Where Walzer most clearly and decisively rejects last resort is in his defense of the 1991 Gulf war.[17] Some critics of the US war charged that it failed to meet the last resort criterion, but Walzer argues that the US war was justified because it was a response to Iraq's invasion of Kuwait. Although he says that "it was morally obligatory to canvass [other] possibilities," he goes on to parody the last resort criterion. "Taken literally last resort would make war morally impossible. For we can never reach lastness."[18] Trying to satisfy "last resort," he suggests, creates a Zeno's paradox situation: because the possible alternativess are unlimited, last resort can never be satisfied. And, because satisfying the last resort criterion is impossible, the failure to satisfy it provides no valid objection to the Gulf war or any other war.

Having cast aside last resort, Walzer goes on to affirm the central role of a single criterion version of just-war theory in *Just and Unjust Wars*. He writes:

For reasons explored at length in this book, acts of aggression like the Iraqi invasion ought to be resisted . . . . It is our abhorrence of aggression that is

---

[14] Walzer, *Just and Unjust Wars*, 52.

[15] See ibid., 70–72 where Walzer uses the 1939 Finnish war against the Soviet Union to justify rejecting the "probability of success" criterion.

[16] Walzer, *Just and Unjust Wars*, 84; see too "Terrorism: A Critique of Excuses," in Walzer, *Arguing About War*, 55.

[17] Walzer's important discussion of the Gulf war appears as the preface to the second edition of *Just and Unjust Wars*; it is reprinted in *Arguing About War*, chapter 6. It also appeared in David DeCosse, ed., *But Was It Just? Reflections on the Morality of the Persian Gulf War* (New York: Doubleday, 1992).

[18] Walzer, *Just and Unjust Wars*, 2nd edn., xiv.

operative here, while the maxims of last resort and proportionality play only marginal and uncertain roles.[19]

Walzer's single criterion view puts him (and anyone else who holds it) in a weak position to oppose preventive wars. If defense against aggression is the paradigmatic just cause, then a country that initiates a preventive war because it genuinely fears a future attack does not seem like an aggressor because defending oneself from attack meets the just cause requirement. Such defensive wars appear to be quite different from aggressive wars that are motivated by such things as the desire for resources, power, or the imposition of one's own values.

Walzer could oppose preventive wars if he claimed that "firing the first shot" in a war always constitutes aggression. He rejects this view, however, because he believes that what he calls "pre-emptive" attacks can be morally justified. Unlike preventive wars, which are intended to head off possible future attacks, preemptive wars are launched in response to attacks that are imminent.[20] For Walzer, the distinction between preemption and prevention is all important. Preemption is always justified while preventive war is always wrong. In order to tell, then, whether starting a war is justified, one must be able to say whether it is preemptive or preventive.

According to Walzer, preemptive attacks have three features. The first two are features of the enemy: it must display "a manifest intent to injure" and "a degree of active preparation that makes that intent a positive danger." The third feature is an assessment by the threatened country that "waiting, or doing anything other than fighting, greatly magnifies the risk."[21]

Defenders of preventive war reject the first two features as necessary and see the third as sufficient by itself. Their view, as Walzer describes it, is that "to fight early, before the balance tips in any decisive way, greatly reduces the cost of the defense, while waiting doesn't mean avoiding war ... but only fighting on a larger scale and at worse odds."[22] This does not seem like

---

[19] Ibid., xvi–xvii.
[20] Walzer's model case of justified preemption is Israel's 1967 war. Walzer believes that Israel was justified in attacking because it faced an imminent attack. For fuller accounts of the causes of the 1967 war, see Tom Segev, *1967: Israel, the War, and the Year that Transformed the Middle East* (New York: Henry Holt and Company, 2007); and Robert Stephens, *Nasser: A Political Biography* (New York: Simon and Schuster, 1971), chapters 16 and 17.
[21] Walzer, *Just and Unjust Wars*, 81.   [22] Ibid., 77.

a foolish argument. Why wouldn't a country want to fight in a way that is both less costly to itself and more likely to succeed?

Walzer's basic response is that preventive wars fail to satisfy his three criteria for justified preemption. But he does not say why a fearful nation should accept these criteria. A threat may not be manifest because the enemy has successfully kept its active preparations secret, and if the risk increases by not acting now, it may well be in a nation's interest not to wait. Walzer's appeal for restraint seems weak, especially because he himself asserts that "states may use military force in the face of threats of war, whenever the failure to do so would seriously risk their territorial integrity or political independence."[23]

It is instructive to see how Walzer applied his view to the 2003 US war on Iraq. Walzer opposed the war because it was preventive not preemptive. "No one," he said, "expects an Iraqi attack tomorrow or next Tuesday, and so there is nothing to preempt."[24] To Condoleezza Rice's assertion that "We don't have to wait for them to attack," Walzer replies, "Well, no, we don't but we do have to wait for some sign that they are going to attack." But why, one might ask, should Condoleezza Rice or George W. Bush have to wait "for some sign that [Iraq] is going to attack" if their cause is defensive and hence just? Walzer's single criterion version of just-war theory provides no response to this challenge.

Walzer's only effective reply to proponents of the Iraq war appeals to the last resort criterion that he himself rejects. The problem with preventive war, he says, is that:

the danger . . . is not only distant but speculative, whereas the costs of preventive war are near, certain, and usually terrible. The distant dangers, after all, might be avoided by diplomacy, or the military work of the other side might be matched by work on this side . . . .Whether or not war is properly the last resort – and I don't believe in that doctrine – there seems no good reason for making it the first.[25]

Walzer's half-hearted appeal to the last resort criterion is his strongest response. The fact that he appeals to it shows the weakness of his single criterion version of just-war theory and provides support for the traditional multi-criterion perspective.

---

[23] Ibid., 85.
[24] Walzer's comments were made at a Pew Forum on September 30, 2002; accessible at http://pewforum.org/events/printe.php?EventID=36. The quote from Walzer can be found in *Arguing About War*, 146; see the same volume for other Walzer essays written before the Iraq war.
[25] Walzer, Pew Forum, in *Arguing About War*, 147.

DOES JUST-WAR THEORY SHOW THAT PREVENTIVE WAR IS ALWAYS WRONG?

Although just-war theory includes a strong presumption against war, it avoids making a sweeping judgment about the wrongness of all wars and requires us to base our moral judgments on an examination of the specific features of proposed (or actual) wars. This might suggest that just-war theory leaves open the question of whether preventive wars – seen as a general category – are justified or not.

This conclusion is too hasty. If, for example, all genocidal wars – i.e., wars whose purpose is to exterminate a group – fail to have a just cause, then just-war theory prohibits all genocidal wars. Similarly, if preventive wars necessarily fail to satisfy just-war criteria, then all wars of this sort will be unjustified.

Looking at preventive war from the just-war perspective, it is plausible to assume that such wars could satisfy the criteria of just cause, right intention, legitimate authority, probable success, and proportionality. The one criterion that is impossible for preventive wars to satisfy is last resort. While Walzer claims that last resort can never be satisfied because the number of possible "resorts" is endless, this is an unfair interpretation of the last resort criterion. Last resort requires that reasonable, less destructive alternatives to war be tried before going to war. If country A poses a future threat to country B, we must ask whether there are things that B could do to protect itself without going to war. If there are, then war is not justified.

The last resort criterion is extremely plausible. In fact, it underlies Walzer's own distinction between preventive and preemptive wars. The essential difference between these is the imminence of an attack, and when attacks are imminent, there is no time to pursue other "resorts." Preventive wars are, by definition, not imminent, and, therefore, time remains to explore possible alternatives.

If preventive wars always fail the last resort test and if just-war theory includes last resort as a necessary condition for justifiable war, then just-war theory yields the view that preventive war is always wrong.

One virtue of the last resort criterion is that it has a foothold in moral common sense. Because it is not an esoteric or a legalistic concept, it is less likely to be seen as a mere technicality. People understand that war is an extreme response to a problem and should not be casually entered into. A second virtue of last resort is that it can shift people from focusing exclusively on a perceived threat to considering as well possible responses other than war. Rather than being guided by fear alone, people using the last resort criterion must analyze, deliberate, and compare options and their possible effects. While these processes are no guarantee of right action, they enhance the chances of people making better choices.

LAST RESORT AND THE LIMITS OF SELF-DEFENSE

If just-war theory implies that all preventive wars are wrong, some people may see this as a serious defect of the theory. This negative view is sharply expressed by the sixteenth-century legal theorist Alberico Gentili: "No one ought to wait to be struck unless he is a fool."[26] Gentili mocks the idea that reasonable people would accept principles that require waiting for an attack rather than acting to prevent it from happening.

One could reply to this challenge by arguing that waiting is required because countries have no right to attack in the absence of an actual or imminent attack against them. From a rights-theory perspective, the just-war criteria describe the conditions under which a country has a right to go to war. While defending oneself against threats is a just cause, the remaining just-war criteria impose constraints on using war to promote that cause. These constraints derive from the rights of the people against whom a preventive war would be launched. The potential victims of a preventive war have a right to life that makes them immune to attack, and the just-war theory's multiple criteria protect that immunity.

It is easy to lose sight of these constraints by viewing preventive war only from the perspective of the party that believes it is threatened. This seems to occur in Whitley Kaufman's rights-based defense of preventive war. According to Kaufman:

> preventive war is legitimate for the very same reason that wars and self-defense are legitimate. One is entitled by natural law and natural right (within limits, of course) to protect oneself and one's citizens against unjust harm. In fact . . . the sovereign authority of a nation . . . has a duty . . . to protect one's citizens from harm.[27]

This argument appeals to the part of the right to life that allows actions in self-defense, but it ignores (apart from the parenthetical "within limits, of course") the rights of potential victims not to be attacked.

In evaluating preventive war, we need to consider both the positive and the negative aspects of the right to life and the potential for conflict

---

[26] Quoted by Crawford in "The False Promise of Preventive War," 116–117.
[27] Whitley Kaufman, "What's Wrong With Preventive War?: The Moral and Legal Basis for the Preventive Use of Force," *Ethics and International Affairs* 19:3 (2005), 23–38; 28–29.

between them. If we give greater weight to immunity rights, we will favor restricting the circumstances in which people can use force to defend themselves and will reject preventive war because of the danger it poses to others. If we give greater weight to positive rights of self-defense, we will favor allowing people to protect themselves even by means that endanger others.[28]

If the right to life were unitary rather than complex, this conflict would not arise. It does not arise, for example, in Hobbes' theory about rights in the state of nature. In Hobbes' view, everyone in the state of nature has a right to do whatever protects their lives or promotes their interests. The cost of this expansive right of defense is that there are no immunity rights. Anyone may be attacked because no one has a duty to refrain from attacking others. This view of the right to life implies the permissibility of preventive wars. Pacifists hold a unitary view of the opposite sort. They recognize an absolute right of immunity to attack; but if the right of immunity to attack is absolute, then the right of self-defense no longer exists. Preventive war, from this perspective, is always wrong because all war is wrong.

Unlike either of these views, common-sense morality and most moral theories accept a complex understanding of the right to life and must wrestle with the tension between immunity rights and rights to take defensive action. Kaufman's argument overlooks these tensions by strongly affirming the right to defense but ignoring the competing right to immunity from attack.

As a result, Kaufman's argument makes the preventive war problem look too easy. Not only does it ignore the tensions between aspects of the right to life. It also ignores people's tendency to view these aspects from a partialist perspective.[29] When people are faced with threats, they are likely to feel that the right to defend themselves is dominant. By contrast, people who are potential victims of a preventive war are likely to believe that their immunity rights would be violated by a country that launches a preventive attack. Neither the rights perspective nor common-sense morality provides a way to resolve these competing claims. What we need is a way to determine which of these competing rights (immunity to attack vs. active defense against attack) takes priority.

---

[28] Walzer stresses the rights of potential victims of a preventive war in *Just and Unjust Wars*, 80; Steven Lee develops a rights-based objection to preventive war in "Preventive Intervention," in S. Lee, ed., *Intervention, Terrorism, and Torture* (Dordrecht: Springer, 2007), 119–133; 122–124.

[29] For a vivid example of this phenomenon, see Uri Bronfenbrenner, "The Mirror Image in Soviet-American Relations: A Social Psychologist's Report," *Journal of Social Issues* 17:3 (1961), 45–56.

CAN CONSEQUENTIALISM SOLVE THE PROBLEM?

Richard Brandt proposes a rule-utilitarian method for addressing these kinds of issues. He asks, "What rules would rational impartial people, who expected their country at some time to be at war, want to have as the authoritative rules of war . . .?" As a utilitarian, Brandt believes that rational impartial people would choose rules whose acceptance would "maximize long-range expectable utility for nations at war."[30] We can apply this method to help us determine whether immunity rights or defensive action rights take priority by asking what judgment would be made by rational, impartial people who are choosing the rules to govern war and other forms of conflict.

The rules of war that rational impartial people would choose do not require people at war to be impartial. People may promote their country's interests rather than those of their enemies. In promoting their interests, however, they are required to limit both their recourse to war and their means of fighting according to criteria that rational impartial people would accept. These criteria would be designed with a view to promoting the well-being of all.[31]

While many writers on the ethics of war are hostile to utilitarianism, the relevance of utilitarian arguments is obvious. Walzer describes – without fully endorsing – the rule-utilitarian argument against preventive war: if preventive wars are permitted, this will lead to "innumerable and fruitless wars," wars that are unnecessary for defense and that nonetheless cause death, injury, and destruction.[32] Even if some preventive wars might produce good results, the likely effect of permitting them would be many unnecessary wars. The overall results of permitting preventive wars will be worse than the results of prohibiting them.[33]

In a similar way, a rule utilitarian could argue that Bernhard Goetz was wrong to shoot the men that he feared on the subway even if he was correct that they were going to attack him. The reason is that a rule that permits people to kill others that they fear in the absence of sufficient evidence of an impending attack would lead to more killings, many of which would have occurred needlessly because no attack would ever have

---

[30] Richard Brandt, "Utilitarianism and the Rules of War," in M. Cohen et al., eds., *War and Moral Responsibility* (Princeton University Press, 1974), 25–45; 30.

[31] I discuss partiality and non-combatant immunity in Nathanson, "Patriotism, War, and the Limits of Permissible Partiality," *Journal of Ethics* 13:4 (2009), 401–422.

[32] Walzer, *Just and Unjust Wars*, 77.

[33] Steven Lee develops this consequentialist argument in "Preventive Intervention," 124–131.

been made. Mere fear is not enough to justify an attack because allowing this justification would lead to more harm overall.[34]

David Luban supports this same argument in two impressive papers on preventive war. Luban points out that consequentialist thinking underlies the rules that make up the United Nations Charter. The drafters of the Charter saw it as a means to "save successive generations from the scourge of war, which . . . has brought untold sorrow to mankind."[35]

Having made a utilitarian argument against preventive war, however, Luban expresses disdain for utilitarian reasoning, noting that "One Achilles' heel of consequentialism has always been its creepy willingness to treat losses of human life as simply the cost of doing business."[36] Here he echoes Walzer, who – after presenting the rule-utilitarian argument against preventive war – disparages utilitarian arguments, claiming that they "radically underestimate the importance of the shift from diplomacy to force" and "don't recognize the problem that killing and being killed poses."[37]

These rhetorical jabs at utilitarians are unfair. Since utilitarians make the promotion of human well-being the central goal of morality, they are often especially sensitive to the human costs of practices like war and punishment as well as conditions like poverty and disease. Moreover, while foes of utilitarianism often express fervent support for respecting human rights and dignity, they manage to find reasons that justify doing terrible things to people when they regard these actions as necessary. Luban, in a later essay, works hard to justify aspects of warfare that he acknowledges to be in conflict with humane values and individual rights, and Walzer, after strongly defending non-combatant immunity, goes on to defend the intentional killing of civilians in "supreme emergency" conditions.[38]

UTILITARIANISM AND JUST-WAR THEORY

Utilitarians, like just-war theorists, neither condemn nor approve all wars. Rather, their method is to consider both war and non-war options and evaluate the likely costs and benefits of each option. Table 1 below illustrates how this method might be applied.

---

[34] George Fletcher discusses the clash between objective and subjective standards of justified fear in the Goetz case in *A Crime of Self-Defense*, chapter 3.

[35] David Luban, "Preventive War," *Philosophy and Public Affairs* 32:3 (2004), 207–248; 218.

[36] Ibid., 224.   [37] Walzer, *Just and Unjust Wars*, 79.

[38] David Luban, "Preventive War and Human Rights," in Shue and Rodin, eds., *Preemption*, 179–183; Walzer, *Just and Unjust Wars*, chapter 16. For criticism of Walzer's view, see my *Terrorism and the Ethics of War*, chapters 10–11.

Table 1 *A utilitarian framework of analysis*

	Possible benefits	Probability of benefits	Possible losses	Probability of losses	Most probable sum of benefits and losses
War					
Limited attacks					
Containment					
Diplomacy					
Wait and see					

Table 2 *A just-war framework of analysis*

	Just cause	Competent authority	Right intention	Last resort	Probability of success	Proportionality
Proposed war						

An important feature of this method is that it forces deliberators to consider options other than war. One cannot say that a particular option maximizes utility without comparing it with other options. A second feature is that this method can be applied either from a prudential perspective that counts only the national interest of particular evaluators or from a universalist perspective that counts the benefits and losses to all who will be affected, including the enemy. While Luban describes prudential reasons as "egoistic" and "not properly . . . moral arguments," this comment overlooks the importance of the lives and interests of people in the nation making the decision. One can surely criticize national leaders on moral grounds if they fail to take seriously the interests of their own country and its citizens.

Although utilitarianism is often contrasted with just-war theory, Table 2 above shows that there are important overlaps between these views.

Last resort, probability of success, and proportionality all deal with the consequences of actions, and the rules requiring just cause, competent authority, and right intention could all be accepted by rule utilitarians on the basis of their likely benefits. Given the serious negative consequences of warfare, there are excellent reasons for thinking that human well-being is enhanced both by limiting warfare to especially serious kinds of threats and by limiting the decision-making power to go to war to persons with official status rather than granting it to everyone. Even right intention can have utility because people's intentions affect their actions. Leaders who go to war for ulterior motives are likely to act differently from those who go to war for a publicly stated "just cause."

We can see some further virtues of the utilitarian method by comparing it with deliberations that focus only on best-case and worst-case scenarios. Best-case/worst-case thinking is influential in decision-making about warfare because people's fears and hopes are especially strong. The case for preventive war can look especially strong if we focus primarily on the best case – safety from attack – and the worst case – being victimized by one's enemies. What this method omits are probabilities, other options, and the possible dire effects of the preventive war itself.

While critics see the utilitarian method as calculating and cold-blooded, this emotional distance can serve as a counter-force against the emotional power of pumped up patriotism and traditions that glorify the wartime sacrifices. Focusing on options and consequences can often bring people back to earth so that they can more realistically assess what is at stake in proposals to go to war.[39]

While the rights perspective has difficulty resolving the conflict between immunity rights and rights of active defense, the utilitarian argument tips the balance toward immunity rights and against preventive war. The argument acknowledges that countries may have reason to launch preventive attacks against possible threats. The problem is that preventive wars may be launched against threats that would never materialize. In a threat-filled world, this is not a merely hypothetical worry. During the Cold War, some US officials proposed nuclear attacks against the Soviet Union and against China in order to prevent them from acquiring nuclear weapons. Millions of people would have died in such attacks, and millions of people did die in the Korean and Vietnam wars, victims (in part) of the "domino theory" and the preventive wars it led to. What history shows is that a permissive doctrine of preventive war leads to more wars, many of them unnecessary.[40]

The short answer to the question "why is preventive war wrong?" is that acceptance of a moral rule that permits such wars leads to worse results than recognizing a moral rule that prohibits them. This answer resolves the clash between immunity rights and defensive rights. While immunity

---

[39] I defend and apply the rule-utilitarian method in *Terrorism and the Ethics of War*, especially chapters 14–16 and 291–302.

[40] Richard Betts makes this historical argument in "Striking First: A History of Thankfully Lost Opportunities," *Ethics and International Affairs* 17:1 (2003), 17–24.

rights are forfeited or overridden when a country engages in aggression, defensive rights are overridden by immunity rights when wars are contemplated as preventive measures rather than responses to actual or imminent attacks.

REPLIES TO THREE OBJECTIONS

Luban's "rogue states" exception

Although David Luban argues strongly against preventive war, he supports an exception for threats posed by "rogue states." Rogue states, he says, are characterized by "militarism, an ideology favoring violence, a track-record of violence to back it up, and a build-up in capacity to pose a genuine threat."[41] Given the special threatening qualities of rogue states, preventive wars against them may be justified.

Although Luban's proposal addresses a genuine worry, accepting the rogue state exception would undermine the prohibition of preventive war. Virtually every strong power could be seen as militaristic, having a track record of violent activity, etc. These qualities, however, only appear threatening in enemies even though allies may have the same features. Moreover, because public opinion is always based on limited information, governments that desire war can generally increase public anxiety about the alleged evils of an enemy country. Categorizing the enemy as a rogue state is useful propaganda, and accepting Luban's rogue state exception would simply be an invitation to include this charge in any pro-war propaganda.

Sinnott-Armstrong's "perfect knowledge" exception

Like Luban, Walter Sinnott-Armstrong uses a rule-utilitarian argument to support public laws that prohibit preventive war. Such laws "might have better consequences" than more permissive rules because "actual agents would make too many mistakes in applying public rules formulated in terms of consequences."[42] Fallibility, then, provides the reason why leaders should not be permitted to justify specific wars by citing their expected good results.

---

[41] Luban, "Preventive War," 230–231; Luban addresses the question "Is the United States a Rogue State?" in "Preventive War and Human Rights," 196–199.

[42] Walter Sinnott-Armstrong, "Preventive War, What is it Good For?," in Shue and Rodin, eds., *Preemption,* 202–221; 204.

Although Sinnott-Armstrong defends a rule that absolutely prohibits preventive war, he nonetheless believes that preventive wars can be justified. The rules whose acceptance would produce the best consequences are useful conventions that may conflict with the "deep morality" of war.[43] For Sinnott-Armstrong, the deep (i.e., true) morality is the act-consequentialist view that any action is right if its consequences are best. Hence, even if it is consequentially best to adopt rules forbidding preventive wars, a preventive war that violates this prohibition would be right if going to war in this case has the best consequences.

To explain how one could consistently support both the moral rule that prohibits preventive war and the moral judgment that preventive wars can be morally right, Sinnott-Armstrong imagines a government "that knows its intelligence is much better than the intelligence of most other countries." This government could favor prohibiting preventive wars because it believes that "if any preventive wars were publicly allowed, then countries with inadequate intelligence would be likely to make mistakes and engage in [unjustified] preventive war[s]." The same country could justifiably violate this prohibition because its reason for endorsing the prohibition is "to prevent mistakes of a kind that it knows it is not making."[44]

As an act-consequentialist, it is not surprising that Sinnott-Armstrong holds this view, but there are serious difficulties with it. Although he stresses the factor of superior intelligence capacities, this feature is neither necessary nor sufficient for justifying a preventive war. It is not necessary because act consequentialism implies that any country, whether it has superior intelligence or not, could rightly violate the rule against preventive war so long as the consequences of war are better than the consequences of refraining from war. Moreover, superior intelligence capacities are not sufficient because countries with superior intelligence capacities are still fallible and could wrongly (by act-consequentialist standards) initiate a preventive war.

The deeper problem is that history shows that national leaders are not only fallible but are also often arrogant, reckless, and desirous of war. For Sinnott-Armstrong, these facts are irrelevant to the "deep morality" of war. Yet facts about the behavior of government leaders are so important that it seems absurd to ignore them in determining the ethics of war. As Luban notes, decisions about warfare occur in "situations in which the burdens of judgment and the infirmities of judgment play an ineradicable

---

[43] Sinnott-Armstrong cites Jeff McMahan – "The Ethics of Killing in War," *Ethics* 114:4 (2004), 693–733 – for the distinction between public rules and the "deep morality" of war.

[44] Sinnott-Armstrong, "Preventive War, What is it Good For?," 205.

role." [45] For this reason, an ethic of war that would be appropriate for a world led by officials with nearly perfect knowledge and motivations is not appropriate for the world we live in.[46]

While Luban's "rogue nation" exception justifies preventive war by focusing on the evil of the enemy, Sinnott-Armstrong's exception focuses on the possibility of a country possessing special (cognitive) goodness. The problem is that exaggeratedly negative views of enemies and exaggeratedly positive views of oneself, one's country, and one's own motives are factors that motivate leaders to start unnecessary wars.

Buchanan's critique of the "bad practice" objection to preventive war

Allen Buchanan criticizes the rule-utilitarian argument against preventive war in two ways. First, he claims that it rests on a generalization argument that is defective. The generalization argument says that if it would be bad for everyone to do x, then it would be wrong for any individual to do x. Buchanan argues that actions can be right even if it would be disastrous for everyone to do them. Closing your eyes every day at a particular time, he points out, is morally permissible even though it would be disastrous for everyone to do this.

This objection fails, however. If there actually were a widespread tendency for people to engage in this eye-closing behavior, a moral rule against it would be justified on consequentialist grounds. The action he describes is morally innocent only because widespread instances of it are so unlikely to occur. Because preventive wars are dangerous and frequently appear to be desirable to political leaders, there are good reasons to have a rule that prohibits them.

Buchanan's second objection challenges the argument that if countries engage in preventive wars, this will set precedents for others and increase the number of preventive wars. Buchanan claims that the relevant question is not whether engaging in preventive war increases the probability of more preventive wars. Rather, the relevant question is:

whether it will significantly increase the probability of unjustified preventive wars. To assume that an increase in the probability of any preventive wars, just or

[45] Luban, "Preventive War," 227.

[46] For discussions of the fallibility of national decision-making about war, see Fred Iklé, *Every War Must End* (revised edn., New York: Columbia University Press, 1991); Dominic Johnson, *Overconfidence and War* (Cambridge, MA: Harvard University Press, 2004). For an historical analysis of US thinking about military force, see Andrew Bacevich, *The New American Militarism* (New York: Oxford University Press, 2005). Daniel Ellsberg provides a vivid account of officials' errors and lies in *Secrets: A Memoir of Vietnam and the Pentagon Papers* (New York: Penguin Books, 2003).

unjust, is unacceptable, is to beg the question at hand, namely, "Is preventive war ever justified?"[47]

Buchanan claims that a rule against preventive war might preclude wars that are justified. To assume that decreasing the number of preventive wars is a good thing, he says, begs the question about whether these wars are morally justified or not. There is nothing wrong with an increase in the number of wars if those wars are justified.

Perhaps it is Buchanan who begs the question. He assumes that we can know that there are justified preventive wars independently of knowing whether accepting a rule permitting preventive wars yields worse consequences than a rule that forbids them. Yet, there are many cases in which actions that appear to be innocent are judged to be wrong because the general practice is harmful. In previous eras, people could legitimately dispose of sewage and other waste in water, for example, because this practice had minimal negative impact. As population increased and industrialization created much greater amounts of these substances, we had to revise our judgments about the permissibility of disposing of them in water. In this case and many others, the connection between the morality of individual actions and the consequences of many people engaging in a type of action is widely recognized.

The importance of moral rules about warfare is especially great because of the strong tendency of leaders and nations to see themselves as special cases. Strong feelings of attachment and partiality lead to the "exceptionalist" view that what is wrong for others to do is right for us.

CONCLUSION

My aim in this chapter has been to show that the traditional, multiple-criterion version of just-war theory can play a valuable public role in curbing the resort to preventive warfare. I have also argued that rule-utilitarian arguments can be used to support both the just-war criteria and the prohibition of preventive war. Both just-war theory and rule-utilitarianism allow for partiality toward and defense of one's own country, but they support constraints on the means that nations and other groups may use to defend their interests. The prohibition of preventive war is one part of the ethic of war that would be chosen by rational, impartial people whose aim was to promote overall human well-being.

---

[47] Allen Buchanan, "Justifying Preventive War," in Shue and Rodin, eds., *Preemption*, 129. David Luban responds to Buchanan's arguments in the same volume, 199–201.

CHAPTER 10

Ethics and legality: US prevention in Iran

Alex Newton

INTRODUCTION

The US response to the nuclear threat posed by Iran inhabits territory perennially mired with ethical, legal, and moral quandaries. The public release of the National Intelligence Estimate on Iran's nuclear program in December 2007 (2007 NIE) created somewhat of a watershed for the then Bush administration's counter-proliferation policy on Iran, reinvigorating debates surrounding the justifications for the US policy of preventive force to respond to states posing a nuclear threat.[1] The 2007 NIE concluded that Iran halted its nuclear weapons program in 2003 and that, as of late 2007, the program remained suspended.

However, reading the 2007 NIE in conjunction with contemporaneous (and subsequent) findings of the United Nations' International Atomic Energy Agency (IAEA) has created more concerns and confusion than it has allayed.[2] While IAEA reports have vindicated the 2007 NIE in certain respects, they have also stated that, since early 2006, "the Agency's knowledge about Iran's current nuclear programme is diminishing."[3] More recently, a new National Intelligence Estimate circulated among the US intelligence community in February 2011 (2011 NIE) – although not

---

[1] The National Intelligence Estimate, "Iran: Nuclear Intentions and Capabilities," November 2007 (hereafter "2007 NIE"), issued by the Office of the Director of National Intelligence Council, the principal intelligence body advising the president and other senior policy-makers.
[2] For example the IAEA's report on Iran's compliance with its obligations under the Nuclear Proliferation Treaty Safeguards Agreement, "Implementation of the NPT Safeguards Agreement and relevant provisions of Security Council resolutions 1737 (2006) and 1747 (2007) in the Islamic Republic of Iran," GOV/2007/58, November 2007 (hereafter "IAEA Report 2007").
[3] Ibid., 8. In his statement issued at the same time as the IAEA Report 2007, former IAEA Director General, Dr Mohamed ElBaradei, stated that IAEA's knowledge about Iran's current program diminished since 2006, "when Iran ceased to provide the Agency with information under the additional protocol and additional transparency measures. This relates especially to current procurement, R&D and possible manufacturing of centrifuges."

available in declassified form – concluded that it is likely that Tehran has resumed work on nuclear weapons research in addition to expanding its program to enrich uranium. This has been substantiated by the IAEA's May 2012 report, which stated that IAEA inspectors had found traces of uranium being enriched at 27 percent at Iran's Fordow site – a higher level of enrichment than previously found.[4] While US officials report that at least some of the 2007 assertions have been revised in the new NIE, the new assessment stops short of rejecting the earlier findings.[5]

This lack of clarity around the possible military dimensions to Iran's nuclear program is explicable given that, as of mid-2011, Iran had not engaged with the IAEA on the substance of these issues since August 2008.[6] Likewise, by not implementing the obligations of its Additional Protocol, Iran has rendered it impossible for the IAEA to provide credible assurance of the absence of undeclared nuclear materials and activities.[7] Meanwhile, based on the findings of its own investigations, the IAEA has ongoing concerns that undisclosed nuclear-related activities have, in fact, continued in Iran beyond 2004.

In the context of these contemporary developments, this chapter examines US policies of preventive action as they have recently been employed in response to the threat posed by Iran's nuclear capabilities. With the Obama administration evincing its intention to pursue a more conciliatory, diplomatic approach to the Iran nuclear issue – despite the continuing opacity about the scope and imminence of the threat involved – the justifications for and against a US preventive response to Iran are as contested as ever.

This chapter considers its origins and rationale, and whether a policy of preventive action is justified – legally or ethically – in the case of Iran. To achieve this task, US justifications for the use of preventive force will be interrogated, first against the current standards of international law and state practice, and second, against more contemporary (and comprehensive) standards recently proposed by leading international relations theorists. After considering the extent to which preventive action by the US to avert

---

[4] IAEA, Board of Governors, "Implementation of the NPT Safeguards Agreement and relevant provisions of Security Council resolutions in the Islamic Republic of Iran," GOV/2012/23, 25 May 2012.

[5] Adam Entous, "US Spies: Iran Split on Nuclear Program," *The Wall Street Journal*, February 17, 2011.

[6] IAEA, Board of Governors, "Implementation of the NPT Safeguards Agreement and relevant provisions of Security Council resolutions in the Islamic Republic of Iran," GOV/2011/29, May 24, 2011, 7.

[7] Ibid., 8.

the Iranian nuclear threat would be justified against both these sets of standards, I will then explore whether comparisons can be drawn between the threat posed by Iran's nuclear capabilities, and that previously perceived by Iraq's weapons of mass destruction (WMD) at the time of the US invasion of Iraq in March 2003. From this, I will suggest an approach to the Iranian nuclear threat, based on mistakes and lessons learned from the US approach to the war in Iraq.

IRAN'S NUCLEAR CAPABILITIES

Before this analysis is undertaken, however, it is useful to situate this discussion within the context of the evidence verifying Iran's actual nuclear capabilities. While the 2007 NIE concluded that Tehran halted its nuclear weapons program in fall 2003, the 2011 NIE, without contradicting it, diluted this conclusion. Despite the lack of clarity as to whether Iran has made the strategic decision to build a nuclear weapon, it is apparent that the country is working on the components of such a device.[8] Interestingly, at the time the 2007 NIE was issued, it was adjudged that the *earliest possible* date Iran would be technically capable of producing enough highly enriched uranium ("HEU") for a weapon was late 2009. However, the NIE assessed that a much more likely time frame for Iran to be technically capable of producing sufficient HEU for a weapon would be during the period from 2010 to 2015. In 2011, though, intelligence officials seem to have reached the consensus that Iran appears to be at least four years away from being able to produce a nuclear weapon.[9]

However, despite the reported halt to the weaponization elements of its nuclear program, and in defiance of seven United Nations Security Council resolutions to the contrary,[10] Iran continues to pursue its centrifuge enrichment-related activities. The IAEA Board of Governors' periodic reports on Iran, issued in 2011 and 2012, noted that Iran was making significant advances in developing and operating its nuclear centrifuges for enriching uranium.[11] For example, as of May 2011, 8,000 centrifuges (in 53 cascades) were installed at the Natanz Fuel Enrichment Plant – a significant increase on the number of centrifuges reported by the IAEA at the same

---

[8] Josh Rogin, "Exclusive: New National Intelligence Estimate on Iran Complete," *The Cable*, February 15, 2011.

[9] IAEA Report 2011.

[10] The United Nations Security Council has adopted the following resolutions on Iran: 1696 (2006); 1737 (2006); 1747 (2007); 1803 (2008); 1835 (2008); 1887 (2009); and 1929 (2010).

[11] IAEA Report 2011 and 2012, 3.

plant in late 2009, being less than 4,000.[12] It has also been argued that revelations of Iran's secret uranium enrichment facility at Qom, which occurred after the release of the 2007 NIE, are further proof that the Iranian regime is pursuing nuclear weapons.[13]

These would appear to be worrying developments, particularly on the basis of the 2007 NIE's finding that centrifuge enrichment is the most probable means by which Iran could first produce enough fissile material for a weapon.[14] Significantly too, the IAEA has highlighted Iran's past and current centrifuge enrichment program as one of the key "remaining major issues relevant to the scope and nature of Iran's nuclear programme."[15]

Therefore, despite the obfuscation and lack of information, many serious concerns persist in relation to Iran's current and potential nuclear capabilities. Nonetheless, the recent findings present a far more nuanced picture of Iran's nuclear ambitions than the one some US administrations have espoused to date.[16] Indeed, it now seems that "Teheran's decisions are guided by a cost-benefit approach rather than a rush to a weapon irrespective of the political, economic and military costs."[17] These findings provide a crucial backdrop against which the current US strategy to the Iranian nuclear threat can be investigated.

THE BASIC MECHANICS OF NUCLEAR WEAPONS PRODUCTION

The complex science of nuclear weapons production is well beyond the scope of this chapter. However, before I turn to examine the origins, rationale, and justifications for the US policy of prevention, it is helpful to take a brief detour into the basic mechanics of the nuclear fuel cycle itself. Mined uranium ore is sent to a mill where it is crushed, ground, and reconstituted in a solid form as uranium oxide (also known as "yellow-cake"). As an intermediate step, yellowcake then undergoes a process of conversion, transforming it into the gas uranium hexafluoride. This is

---

[12] IAEA, Board of Governors, "Implementation of the NPT Safeguards Agreement and relevant provisions of Security Council resolutions 1737 (2006), 1747 (2007), 1803 (2008) and 1835 (2008) in the Islamic Republic of Iran," GOV/2009/74, November 16, 2009.

[13] Josh Rogin, quoting House Foreign Affairs ranking Democrat Howard Berman, in Rogin, "Exclusive," n. 8.

[14] NIE Report 2007, at C.   [15] IAEA Report 2007, 8.

[16] During a press conference at the time of the 2007 Estimate's publication, President Bush stated, "Look, Iran was dangerous, Iran is dangerous, and Iran will be dangerous, if they have the knowledge necessary to make a nuclear weapon … What's to say they couldn't start another covert nuclear weapons program?," Steven Lee Myers and Helene Cooper, "Bush Insists Iran Remains a Threat Despite Arms Data," *New York Times*, December 5, 2007.

[17] NIE Report 2007, at E.

necessary in order for it to proceed to the next step: enrichment. Put simply, enrichment increases the proportion of more powerful atoms within the uranium particles. In Iran, enrichment occurs by the use of a centrifuge process. The enriched uranium can then be fed into a nuclear reactor to generate electricity. Lastly, spent fuel from a nuclear reactor (which still contains approximately 96 percent of its original uranium)[18] can be reprocessed to separate potentially valuable uranium and plutonium, from other (non-valuable) nuclear waste.

Building a successful nuclear weapons program comprises three vital stages: first, a sufficient stockpile of nuclear material (highly enriched uranium or plutonium); second, the construction of bombs out of that nuclear material; and third, assembling missiles to deliver those bombs to their desired targets. Each stage presents its own significant challenges and difficulties for a state. It is notable that the enrichment and reprocessing stages are the most likely points at which nuclear material will be diverted from civilian to military use.[19] This is because, during enrichment, uranium can be enriched to a greater degree with the aim of using it as the basic ingredient in a uranium bomb; and during reprocessing, plutonium can be diverted to bomb-making instead of into civilian energy production.[20] Accordingly, despite Iran's ostensible compliance with its IAEA obligations, its continued development and expansion of its enrichment facilities (as outlined above) – for many critics of the regime – bespeaks its real intentions.

ORIGINS AND RATIONALE OF THE POLICY OF PREVENTION

The Bush administration's stated commitment to a policy of preemption (also known as the "Bush doctrine") was most clearly articulated in the National Security Strategy of the United States of America ("NSS"), issued by the administration in September 2002. However, despite using the rhetoric of "preemption," in promulgating an offensive strategy that targets non-imminent, uncertain, and even unformed threats (such as that currently posed by Iran) the policy was clearly *preventive*, rather than preemptive

---

[18] World Nuclear Association: Nuclear Information, http://world-nuclear.org/education/nfc.htm, accessed on 11/24/2007.

[19] International Network of Engineers and Scientists Against Proliferation, Beyond the NPT: A Nuclear-Weapon-Free World, April 1995, www.inesap.or/beyondNPT.htm. Note also the findings of the IAEA Report 2007.

[20] Benjamin M. Greenblum, "The Iranian Nuclear Threat: Israel's Options Under International Law," *Houston Journal of International Law* 29:1 (2006), 55–112, at 60.

in character. In this vein, William Bradford has asserted that the Bush doctrine was "effectively a unilateral US assertion of the right to engage in preventive war."[21]

The NSS states: "We will cooperate with other nations to deny, contain, and curtail our enemies' efforts to acquire dangerous technologies. And, as a matter of common sense and self-defense, *America will act against such emerging threats before they are fully formed*,"[22] and similarly:

The United States has long maintained the option of preemptive actions to counter a sufficient threat to our national security. The greater the threat, the greater is the risk of inaction – and the more compelling the case for taking anticipatory action to defend ourselves, *even if uncertainty remains as to the time and place of the enemy's attack. To forestall or prevent* such hostile acts by our adversaries, the United States will, if necessary, *act pre-emptively* [emphasis added].[23]

Likewise, President George W. Bush himself espoused a strong personal commitment to the policy of prevention. For example, in his West Point commencement day address in 2002, he stated, "We must take the battle to the enemy, disrupt his plans, and confront the worst threats before they emerge. In the world we have entered, the only path to peace and security is action."[24] In October 2007, he suggested that a nuclear-armed Iran could lead to "World War III."[25] Similarly, former Secretary of State in the Bush administration, Condoleezza Rice, stated that the US and its allies "cannot allow the Iranians to develop a nuclear weapon."[26]

Some ascribe the genesis of the US policy of prevention exclusively to the Bush administration, and more specifically, to its exploitation of the new world climate of fear and uncertainty generated post-September 11, 2001. However, as asserted by the NSS (as extracted above), and attested to by various academic commentators, rather than being anomalous to the Bush administration, prevention and/or preemption (in one form or another) has been a recurring feature of much US foreign policy throughout the twentieth century.

---

[21] William C. Bradford, "The Duty to Defend Them: A Natural Law Justification for the Bush Doctrine of Preventive War," *Notre Dame Law Review* 79:4 (2004), 1365–1492.

[22] National Security Strategy of the United States of America, September 2002, v.

[23] Ibid., 15.

[24] George W. Bush, "Graduation Speech at West Point," June 1, 2002: www.whitehouse.gov/news/releases/2002/06/20020601–3.html.

[25] Mark Mazzetti, "US Finds Iran Halted Its Nuclear Arms Effort in 2003," *New York Times*, December 4, 2007.

[26] David E. Sanger, "Rice Says Iran Must Not Be Allowed to Develop Nuclear Arms", *New York Times*, August 9, 2004, A3.

For example, Marc Trachtenberg has argued that (even in the pre-nuclear world) a preventive war strategy played an influential role in shaping US foreign policy. In particular, he claims that the policies pursued by the Truman, Eisenhower, Kennedy, and Clinton administrations, at different junctures, were each preventive in character.[27] Trachtenberg's central claim is not that there is no difference between the Bush doctrine and the policies of his predecessors. Rather, he argues "simply that there is a greater element of continuity here than people realize."[28]

Whether President Obama will break this line of continuity in relation to Iran remains to be seen. From the outset of his presidency, Obama expressed his intention to open direct talks with Iran about its nuclear program and, in conjunction with other major powers, has taken steps towards commencing negotiations with Iran. The five permanent members of the UN Security Council – China, France, Russia, the United Kingdom, and the United States – and Germany, known as the "P5+1," have been engaged in off-and-on discussions with Iran over its nuclear program over the past several years. However, with growing evidence that Iran's nuclear-enrichment program is proceeding briskly, quickly outpacing the progress of diplomatic talks, it is possible that the president's best laid plans for direct engagement may need revision. Indeed, in Washington DC in March 2012, at a major pro-Israeli conference, he stated, "Iran's leaders should know that I do not have a policy of containment . . . I have a policy to prevent Iran from obtaining a nuclear weapon."[29]

Consideration of the *origins* of US preventive force is instructive to an evaluation of its *justifications*. While history is not a predictor of the present, it may, to a certain extent, assist us to understand the natural precursors and underlying foundations upon which contemporary national policy and international politics are based. Viewed against this background, it is arguable that the Bush administration's preventive approach to the threat posed by a nuclear Iran was more comprehensible (albeit not justifiable) given the strategies of previous administrations. While the power of such "systemic forces" should not be overstated,[30] their influence, at the least, bears some consideration in assessing the various (and complex) contributory factors informing recent US policies of prevention.

---

[27] Marc Trachtenberg, "Preventive War and US Foreign Policy," *Security Studies* 16:1 (January–March 2007), 1–31.

[28] Ibid., 20.

[29] Jon Swaine and Phoebe Greenwood, "Obama: I will not hesitate in using force to block Iran's nuclear threat from Iran," *The Telegraph*, March 4, 2012.

[30] Mazzetti, "US Finds Iran Halted Its Nuclear Arms Effort in 2003," 29.

THE DIFFERENCE BETWEEN PREEMPTION AND PREVENTION

Before the justifications for and against US prevention in response to the nuclear threat posed by Iran are extrapolated, it is important to first delineate the distinction between "preemptive" and "preventive" use of force. Stated most simply, "preemption" describes the response to an *imminent* threat, while "prevention" describes the response to a *non-imminent* threat.[31]

Some academic commentators have elided the two concepts by arguing that the difference between preventive and preemptive force is only a matter of degree.[32] Similarly, by using the words interchangeably, in recent times some US government policy-makers have attempted to extend the scope of anticipatory action encompassed by the notion of *preemption*, such that it now also includes *preventive* action, that is, the response to non-imminent threats.[33] Both these approaches, however, diminish important qualitative differences in the concepts' meanings.

Michael W. Doyle, for example, argues that the most important distinction between the two terms is captured by likelihood.[34] He states, "Preemption is motivated by wars that are expected to occur imminently; prevention by wars that, if they must be fought, are better fought now than later. Certainty and uncertainty are what connects them."[35] Similarly, preventive action has been defined as "the initiation of military action in anticipation of harmful actions that are neither presently occurring nor imminent"[36] and "attacking to forestall a rising threat".[37]

Following the release of the NIE and IAEA reports, there can be little doubt that, based on current intelligence, US military action in response to the Iranian nuclear threat would be *preventive*, rather than preemptive. While the potential threat posed by Iran's nuclear program remains very real, it is clearly not imminent in the sense used to justify preemptive action. While Iran's future capabilities and intentions remain shrouded in

---

[31] Gareth Evans as cited in Alan M. Dershowitz, *Preemption: A Knife that Cuts Both Ways* (New York: W. W. Norton, 2006), 204.

[32] Whitley Kaufman, "What's Wrong with Preventive War?: The Moral and Legal Basis for the Preventive Use of Force," *Ethics and International Affairs* 19:3 (2005), 23–38; 30.

[33] National Security Strategy of the United States of America, September 2002, 13. For example, the NSS states, "To forestall or *prevent* such hostile acts by our adversaries, the United States will, if necessary, act *preemptively*" [emphasis added].

[34] Michael W. Doyle, *Striking First: Preemption and Prevention in International Conflict*, ed. Stephen Macedo (Princeton University Press, 2008), 55.

[35] Ibid.

[36] Allen Buchanan and Robert O. Keohane, "The Preventive Use of Force: A Cosmopolitan Institutional Proposal," *Ethics and International Affairs* 18:1 (2004), 1–22, 1.

[37] Dan Reiter, *Preventive War and its Alternatives* (Carlisle, PA: Strategic Studies Institute, 2006), 2.

uncertainty and characterized by a "confidence deficit" in the international community,[38] there is no "concrete information"[39] to verify presently existing undeclared nuclear material and activities in Iran and, indeed, there are some strong reasons to believe that the entire program may have been suspended since 2003.[40] Indeed, until Iran provides the IAEA with the access and information it requires to resolve its outstanding issues and concerns, any conclusions the agency can make about the absence of undeclared nuclear material and activities in Iran will remain tentative at best.

JUSTIFICATIONS

The current legal framework

Having ascertained these distinctions, I turn now to consider whether, and in what circumstances, the use of preventive force by the US to combat Iran's nuclear threat would be justified, on the basis of existing law.

Article 51 and self-defense

Unequivocally, unilateral preventive action against Iran would *not* be justified pursuant to Article 51 of the UN Charter. According to Article 51, "Nothing in the present Charter shall impair the inherent right of individual or collective self-defense *if an armed attack occurs* against a Member of the United Nations, until the Security Council has taken measures necessary to maintain international peace and security" [emphasis added].[41] This article operates coterminously with the notions of territorial integrity and political independence, as articulated in Article 2(4).[42] The use of the words "if an armed attack occurs" necessarily implies that *preventive* self-defense against a non-imminent or uncertain attack is unlawful according to the terms of Article 51.[43] Accordingly, under the UN Charter, the legality of unilateral, anticipatory use of force, such as by the US against Iran, in any circumstances other than *actual* self-defense, would be vitiated.

---

[38] Dr Mohamed ElBaradei, former IAEA Director General, Introductory statement to the Board of Governors, November 22, 2007, accessed at www.iaea.org/NewsCenter/Statements/2007/ebsp2007n019.html.

[39] IAEA Report 2007, 9.   [40] NIE Report 2007.   [41] UN Charter, Article 51.

[42] UN Charter, Article 2(4) states: "All Members shall refrain in their international relations from the threat or use of force against the territorial integrity or political independence of any state, or in any other manner inconsistent with the Purposes of the United Nations."

[43] Dershowitz, *Preemption*, 202.

However, while Article 51 clearly does not sanction *prevention*, the "*inherent right*" of individual or collective self-defense" [emphasis added] is generally understood to incorporate *preemption* in certain circumstances. For example, in its December 2004 report ("UN Report"), the UN's High-Level Panel on Threats, Challenges and Change, stated that, despite the "restrictive" language of Article 51:

A threatened state, according to long established international law, can take military action as long as the threatened attack is *imminent*, no other means would deflect it and the action is proportionate. The problem arises where the threat in question is not imminent but still claimed to be real: for example the acquisition, with allegedly hostile intent, of nuclear weapons-making capability.

. . .

in a world full of perceived potential threats, the risk to the global order and the norm of non-intervention on which it continues to be based is simply too great for the legality of unilateral preventive action, as distinct from collectively endorsed action, to be accepted. Allowing one to so act is to allow all.[44]

Customary law and preemption/prevention?

Therefore, as the above UN Report alludes, Article 51 incorporates the customary law principle of preemptive self-defense, as set out in the *Caroline* case. The scope of the customary law standard is limited to authorizing the use of force in cases where the relevant threat is *imminent*. That is, like Article 51, it only extends to authorizing *preemption*, not prevention. The seminal principle emanating from the *Caroline* case is encapsulated in the statement of former US Secretary of State, Daniel Webster, that the use of anticipatory force could only be justified where the necessity for self-defense is "instant, overwhelming and leaving no choice of means, and no moment for deliberation."[45] In the case of Iran as it stands in mid-2012, none of these criteria are satisfied. Accordingly, under the *Caroline* test, US preventive action in response to the Iranian nuclear threat must be firmly rejected at this point in time.

It has been argued that the *Caroline* standard is too extreme and that, as such, its conditions are very rarely found in reality.[46] In commenting on the adequacy of the *Caroline* standard, and how it compares to more

---

[44] United Nations High-Level Panel on Threats, Challenges and Change, "A More Secure World: Our Shared Responsibility" (2004), 63; accessed at www.un.org./secureworld/ (hereafter "UN Report 2004").

[45] Michael Walzer, *Just and Unjust Wars* (New York: Basic Books, 2000), 74.

[46] Trachtenberg, "Preventive War and U.S. Foreign Policy," 15.

contemporary US doctrines of prevention, Doyle has stated, "traditional preemption is too strict and the Bush Administration's expansive prevention is too loose."[47]

Article 39 and prevention

Accordingly, while a *preemptive* attack on an imminent threat posed by a state may well be lawful under customary international law, the only mechanism by which *preventive* force against a non-imminent, latent, or uncertain nuclear threat (such as that currently posed by Iran) would be lawfully justified is by the authorization of the Security Council, by resolution under Article 39. Article 39 states as follows:

The Security Council shall determine the existence of any threat to the peace, breach of the peace, or act of aggression and shall make recommendations, or decide what measures shall be taken in accordance with Articles 41 and 42, to maintain or restore international peace and security.[48]

In commenting on the use of preventive force under this article, the UN Report stated:

The question is not whether such action can be taken: it can, by the Security Council as the international community's collective security voice, at any time it deems that there is a threat to international peace and security. The Council may well need to be prepared to be much more proactive on these issues, taking more decisive action earlier, than it has been in the past.[49]

Further, the UN Report elaborated on the rationale behind Article 39:

[I]f there are good arguments for preventive military action, with good evidence to support them, they should be put to the Security Council, which can authorize such action if it chooses to. If it does not so choose, there will be, by definition, time to pursue other strategies, including persuasion, negotiation, deterrence and containment – and to visit again the military option.[50]

Accordingly, within the current legal framework, Article 39 provides the *only* mechanism by which *lawful* preventive action could be taken to respond to the threat posed by Iran's nuclear capabilities. However, under no circumstances would this article justify the use of *unilateral*, preventive force by the US against Iran of the kind foreshadowed in the recent past under the Bush doctrine.

---

[47] Doyle, *Striking First*, 43.   [48] UN Charter, Article 39.   [49] UN Report 2004, 55.
[50] Ibid.

Alternative frameworks for assessing justifications for prevention

As I have outlined above, based on our current knowledge of the nature and scope of Iran's nuclear program, the use of unilateral, preventive force by the US to counter this threat would be unlawful and, therefore, unjustifiable under the existing legal framework. However, dissatisfaction with the current legal framework is widespread among academics, politicians, and policy-makers alike. In practice, this is evidenced by the plethora of occasions (most recently in Iraq) in which states have adopted preventive action to oppose a threat, in the absence of Security Council authorization.[51] Accordingly, I now examine two alternative paradigms under which the use of unilateral preventive force (without Chapter 7 authorization) may be justified as legitimate, albeit unlawful. By broadening the scope of the discussion, in this way, I hope to highlight some of the relevant *ethical* considerations that bear on an overall assessment of the justification for US preventive action in Iran.

A duty to prevent?

By leveraging on the UN's "Responsibility to Protect" doctrine[52] and drawing a corollary between humanitarian interventions and global security, international scholars Lee Feinstein and Anne-Marie Slaughter claim that the international community has a collective "duty to prevent" dictatorships and closed societies, lacking internal checks on their power, from acquiring or using WMDs.[53] By reconceptualizing the traditional principle of state sovereignty such that, in certain circumstances, the principle of non-intervention yields to the "duty to prevent," they argue that, "Like the responsibility to protect, the duty to prevent begins from the premise that the rules now governing the use of force, devised in 1945 and embedded in the UN Charter, are inadequate."[54] Likewise, they state that, "We live in a world of old rules and new threats."[55]

Underlying their proactive "duty to prevent" is a moral obligation on the international community, collectively, to act promptly and effectively to obviate nuclear threats when and where they arise. Indeed, under the

---

[51] The UN Report 2004 states further, "For the first 44 years of the United Nations, Member States often violated these rules and used military force literally hundreds of times, with a paralyzed Security Council passing very few Chapter VII resolutions," ibid., 54.

[52] "The Responsibility to Protect" doctrine was issued by the UN in late 2001. It can be accessed at www.iciss.ca/report-en.asp.

[53] Lee Feinstein and Anne-Marie Slaughter, "A Duty to Prevent," *Foreign Affairs* 83:1 (January–February 2004), 136–150.;137.

[54] As above.   [55] Ibid., 138.

Feinstein/Slaughter model, it is arguable that preventive action by the US in Iran is not only justified, it is *demanded*.

Rather than a personal dictatorship, President Mahmoud Ahmadinejad's Iran is perhaps best characterized as an unusual combination of Islamic theocracy with elements of democracy. While, in theory, the Iranian system combines a popularly elected president and parliament with a network of unelected institutions headed by the all-powerful Supreme Leader, in practice, the democratic aspects of the regime are scarcely discernible in 2012. Since Ahmadinejad's election in June 2005, all state power has been concentrated in the hands of a few so-called "divine representatives" who have propagated a return to the fundamentalist principles of the Islamic Revolution. In the current regime, the unelected Supreme Leader of Iran, Ayatollah Sayyid Ali Khamenei, plays an enormous role. A hard-line conservative, he controls the armed forces and judiciary, and is responsible for making decisions on security, defense, and foreign policy issues.[56] In addition to the complete absence of checks and balances on governmental power, the danger posed by the Iranian regime is infinitely heightened by its alliances with Hezbollah and other terrorist organizations. For example, the Islamic Revolutionary Guard Corps ("IRGC"), the group responsible for the day-to-day control of Iran's nuclear facilities, is known to have terrorist ties.[57] Further, the nature of the Iranian regime is such that any opposition – perceived or actual – wherever it arises, is quickly and decisively crushed.[58] Accordingly, Ahmadinejad's Iran would seem to represent the archetypal closed society within the Feinstein/Slaughter paradigm.

However, despite the weighty demands their model places on states to "prevent" and its (potentially) immense implications for states that are the subject of the prevention, it sets no conclusive guidelines or parameters for the circumstances in which it will actually operate. Instead, under this model, the assessment of the relative danger posed by states and their rulers appears to be highly subjective and, to a certain extent, based on inconsistent value judgments as to what constitutes a so-called "open" or "closed" society. As a result, the determination of which states are deserving of sovereignty is extremely problematic. For example, in discussing their model's selective application, Feinstein and Slaughter affirm that, "It

---

[56] See: "Iran: Who Holds the Power?," BBC News, http:news.bbc.co.uk/2/shared/spl/hi/middle_east/03/iran_power/html/default.stm accessed on July 6, 2012.

[57] Scott D. Sagan, "How to Keep the Bomb From Iran", *Foreign Affairs* 85:5 (September–October 2006), 45–59.

[58] Negar Azimi, "Hard Realities of Soft Power," *New York Times*, June 24, 2007.

applies to Kim Jong Il's North Korea, but not to Hu Jintao's (or even Mao's) China."[59] Further, they state that, "regimes such as Iran's, because they sponsor terrorism, suppress democracy, and have clear nuclear designs, are not entitled to the same rights as other NPT members."[60] Without a clearer delineation of the selection criteria on which these assessments are based, this differential application is concerning.[61] To a large extent, it undermines the model's usefulness as a normative framework by which US preventive force in Iran could possibly be justified.

Another difficulty with the "duty to prevent" is that – unlike the Responsibility to Protect – it targets rulers and states largely based on *who* and what they *are*, not on what they have *done* (or failed to do). The logical implication of this approach is that eligibility for national sovereignty would be determined on the basis of a state's ideological acceptability to the world's dominant hegemonic powers: a situation anathema to the general principles of international diplomacy and the comity of nations, which is potentially rife for abuse, politicking, and horse-trading.

While I would not advocate the adoption of the Feinstein/Slaughter model of prevention, its weaknesses do suggest two important ethical principles to be applied to testing the validity of justifications for US preventive action in Iran. First, prevention must be based on *clear, objective*, and *justifiable* criteria, to ensure consistency with the US response to other countries possessing similar nuclear capabilities. And second, preventive action must be based on a state's actions (or omissions to act), rather than on the idiosyncrasies of its leader or ruling party's political ideology. Ultimately, US unilateral prevention in Iran will only be valid if it serves universal, rather than statist or particularist, values and interests.

Lethality, likelihood, legitimacy, and legality
Drawing on "just-war" theory, a much more comprehensive model for assessing the justifiability of prevention has been proposed by Michael W. Doyle. He argues that the standards for unilateral prevention should "look beyond imminence and active preparations to four wider considerations of *lethality, likelihood, legitimacy* and *legality*" [emphasis in the original].[62] Assessed against this broader framework, it is clear that US

---

[59] Feinstein and Slaughter, "A Duty to Prevent," 143.   [60] Ibid., 145.
[61] This concern is also shared by Anthony Burke, "Against the New Internationalism," *Ethics and International Affairs* 19:2 (2005), 73–89; 77.
[62] Doyle, *Striking First*, 46.

preventive action against Iran, at the current time, based on the most
recent intelligence, would *not* be justified. Dealing with each substantive
consideration in turn, I outline the reasons for this conclusion below.

Lethality identifies the amount of anticipated harm if the threat is not
eliminated, discounted by the reversibility of the harm.[63] While not
persuasively satisfied in the case of Iran, this measure (more than the three
that follow) would seem to provide the best justification for the US use of
preventive force against Iran. The scale and scope of destruction that
would be likely to result from Iran's use of nuclear weapons is immense,
and, in most respects, irreversible. Condemning Israel as a "filthy Zionist
entity which has reached the end of the line,"[64] Iranian President Ahmadinejad has threatened to "wipe Israel off the map."[65] Likewise, his predecessors have boasted that Iran's missiles have the capacity to destroy Jewish
and Christian civilization,[66] based on their predictions that an Iranian
attack would kill as many as five million Jews.[67] However, whether or not
these threats are, in fact, credible in light of the recent conclusions of the
NIE and IAEA reports, is open to question. Particularly notable for the
assessment of lethality, is the 2007 NIE's finding that Iran does not have a
nuclear weapon.[68]

Likelihood assesses the probability that the threat will occur.[69] As well as
being indications of the *lethality* of an Iranian missile strike, the threats of
Iranian leaders past and present, as noted above, also bear significantly on
the *likelihood* of such a threat. Likewise, the election of the aggressive
Ahmadinejad government in 2005, viewed in combination with its strong
terrorist alliances, serves to intensify the force of these threats and their
impact on the likelihood of a nuclear strike. However, taking into account
Iran's overall capacity and its technical feasibility,[70] the current likelihood
of an Iranian nuclear attack seems minimal. In addition to the strong
probability that Iran does not currently possess a nuclear weapon, this
conclusion is supported by assessments that found the Iranian nuclear
program has been suspended since 2003 and, if restarted, would, in all

---

[63] Ibid., 46–47.
[64] Nazila Fathi, "Ahmadinejad Sees Nuclear Energy in Iran by 2009," *New York Times*, January 31,
2008.
[65] Nazila Fathi, "Iran's New President says Israel 'Must Be Wiped Off the Map'," *New York Times*,
October 27, 2005.
[66] President Mohammad Khatami, as cited in Dershowitz, *Preemption*, 175.
[67] President Hashemi Rafsanjani, as cited in ibid., 175.
[68] NIE Report 2007, at A. This assessment is made with "moderate-to-high confidence."
[69] Doyle, *Striking First*, 46.
[70] These are two of the standards adopted by Doyle to assess likelihood. Ibid., 54.

likelihood, not be in a position to produce enough HEU for a weapon before around 2015.[71] Accordingly, based on current information indicating that the *likelihood* of an Iranian nuclear strike is reasonably weak, US unilateral, preventive action in Iran could not be justified on this basis.

The third consideration in Doyle's framework, *legitimacy*, incorporates the traditional just-war criteria of proportionality, necessity, and seeking relevant deliberations.[72] Applied to the Iranian nuclear threat, this standard would *not* justify a US preventive action in Iran at the present time. Unlike the 1981 Israeli attack on the Iraqi Osirak nuclear reactor, which caused minimal loss of life and is considered an archetype of proportionality by many,[73] a preventive attack on Iranian nuclear facilities would be likely to result in enormous civilian casualties and loss of life. Based on recent intelligence reports, Iran, learning from the Osirak experience, has deliberately dispersed its nuclear facilities broadly around the country (many in deep underground bunkers), including in densely populated areas.[74] Commenting on the horrifying moral conundrum this produces, Dershowitz has stated:

This could force Israel and the United States into a terrible choice: either allow Iran to complete its production of nuclear bombs aimed at their civilian population centers and other targets, or destroy the facilities despite the inevitability of Iranian civilian casualties.[75]

Similarly, the question of necessity is acutely problematic in attempting to justify the legitimacy of a US preventive action on Iran's nuclear facilities. Based on the findings of the 2007 and 2011 NIE reports and recent IAEA reports (as I have outlined above), there would seem to be no necessity in the immediate to mid-term future for authorizing such an attack. However, as Dershowitz points out, "The longer they wait, the greater the risks to civilians, especially if they wait until an attack on the reactors might spread radiation."[76] Accordingly, it would seem problematic to claim that a preventive attack against Iranian nuclear facilities (to forestall the production of weapons that currently do not exist and the recommencement of processes that are presently stalled) is necessary (and justifiable under customary law) now rather than later on the basis that such action would at this point in time only cause massive, rather than cataclysmic, loss of civilian life. Therefore, on both the necessity and proportionality arms of the legitimacy paradigm, justifications for US preventive action in Iran must be rejected.

---

[71] NIE Report 2007, at B.   [72] Doyle, *Striking First*, 46 and 57.
[73] Dershowitz, *Preemption*, 180.   [74] Ibid., 181.   [75] Ibid.   [76] Ibid.

The last standard, *legality*, asks whether the proposed remedy (that is, US preventive action) is more or less legal than the threatening situation which has precipitated the preventive action (that is, Iran's nuclear threat).[77] Based on IAEA reports, Iran is substantially in compliance with its obligations under the Non-Proliferation Treaty (NPT). In particular, the IAEA has verified the non-diversion of declared nuclear material and that Iran's reprocessing and uranium conversion activities are within the scope of its obligations under its safeguards agreement (although not in compliance with United Nations Security Council resolutions).[78]

However, the IAEA has characterized Iran's cooperation as "reactive rather than proactive"[79] and these recent findings must be counter-balanced with the illegality of Iran's past international deviance in nuclear matters[80] and its continued reluctance to implement the Additional Protocol to the NPT, which would afford greater transparency in its programs. Without greater cooperation from Iran, the IAEA cannot provide credible assurance about the absence of *undeclared* nuclear material and activities in Iran. Further, Iran's continued threats of belligerence (for example, to "wipe Israel off the map"), in themselves, constitute violations of Article 2(4) of the UN Charter.[81] In addition, by not suspending its enrichment-related activities, Iran continues to contravene Security Council resolutions 1737, 1747, 1803, and 1835.

According to Doyle's framework, the legality of these aspects of Iran's current and past behavior will need to be weighed in the balance with the legality of US preventive action in Iran. In assessing its justification, he highlights that a strict requirement of proportionality must be imposed in preventive actions.[82] By way of explanation, he states, "Greater uncertainty, which is equivalent to lesser imminence, justifies this safeguard."[83] Accordingly, irrespective of its previous and ongoing violations of international law and IAEA standards, it is clear that Iran's current activities would not meet the high threshold for illegality to justify the extraordinary (and also illegal) remedy of US preventive action.

As a systemic framework for assessing whether US prevention would be justified in response to Iran's nuclear capabilities, the "four *Ls*" provide an

---

[77] Doyle, *Striking First*, 46 and 59.   [78] IAEA Report 2007, at C, E1 and F; IAEA Report 2012.
[79] IAEA Report 2007, at F.42.
[80] Iran pursued a covert, undeclared nuclear program for almost two decades until its breaches of the NPT were detected in the 1990s. For example, see: "Iran and Nuclear Weapons," *New York Times*, June 22, 2003, located at: http://query.nytimes.com/gst/fullpage.html?res=9803E0D8163BF931A157 55C0A9659C8B63.
[81] Doyle, *Striking First*, 92.   [82] Ibid., 60.   [83] Ibid., 61.

invaluable guide and, to a large extent, mitigate the previous challenges of using old rules to deal with new threats in the realm of nuclear proliferation. Assuming that "each is necessary and all are interrelated,"[84] the failure of the US to justify preventive force in Iran on the basis of *all four* standards means that, at the present time, prevention in Iran must be unequivocally rejected.

WOULD US PREVENTIVE ACTION IN IRAN RISK REPEATING MISTAKES MADE IN IRAQ?

A number of comparisons can be drawn between the US response to the threat currently posed by Iran's nuclear capabilities, and to that previously perceived by Iraq's WMDs. I turn now to consider the extent to which correlations can be drawn between these two examples and, accordingly, whether any lessons learned from the US experience of prevention in Iraq can be applied to Iran. I examine these two cases in juxtaposition by highlighting several relevant corollaries.

Iraq: also an example of unilateral preventive force?

The US invasion and occupation of Iraq in March 2003 has been broadly condemned as contrary to international law. While a few commentators have endorsed the Bush administration's claim that the action was lawfully justified by its enforcement of UN Security Council Resolutions,[85] by far the majority argue that it was a classic example of unilateral preventive war, pursuant to the Bush doctrine.[86] While the Security Council was prepared to enforce Iraq's compliance with UN inspections, it refused to sanction the US invasion. Michael Ramsey states that the failure of the UN Security Council to authorize the Iraq war represents a "breakdown in the UN system," that justified the US pursuing a unilateral preventive war against Iraq.[87] Whitley Kaufman, on the other hand, considers that as a case of preventive war, the US invasion was not justified.[88]

---

[84] Ibid., 63.

[85] Specifically, UN Security Council Resolutions 1441 (2002), 678 (1990), and 687 (1991). These resolutions were passed in the context of the first Gulf war and required Iraq's disarmament.

[86] For example, see Bradford, "The Duty to Defend Them," 2. Doyle, *Striking First*, 90 states: "In March 2003, however, the lack of evidence that Saddam was successfully developing nuclear weapons ... made an invasion and occupation illegitimate, radically disproportionate, and unjustifiable."

[87] Michael Ramsey, "Reinventing the Security Council: The UN as a Lockean System," *Notre Dame Law Review* 79:4 (July 2004), 1529–1562.

[88] Kaufman, "What's Wrong with Preventive War?," 35 and 38. Kaufman states that the UN Security Council was within its rights to determine that a war was not justified in Iraq.

Similarly, as I outline above, the prospect of the use of anticipatory force by the US against the Iranian nuclear threat, at the present time, based on the available evidence, would also constitute a clear case of unilateral prevention. For the reasons I set out above, such action would be ethically unjustifiable, as well as unlawful under international law and accepted state practice.

Lack of evidence: uncertainty and likelihood of the nuclear threat

Second, it is relevant to compare the nuclear threat currently posed by Iran with that previously alleged against Iraq, by reference to the intelligence used by the US to justify the existence of the threat. Despite the presence of significant uncertainty in the intelligence surrounding the existence and scope of both threats, the Bush administration continued to advocate preventive action as the appropriate response, largely on the basis of the nature of the *threat* and the *regime* controlling it. For example, in 2002 President Bush justified preventive action in Iraq, stating, "Understanding the threats of our time, knowing the designs and deceptions of the Iraqi regime, we have every reason to assume the worst, and we have an urgent duty to prevent the worst from occurring."[89] In relation to Iraq, this position was maintained by the Bush administration, despite its notable lack of substantiating evidence in support,[90] until the release of chief US weapons inspector David Kay's interim report in January 2004, verifying that Iran, in fact, possessed no WMDs.

Similarly, British Prime Minister Tony Blair justified the invasion of Iraq, despite the weak evidence supporting this course of action. He argued, "the risk of this new global terrorism and its interaction with states or organizations or individuals proliferating WMD is one I am simply not prepared to run ... this is not the time to err on the side of caution; not a time to weigh the risks to an infinite balance."[91]

Likewise, following the release of the NIE in late 2007, the Bush administration interpreted its findings, that Iran's nuclear program had

---

[89] Amy Gutmann and Dennis Thompson, eds., *Ethics and Politics* (Chicago: Nelson Hall, 2005), 49.

[90] For example, while the 2002 NSS states, "[a]t the time of the Gulf War, we acquired irrefutable proof that Iraq's designs were not limited to the chemical weapons it had used against Iran and its own people, but also extended to the acquisition of nuclear weapons and biological agents" (14), David Kay commented on the evidence for WMDs, that "[t]he more you look at it, the less that is there." Quoted in Bob Woodward, *State of Denial* (New York: Simon & Schuster, 2006), 217, as cited in Doyle, *Striking First*, 91.

[91] 10 Downing Street Press Release, "Prime Minister Warns of Continuing Global Terror Threat," March 5, 2004, cited by Burke, "Against the New Internationalism," 75.

been suspended since 2003, as a vindication of the US government's aggressive strategy of prevention, rather than as a reason for re-evaluating their approach or assessment of the nuclear threat Iran posed. For example, on the day of the release, the National Security Advisor, Stephen Hadley stated, "It confirms that we were right to be worried about Iran seeking to develop nuclear weapons . . . But the intelligence also tells us that the risk of Iran acquiring a nuclear weapon remains a very serious problem."[92] Likewise, in light of the information, President Bush stated at the time that the new assessment underscored the need to intensify international efforts to prevent Iran from acquiring a nuclear weapon.[93]

Nature of the regime: repressive dictatorships and international delinquency

Like Iran, until the overthrow of the government in 2003, Iraq had a long history of authoritarian rule by an oppressive and violent dictator.[94] Further (and also like Iran), the Iraqi government propagated strong connections between the state and terrorist groups. As a former chief weapons inspector of the UN commented, "The fundamental problem with Iraq remains the nature of the regime, itself. Saddam Hussein is a homicidal dictator who is addicted to weapons of mass destruction."[95] Similarly, in relation to Iran, former Secretary of State, Condoleezza Rice, stated that the "Iranian regime remains a problematic and dangerous regime and that the international community must continue to unite around the Security Council resolutions that it has passed."[96]

Additionally, with regard to their nuclear armories, both regimes have been characterized by a record of international delinquency, contravention of their declared international commitments, and non-cooperation. For example, Iraqi non-compliance with their obligations under the 1991 Gulf war cease-fire agreement, relating to the immediate destruction of all WMDs and long-range missiles, climaxed in December 1998 with the withdrawal of UN inspections teams and a four-day retaliatory bombing campaign by the US and UK against Iraqi weapons facilities.[97] Likewise,

---

[92] Statement of National Security Advisor, Stephen Hadley, accessed at: www.whitehouse.gov/news/releases/2007/12/20071203–5.html.

[93] Myers and Cooper, "Bush Insists Iran Remains a Threat."

[94] Saddam Hussein had governed Iraq since 1979. An example of the violence of his regime and its disdain for human rights is the 1988 mass slaughter of an estimated 5,000 Iraqi citizens and Kurds.

[95] Greenblum, "The Iranian Nuclear Threat," 48.

[96] Nazila Fathi, "Iranian Leader Calls Report US Confession of 'Mistake'," *New York Times*, December 6, 2007.

[97] Gutmann and Thompson, eds., *Ethics and Politics*, 46.

Iran's covert nuclear program, which remained undeclared from the mid 1980s until approximately 2003,[98] was in breach of its obligations under the NPT. While the NIE indicates that Iranian compliance with their international obligations has substantially improved in recent years, the regime's cooperation with the IAEA has been "reactive rather than pro-active."[99] As the IAEA's June 2011 report on Iran's compliance stated:

As Iran is not providing the necessary cooperation, including by not implement-ing its Additional Protocol, the Agency is unable to provide credible assurance about the absence of undeclared nuclear material and activities in Iran, and therefore to conclude that all nuclear material in Iran is in peaceful activities.[100]

CONCLUSION

It may be true that the "threat or use of preventive force is neither a magic bullet nor an anathema."[101] However, based on the recent evidence of the NIE and IAEA reports, there is clearly no justification – legal or ethical – for the use of preventive force by the US in Iran at this stage. Evaluating the possibility of US preventive force against the current standards of international law reveals that the use of unilateral, preventive action to avert the Iranian nuclear threat, would patently breach the UN Charter and customary international law. Further, an analysis of the Bush doctrine against the broader framework formulated by Doyle – based on the standards of lethality, likelihood, legitimacy, and legality – leads to the same conclusion: unilateral preventive action in Iran is *not* justified in response to Iran's current nuclear capabilities.

There are numerous parallels that can be drawn between the previous US administration's preventive approach to dealing with the perceived WMD threat in Iraq, and its strategies to counter the threat posed by Iran's nuclear program. In particular, clear corollaries exist in terms of the certainty and likelihood of the threat; and the nature of the regimes themselves. Perhaps the greatest lesson we can draw from Iraq is that any policy of prevention must be based on comprehensive, substantiated, and reliable intelligence. Without this solid foundation, any prospect of US preventive action in Iran is gravely at risk of replicating past mistakes.

---

[98] IAEA Report 2007.   [99] Ibid., at F.42.   [100] IAEA Report 2011, 9.
[101] James Steinberg, "The Use of Preventive Force as an Element of US National Strategy," www.wws.princeton.edu/ppns/papers/Steinberg_Preemption.pdf

PART IV

Beyond preventive war: exploring other options

CHAPTER 11

Preventive violence: war, terrorism, and humanitarian intervention

C. A. J. Coady

An important and rather surprising development in much recent philosophical and public discourse about war has been the endorsement of preventive war. This is clearly related to the Bush administration's famous (or infamous) enthusiasm for this form of military engagement that they preferred to call preemptive war, a preference which, as many commentators have noted, obscures important moral and political issues.

The widespread discussion of this topic is also bolstered by a concern for two prominent phenomena of the late twentieth and early twenty-first centuries, namely terrorism and extreme political persecution. The first worry gained additional momentum from the attacks in the United States on September 11, 2001 that provoked "the war on terror," and the second was given additional urgency by the ghastly slaughter in Rwanda during 1994 that helped stimulate a huge debate on the value of armed humanitarian intervention which, having failed to occur in Rwanda, then took place to some extent in Bosnia and fully in Serbia and Kosovo, and was cited by some as justification for the intervention in Iraq. It was also cited in the more recent air power intervention in Libya. In what follows, I want to consider not only the issue of preventive war in the context of state-on-state hostility and political tension, but in the context of contemporary terrorism and, more briefly, humanitarian disaster.

A common thought behind advocacy of preventive war is captured in the sayings: "Prevention is better than cure" and "An ounce of prevention is worth a pound of cure." Nipping some bad development in the bud, or even forestalling the budding altogether, has an obvious appeal in some areas, most notably health care, where preventing the development of cancer is clearly better than trying to deal with the malignancy once it is present. But I shall argue later that these slogans and examples are quite misleading in the context of war. This is despite the fact that the basic thought is present in ancient defenses of preventive war and in the balance of power doctrine so fashionable in the eighteenth and nineteenth centuries.

189

Cicero puts it pithily in countenancing preventive war: "every evil is easily crushed at its birth; become inveterate, it as a rule gathers strength."[1]

BACKGROUND TO THE MORAL ASSESSMENT OF WAR

First, I want to set in place a context for the discussion to follow. This is important because the background to considering preventive war is crucial to the forms of argument that are developed and can be considered cogent.

To begin with, there is the obvious fact that war has been a significant part of human history since the earliest times. Warrior roles may have initially developed, as some writers believe, as a defense for small communities against the depredations of wild animals, but they rapidly evolved to both attacking and defensive roles against other human groups. No doubt some groups were less prone to the paths of violence than others, but the constancy of violent conflict in the history of our species is undeniable. This fact leads some to declare that the tendency to such violence is inherent in our make up and that, in this sense, war is natural, indeed normal. Such terms as "natural" and "normal" give rise to nervousness amongst many philosophers, and, in the present context, I think they should. It is one thing to declare as the Australian historian Geoffrey Blainey did in his fascinating book, *The Causes of War*, that war is so normal in history that what needs explaining is not so much why wars occur but why that exceptional thing peace occurs.[2] Here "normal" is doing service for "common" or "preponderant" and it contains no direct evaluative element, though perhaps Blainey thought it might. Nonetheless, the tendency to think of war as normal goes hand in hand with Clausewitz's dictum that war is "the continuation of political activity by other means."[3] Clearly this dictum can be read as the view that warfare as political activity is both normal and legitimate: war is just one more of those legitimate, everyday civic activities on a par with voting or negotiating.[4] Yet this assimilation

---

[1] Cicero, *Works*, XIV, Loeb Classical Library (London and Cambridge MA: Harvard University Press, 1979), 16–17 *Pro Milone*, 10–11. This is cited by David Rodin in his "The Problem with Prevention," in Henry Shue and David Rodin, eds., *Preemption: Military Action and Moral Justification* (Oxford University Press, 2007), 143–170.

[2] Geoffrey Blainey, *The Causes of War* (London: Macmillan, 1973).

[3] Carl von Clausewitz, *On War*, ed. and trans. Michael Howard and Peter Paret (Princeton University Press, 1976), 87.

[4] On another interpretation, Clausewitz can be seen as insisting that war must have a political dimension and that the ignoring or downgrading of this aspect can be disastrous. Both readings are available in the text, and indeed Clausewitz may have intended both since they are not strictly incompatible.

disregards two related things. One is the sheer horror and abnormality of war when it is compared to conduct in settled, political circumstances, and the other is the way that responses to war have always contained elements of critique and rejection and these responses have in recent centuries come to carry increased weight.

Both of these things, especially the first, are present in the following moving quotation from Franklin Delano Roosevelt reflecting on his participation in the First World War:

> I have seen war.
> I have seen war on land and sea,
> I have seen blood running from the wounded . . .
> I have seen the dead in the mud.
> I have seen cities destroyed . . .
> I have seen children starving.
> I have seen the agony of mothers and wives . . .
> I hate war.

These words are engraved in stone on the Roosevelt Memorial in Washington DC. They were spoken in 1936 and encapsulate what is morally problematic, to say the least, about the waging of war. Of course, Roosevelt's hatred did not amount to a total rejection of war as is evident in his efforts to involve the United States in the war against Hitler a few years after these comments were made. But he clearly thought that war was not just a normal part of political operations in the fashion suggested by Clausewitz's comments.

Others, notably adherents to the pacifist tradition, have gone further and rejected war altogether on moral grounds. Others again, notably many of those in the just-war tradition, adopt a very restrictive approach to the moral permissibility of war that shares part of the outlook of the pacifist case, but allows for the resort to war in some circumstances. The joint effect of these critical and negative attitudes to war is to counter the implicit acceptance of war as normal with a perspective that looks to the reduction and even the eventual elimination of war as a political tool. This stance is present in the UN Charter's Preamble, the first statement of which expresses a determination "to save succeeding generations from the scourge of war, which twice in our lifetime has brought untold sorrow to mankind."[5]

In addition to the revulsion from war that followed the two World Wars of the twentieth century, the shift away from the treatment of war as

---

[5] See www.un.org/en/documents/charter/preamble.shtml.

"normal" is also influenced by the increase throughout most of the developed world and much of the undeveloped world of those "settled political circumstances" that I referred to earlier. War is still an alarmingly present reality in many places, but the more settled political and economic circumstances of so many people make the prospect of the grave disturbance of warfare unwelcome in their parts of the world. Of course, it is a sad fact that nations that are prosperous and confident of the superior power of their military and economic forces are less reluctant to enforce war on people in distant lands with fewer such resources on the assumption that the costs to the enforcers will be slight. It is however the task of any serious ethic to oppose this discounting of the horrors that others must endure. Fortunately, moral reminders are often supported, in the event, by the fact that the costs to the invaders often turn out to be a good deal more than slight, as the Americans and their allies have found in Iraq and increasingly in Afghanistan where the Soviets previously learned the same lesson.

These considerations give particular point to the just-war condition of war as "a last resort." There are indeed various ambiguities in the expression "last resort" but the basic message the condition sends is one of reluctance to embark on the horrors attendant even on a war with a just cause when there remain feasible political alternatives unexplored. No amount of casuistry or anxiety about the meaning of "last resort" should obscure this message. Yet this marks a striking contrast with the slogans about prevention mentioned above and the most obvious cases to which they apply. When we advocate spending money on prevention of some dire disease rather than concentrating upon treatment and cure after it develops, we do not think in terms of such prevention being anything like a "last resort," even though in practice it has had a low priority in many communities. The policy of prevention offers itself as a benign alternative to later medical intervention.

So the initial appeal of the slogans in the context of war is not, on reflection, fully convincing. Supporters of prevention argue as follows: if some nation A is going to wage an unjust war that will cause untold misery and undeserved injury, surely it is better to stop it before it begins its campaign of slaughter; responding to its evil when it is in full progress will very likely compound the loss of lives and the damage done. Indeed, but there are at least two obvious problems with this insight. One is the mode of prevention proposed, another is the solidity of the predictive knowledge that A is going to wage an unjust war. There can be no similar quarrel with the insight where the prevention is non-violent, such as diplomatic pressure, guarantees, etc., and where the dangerous intentions of A are palpable. But preventive war is standardly a very violent measure and the predictions involved are commonly hazardous. At least, they are hazardous if we are concerned with prevention rather than preemption. Here I invoke a useful distinction developed by Michael Walzer, though muddied in the enthusiastic Bush doctrine of preemptive war.[6]

Following precedent, Walzer reserves the term preemption for those cases where one side strikes the first blow in anticipation of an imminent attack, whereas preventive war is aimed at forestalling a more remote prospect of war, related, for example, to anticipated changes in political and military balances of power. I say "broadly" because the clarity of Walzer's discussion is blurred somewhat by his desire to show that the Israeli anticipatory attack on Egypt was legitimate, even though he admits that it occurred "in the (probable) absence of any immediate intention (by Egypt) to launch such an attack or invasion."[7] He admits that this constitutes "a major revision" of the legalist paradigm regarding preemption that he had previously taken himself to be expounding. His position seems to be that this case of Israeli first strike is in a grey area between preemption and prevention, though nearer to preemption.

More recently, in a discussion of the Bush administration's plans for invading Iraq, Walzer used his distinction to cast doubt on the moral legitimacy of such an invasion.[8] He argued that, in the circumstances then prevailing (in late September 2002) the war proposed would be, at best, preventive and not preemptive, and hence "neither just nor necessary."[9] Even so, Walzer has some doubts, connected with his sympathy with the Israeli preventive strike against Iraq's nuclear reactor in 1981. This is adduced as an illustration of what seems a further "revision" of his earlier account. He now says, "the old argument for preventive war did not take into account weapons of mass destruction or delivery systems that allow no time for arguments about how to respond. Perhaps the gulf between preemption and prevention has now narrowed so that there is little strategic (and therefore little moral) difference between them."[10] Walzer's final position is not entirely clear but he seems to be saying that there remains a significant difference between preemption and prevention even

---

[6] Here and in the next section I reprise with some modification arguments from my book, C. A. J. Coady, *Morality and Political Violence* (Cambridge University Press, 2008), 100–106.
[7] Michael Walzer, *Just and Unjust Wars: A Moral Argument With Historical Illustrations* (4th edn., New York: Basic Books, 2006), 85.
[8] Michael Walzer, "No Strikes: Inspectors Yes, War No," *The New Republic*, September 30, 2002, 19–22.
[9] Ibid., 22.   [10] Ibid., 21.

though, in view of changed military and political circumstances, it is not as great as he previously thought.

OBJECTIONS TO PREVENTIVE WAR

Yet weapons of mass destruction and rapid delivery systems really do nothing to repair the defects in the "old arguments" for preventive war. These were well sketched earlier by Walzer and even earlier by the great nineteenth-century moral philosopher Henry Sidgwick. As Sidgwick pointed out, even the legitimate preemption ". . . easily passes over into anticipation of a blow that is merely feared, not really threatened. Indeed this enlarged right of self-protection against mere danger has often been further extended to justify hostile interference to prevent a neighbour growing strong merely through expansion or coalescence with other states."[11] We might add that the resort to preventive war by one nation provides a pattern for other strong nations to emulate so that the dangers instanced by Sidgwick are multiplied.

Once we get beyond immediate threat of attack by an enemy, we are in the realm of pretty much untrammelled speculation. Another nation's development of weapons, including weapons of mass destruction, may create various worries and uncertainties, but there is so much that can come between that development and its hostile use, that we should not risk the hazards of war on behalf of the alarming prediction. After all, numerous nations now have such weapons, especially nuclear weapons, and so far only the United States has used nuclear weapons, and poisonous gas has been used very rarely since international law forbade it, Iraq under Saddam being a notable exception. Moreover, the existence of rapid delivery systems does not eliminate the space for arguments about response since these arguments will have been canvassed, and policies put in place, long before any attack. Widespread knowledge of military potential has become as swift and comprehensive as the speed of delivery systems though fallibility still attaches to both. In addition, those with, or developing, such weapons are increasingly alert to the risks they face from preventive military action (especially when it is loudly advocated) and take steps to make it more difficult for enemies to destroy their facilities with speed and precision; hence awareness of the likelihood of preventive military attacks increases the probability that they will be thwarted.

[11] Henry Sidgwick, "The Morality of Strife," in his *Practical Ethics* (London: Swann Sonnenschein and Co., 1898), 47–62; 56.

I do not mean to dismiss the dangers of WMD, especially nuclear weapons, but there is irony in the fact that the loudest advocate of war to eliminate nuclear threats has been the one nation that has actually used nuclear weapons to devastating effect, has made the threat of using them a cornerstone of its foreign policy for over sixty years, and, in spite of some reduction in capacity, still possesses a huge nuclear stockpile at the ready. It is hardly surprising that nations branded as evil enemies by the USA are anxious to achieve a nuclear deterrent of their own, and the enthusiastic Western advocates of the benefits of the nuclear umbrella are ill-placed to denounce their ambitions. The spread of nuclear weapons is indeed a bad thing, but so is the possession of them by the existing nuclear club which includes at least America, France, Britain, Pakistan, Israel, India, and China, several of whom are already involved in political and military situations that could be described as precarious. Reducing the incentives to acquire nuclear armaments by serious and continuing reductions in the existing stock to the point of voluntary elimination, is the best way to combat proliferation. It is significant that even hard-core political pragmatists like Henry Kissinger have come to see this light.

Against this scenario, namely, one of negotiated prevention of WMD proliferation, weapons inspection regimes, and eventually general WMD disarmament, there are those who continue to believe that there is a better, and even more realistic, course. This is to make use of the massive military might of the United States to prevent the spread of such weapons by military threats and actions against those who are suspected of ambitions to develop them, have begun to develop them, or have recently become possessed of them. America's more belligerent posture in world affairs during the reign of George W. Bush seemed to make this option a live one. The advantage of this course is that US military superiority, especially in its technical aspects, is now so great that the costs of preventive war seem to be much less than critics like Sidgwick could have envisaged. But most of this is mere appearance and there are great and evident disadvantages as well. Much of the appearance of low cost warfare is related to the supposed low costs to the attackers in the wars in Serbia, Afghanistan, and Iraq, but these are not of course the only costs of those wars, since they have together cost an overall loss of life that very probably considerably exceeds 100,000, not to mention the political and economic disturbances that the wars entailed. In the case of Iraq, the cost in lives to the invaders, initially low, has gathered momentum with the development of insurgent warfare, and, at the time of writing, the Afghan conflict is going the same way. By the time the official American forces, or the majority of them, fully quit both scenes their death toll is likely to be close to double those killed in the terrorist attacks of 9/11. And this is not to mention the scarring psychological effects on so many American soldiers who physically survived these conflicts. Moreover, the huge financial cost is soaring and seems to have no obvious horizon, and, whatever the intervention may have prevented, it has clearly stimulated terrorist activity in the region and beyond. In addition it has probably reduced America's political prestige markedly and hence its capacity for soft power and diplomatic heft. President Obama's efforts to repair this inherited damage have been partially successful, but Iraq and Afghanistan still hang around his neck like an albatross. Furthermore, his failure to fulfil election promises to close down Guantanamo Bay and startling revelations about his hands-on role in the controversial campaign of targeted killing by drones have further eroded confidence in America's capacity to deal preventively with threats to its security.[12]

The traditional justification for preemptive war turned on the idea that the harm to be dealt with was grave and imminent, and Walzer's distinction between preemption and prevention is principally made in terms of the test of imminence. David Luban has argued that imminence should be seen as a special case of high probability (highly probable and temporally near), and he uses this to allow for preventive wars in special cases against "rogue states" whose nature is such that they are "all but certain" to engage in an attack, even though such an attack is not imminent.[13] Although Luban is right that imminence is a special case of probability, it is actually a very special case, and his extension of the test beyond temporal imminence is fraught with danger, a danger that is multiplied by his resort to the fashionable but dubious notion of "rogue states." The point about imminence is that it is excellent evidence that an attack is "all but certain" whereas other indicators such as the character of the regime, its public rhetoric, information from disgruntled émigrés, intelligence reports, and even the regime's past record are much less secure. A considerable gap in time between bellicose behavior or past wrongdoing or other indicators of alarm still allows plenty of room for hesitation, reconsideration, or reform on the part of the potential aggressor, and for non-military efforts at diplomacy or other interventions short of war, including deterrence by

---

[12] See Jo Becker and Scott Shane, "Secret 'Kill List' Proves a Test of Obama's Principles and Will," *New York Times*, May 29, 2012. www.nytimes.com/2012/05/29/world/obamas-leadership-in-war-on-al-qaeda.html?pagewanted=all.

[13] David Luban, "Preventive War," *Philosophy and Public Affairs* 32:3 (2004), 207–248, 230.

credible threats. What Luban calls the "rule consequentialist" objection to preventive war still has force against his proposed extension.[14]

Indeed, the talk of rogue states makes this even clearer. It has been argued by Michael Klare that the currency of the category of rogue states originated in the Pentagon's desire to resist spending cuts and other reductions as a result of the ending of the Cold War.[15] Whatever the truth of this claim, the category of "rogue states" has proved an elusive and dangerous tool of world politics. The original description was applied to Libya which later graduated to respectable status, partly through a shrewd renunciation of nuclear weapon ambitions, and then relapsed into something like rogue status, in the face of citizen rebellion, though nuclear weapons were not an issue. The rogue odium still applies to Cuba which also has no nuclear ambitions. The idea was given additional impetus by the attacks of September 11, though the Bush doctrine of an "axis of evil," predating those attacks, is also part of the same mindset. The fact is that the September 11 attacks had nothing to do with designated "rogue states" such as Iraq, North Korea, or even Iran, and it is unlikely that the Taliban government of Afghanistan had anything directly to do with the attacks.

Luban defines a "rogue state" as having the following "important characteristics": "militarism, an ideology favouring violence, a track-record of violence to back it up, and a build-up in capacity to pose a genuine threat." All of these palpably apply to the United States itself, a society with a huge military budget and capacity (including large stocks of WMD), a unique gun culture, a record of military and undercover adventurism in various parts of the world, and an ever-increasing military capacity that many other states view, not unreasonably, as threatening. There will, of course, be numerous other countries beyond the "axis of evil" that might plausibly fit the category, including China and Israel. Admittedly, some regimes are worse than others on some of the indicated criteria and there is much room for debate and interpretation, but these

---

[14] The idea is that we should have a rule against preventive war because such a rule would have the best overall consequences, in particular, it would prevent the sort of bad consequences that I have earlier discussed. I prefer not to speak of rule consequentialism in this context because that suggests that the justification of rules by reference to consequences is somehow the preserve of consequentialist philosophers, whereas it is obviously available to any moral theorist to make use of consequences, while believing that this is not the only resort available. See ibid., 225.

[15] Michael Klare, *Rogue States and Nuclear Outlaws: America's Search for a New Foreign Policy* (New York: Hill and Wang, 1995). The category is taken more seriously by Robert Litwak in *Rogue States and U.S. Foreign Policy: Containment After the Cold War* (Washington, DC: Woodrow Wilson Centre Press; Baltimore: Distributed by the Johns Hopkins University Press, 1999).

facts themselves indicate how obscure and dangerous an instrument the concept of a rogue state is, especially in the context of a discussion of preventive war.

RESPONDING TO "WRONGFUL IMPOSITIONS OF DIRE RISK"

I have concentrated upon the likely bad consequences of preventive war, but, real as these are, there is a deeper, though connected, objection. That is the objection that the horrible recourse to war needs as a justifying cause, the commission of some grave wrong. This is the intrinsic problem with the preventive project, viewed as an exercise that comes under the scope of justice. Within the state, the need to deal with wrongdoers may extend occasionally to those who are about to commit a crime or are actively conspiring to do so, but it is unjust for the state to exercise "the right of the sword" against those whom it suspects might be wrongdoers some time in the future. In the international order, the same principle applies. Unless the wrongdoing or attack is palpable and imminent, there can be no justification for unleashing the horror of war. In this respect, there is something deeply misleading about Clausewitz's dictum that war is "the continuation of political activity by other means."[16] One useful point he is trying to make is that resort to warfare must, in a broad sense, be governed by non-military objectives since there is no moral sense in merely pursuing victory or conquest as ends in themselves. These governing objectives must, in a broad sense, be political, but not just any political objective will be significant enough to justify war. Clausewitz's dictum makes the justification look too easy, since there are all sorts of circumstances in which political activity is unsuccessful or stale-mated and we just have to live with it, rather than resort to the mayhem of war. Few worthy objectives can constitute specific just cause for war, and the worthy objective of removing conditions that might lead to future crimes is not one of them.

Against this, it has been argued that preventive war may be legitimate when it is seen as a response to a crime that is already in progress: the analogy with domestic crimes of conspiracy or attempt has been cited by Allen Buchanan in this connection.[17] Buchanan thinks of these deeds as "wrongful impositions of dire risk." The attempt analogy is hardly relevant

---

[16] Clausewitz, *On War*, 87.
[17] Allen Buchanan, "Institutionalizing the Just War," *Philosophy and Public Affairs* 34:1 (2006), 2–38; 9–11.

since an attempt is an action that is fully underway in the appropriate sense but fails in its objective. The traditional doctrine of legitimate preemption allows that defensive violence may be used when an attack is actually being attempted. This is one reason why "imminence" cannot be collapsed into mere "probability"; it involves a high degree of probability but the more significant fact is that it indicates that an attack is all but underway. The "attempt" phase has already begun. But the conspiracy analogy is more interesting and pertinent. Certainly in domestic legal contexts, it can make sense to criminalize the planning of crimes, but, as Buchanan is aware, the analogy with the international order limps in several ways. For one thing, since conspiracy is a charge that is manifestly open to abuse by prosecuting agencies, it is more than usually important that allegations of conspiracy can be tested by authoritative, independent tribunals, especially where the conspiracy involves political issues. Yet this is exactly what is conspicuously lacking in the international scene, though present, with some fragility, in the more constitutionally stable domestic jurisdictions. Given the strong tendencies of national leaders to spring to conclusions about the conspiratorial behavior of other states, resort to the conspiracy model to reject the criticism that preventive war wrongly responds to possibilities of offence rather than actual offences is hardly compelling.

Buchanan realizes that there are dangers in the model, but thinks them merely contingent, so that preventive war against a conspiracy is not *necessarily* a violation of the rights of those targeted. He and Jeff McMahan, in another context, support this point by producing highly artificial examples in which intuitions allow for preventive violence. McMahan has a Paralysis example where you discover that a villain has a fiendish plan to murder you when you become paralysed and unable to defend yourself a few weeks hence; surely if you cannot somehow alert the police or provide for others to protect you nearer the event, you are entitled to kill the fiend now even though he has done nothing to implement his plan.[18] The idea is that there might be an extrapolation from this to the collective case. Buchanan has a collective example, namely, a Lethal Virus example, where country A knows that a terrorist group which has already committed several deadly attacks on innocent populations has a lethal, highly contagious, and untreatable virus which it plans to release on a city of country A. A missile strike against a remote mountain

---

[18] Jeff McMahan, "Preventive War and the Killing of the Innocent," in Richard Sorabji and David Rodin, eds., *The Ethics of War: Shared Problems in Different Traditions* (Aldershot: Ashgate, 2006), 173–174.

stronghold will destroy the virus and only kill members of the terrorist group. Surely, it is justified.[19] The construction of such examples (reminiscent of the "ticking bomb" extravagances in the torture debate) as well as the "not necessarily" emphasis may be thought typically philosophical in a sense that is hardly flattering. Such manoeuvres provide small comfort for those whose rights are highly likely to be violated in the real world where the philosophers' epistemic certainties and cheerfully constructed restrictions never apply. Moreover, if we are talking of the right not to be killed, then Buchanan's argument is a giant stride away from the restrictive impulses of just-war theory that were outlined earlier as background to this discussion. If the self-defense model has application at all, it should not stretch in either the individual or the national case to killing those you believe are planning an attack in some relatively remote future. Self-defense should not be confused with self-preservation; self-defense is a very specific form of self-protection and involves rights to inflict harm that do not apply to other forms of self-preservation.[20]

In fairness, it should be stressed that Buchanan regards at least the prudential objections to preventive war as decisive in the world as it now is; his position is that empirical work is required to establish whether institutions might now be developed that would make resort to preventive war (and indeed war to establish democracy) immune to these powerful objections. These institutions include those that might investigate and license a preventive war in advance and those that adjudicate post facto on the legitimacy of a preventive war and sanction those nations whose resort to such war was condemned by this verdict. As he puts it: "My aim is not to show that the institutional approach outlined here is likely to be adapted [sic] by the most powerful states either at present or in the future. If it turns out that the institutional demands for morally permissible decisions to engage in preventive self-defence or forcible democratization will not be met, then my argument supports the conclusion that preventive self-defence and forcible democratization are not justifiable."[21] Given the difficulties in developing international institutions to deal effectively with *actual* crimes and harms, there is something deeply unrealistic in the proposals to adjudicate, license, vindicate, or punish states who decide to engage in preventive war.

---

[19] See Allen Buchanan, "Justifying Preventive War," in Henry Shue and David Rodin, eds., *Preemption: Military Action and Moral Justification* (Oxford University Press, 2007), 127.

[20] For a very good exploration of the differences see Suzanne Uniacke, "On Getting One's Retaliation in First," in Shue and Rodin, eds., *Preemption*, 69–88.

[21] Buchanan, "Institutionalising the Just War," 35–36.

Buchanan's Lethal Virus example does, however, raise an interesting point about the ambiguous scope of the term "prevention." As he describes the case, the group with the virus is already known as a terrorist group "which has already committed several deadly attacks on innocent populations." Hence the attack upon the group is more like the sort of prevention that is involved in normal military operations during a continuing war; one side will commonly be striving not merely to defeat a current enemy attack, but to take military measures to prevent further attacks at later times. Indeed, even the current fighting is aimed at preventing certain things happening. But a critique or a defense of "preventive war" must primarily address justifications for military measures against those who have not yet taken violent steps themselves or embarked upon preliminaries that amount to imminent attack. This is important for the status of Buchanan's example, but it is also relevant to my discussion below of preventive war against terrorism, since military measures to prevent terrorist acts will usually take place in contexts that partly resemble an ongoing war and partly don't. Hence the plausibility of talk about a "war on terror" and also its capacity to mislead. It is plausible because there is something warlike about campaigns of terrorism (and military responses to them) but it can mislead because invocation of the "war on terror" (like resort to the slogan "war on drugs") can obscure the need for other ways of conceptualizing terrorist threats and for non-violent responses to them. So my discussion of preventive war on terrorism will need to acknowledge the ambiguity of "prevention" that Buchanan's example highlights.

It is worth noting here that the Bush administration's fascination with preventive war was not the radical departure from traditional US military policy that both critics and proponents have often assumed it to be. The emergence of the Cold War after 1945 and the various crises that it created in subsequent decades were met by much talk in influential circles about the merits of preventive military action. This ranged from advocacy of nuclear bombing against the Soviets to prevent their developing a nuclear capacity, and strikes against China for the same reason, to preventive attacks upon Cuba during the Cuban missile crisis and attacks upon North Korea to prevent its development of nuclear weapons.[22] What is fascinating about all of these is that they were aimed precisely at the perception of what Buchanan calls "wrongful imposition of risk" and fears of the risk were not totally fanciful, though distorted in various ways. In

---

[22] These arguments are well documented by Marc Trachtenberg in his "Preventive War and US Foreign Policy," in Shue and Rodin, eds., *Preemption*, 40–68.

the event, many of the risks proved insignificant and what risk there was turned out to be manageable by other means. Those who rejected prevention in most of these cases were surely right to do so.

DOES MODERN TERRORISM MAKE A DIFFERENCE?

This seems to me the right conclusion to draw but I want to test it against two scenarios that present rather different challenges from the standard model of state versus state hostility. These scenarios are those of terrorism and humanitarian intervention. These are amongst two of the contemporary political crises that make some theorists insist that we now face quite novel forms of warfare that require abandonment or revision both of prevailing international law regarding warfare and of received understanding of just-war theory. A variety of voices call for revision of legal and moral norms against torture, extraordinary rendition, attacks upon noncombatants, assassination, various protections for combatants captured in war, and, of course, preventive war.[23] My own view is that all these pleas are ill-founded and dangerous. They exaggerate the novelty of present circumstances and tend to base moral recommendations either solely on military necessity or upon conventional arrangements grounded in mutual self-interest rather than on more basic moral premises. Indeed much of the reaction to the phenomena of rogue states and transnational terrorism echoes the fear and posturing that marked reactions to the Soviet Union, China, and later North Korea moving towards gaining access to nuclear weapons. Prominent American policy advisers, Brent Scowcroft and Arnold Kanter wrote in 1994 when the Clinton administration was issuing belligerent warnings to North Korea that "if war is unavoidable, we would rather fight it sooner than later, when North Korea might have a sizable nuclear arsenal."[24] Asymmetric warfare (which is often cited in this connection) and terrorism are situations with long historical precedents, either exact or similar, as are hostage-taking, torture, and attacks upon civilian populations.[25] Although arguments for revision of existing norms must be considered case by case on their merits, the mood behind them seems to

---

[23] One of the most detailed and comprehensive arguments for such revisions is contained in Michael L. Gross, *Moral Dilemmas of Modern War* (New York: Cambridge University Press, 2010). For further discussion of the book see my review of it in C. A. J. Coady, *Ethics and International Affairs* 25:1 (March 2011), 90–92.

[24] Quoted by Trachtenberg, "Preventive War," 54.

[25] I have discussed these issues more fully in C. A. J. Coady, "How New Is the 'New Terror'?," *Iyyun: The Jerusalem Philosophical Quarterly* 55:1 (2006), 49–65.

me to be a product of frustration and sometimes panic. But here I shall consider only the case of preventive war as a morally licit response to terrorism or humanitarian crises.

First, let us consider terrorism. Walzer's reference to the difference made by WMD which I argued against earlier can be adapted to make a similar and even more plausible point about changed circumstances with regard to terrorist threats. Terrorism, it might be said, makes the distinction between preemption and prevention morally irrelevant because where states do not exist primarily to deliver violence against other states, though they have the potential to do so, and some are more ready to do it than others, terrorist groups are defined by their orientation to deliver violence, and violence of a particularly reprehensible nature.

My own definition of terrorism is a restricted one whereby terrorist acts are violent attacks upon non-combatants (or their property) normally by groups, or individuals representing or claiming to represent groups, who launch the attacks for political purposes. By non-combatants I mean those who are innocent of any purported wrongdoing that might serve to legitimize the resort to political violence against the wrongdoers. This style of definition I call a tactical definition because it concentrates not upon anti-state violence in general, or even politically motivated anti-state violence in general, but upon the specific tactic of targeting non-combatants (or, if you like, innocents). Other versions of a tactical definition can be more expansive than mine by including the motive of creating fear, or other features such as targeting one group in order to influence the policies of another. One might also include the threat of harming non-combatants as part of the definition. But these variations will not matter greatly for what follows. Broader definitions of terrorism will include all violent attacks upon the state, or upon a legitimate state, as terrorist. Even broader definitions that take the terror reference in the term "terrorism" over-seriously will not bother to include violence in the account, so making any politically motivated fear campaign terrorist. Much of what I say about the use of preventive violence against terrorists will apply whichever definition we use, but I shall have in mind a tactical understanding of the phenomenon. I am also thinking of terrorism in a fairly common way as restricted to sub-state agents. On a tactical definition this is a mistake since states can use terrorism (and use it more dreadfully) and indeed some states might qualify for the title "terrorist state." Nonetheless, there are particular problems posed by sub-state terrorism in the context of preventive war, and we need to consider these. Sub-state terrorism raises the question of prevention in an acute form since the threat posed is not one that is indicated by massive increase in conventional military forces or the conspicuous build-up of armaments.

Yet sub-state terrorism (or simply terrorism, as I shall refer to it subsequently) has distinctive features that make the response of war, whether preventive or not, singularly inept as a way of dealing with it. The war in Afghanistan provides an exemplary contemporary lesson in the follies of large-scale military solutions to terrorism. It is arguable that a "surgical" military strike at Al-Qaeda headquarters and training areas in Afghanistan with the aim of weakening the terrorist organization by killing significant leaders was a legitimate response to the attacks of September 11. This was part of the American response, and, as we know, not particularly successful. Partly because of this lack of success, the project was widened to involve first a partnership with anti-Taliban forces in what was virtually a civil war and then a full-scale attempt to remove the Taliban from power. In the short term this was successful, but it has involved the United States and its dwindling Allied forces in an eleven-year war (at the time of writing) with no clear solution in sight in spite of US declarations about withdrawal dates and training of local forces. This war continues to be justified (mostly) in terms of the response to terrorism even though it has created much more terrorism, revived the Taliban and bound many of them closer to the original terrorists, strengthened sympathy in the Muslim world with the agents of terrorism and, even more importantly, helped radicalize elements in Muslim diasporas within Western countries. Insofar as the attack upon Afghanistan was conceived as an attempt to prevent and curtail future terrorist activity (rather than as a punitive measure) then it has failed dismally.

The aims of the Afghanistan and Iraq wars were unclearly presented and what was presented was open to dispute as to its reality and honesty. On some accounts, the wars were responses to wrongs already inflicted: for Afghanistan the attacks of September 11, 2001, for Iraq the alleged violation of UN prohibitions on the development of weapons of mass destruction or (on some stories) the supposed complicity of Iraq in the 9/11 attacks. But there were elements of a preventive argument for the invasions. One was the prevention of future terrorism, another the prevention of Iraq's use of nuclear weapons against Israel and even the United States. The second is open to the difficulties already discussed (especially given the fact that Iraq did not have nuclear weapons and had apparently given up the quest for them) plus the fact that both Israel and the United States already had nuclear weapons and would have had a vast superiority in such weapons over Iraq for the foreseeable future, so that whatever truth there is in deterrence theory would have militated against any Iraqi use of such weapons. The first however is more pertinent to my concern here.

What forms of military intervention could prevent future (sub-state) terrorism? One problem concerns the dispersed nature of the threat. Even where a terrorist organization exists, its direct agents are not likely to be located where the organization has its headquarters, if indeed it has anything like a stable headquarters. This was clear in the 9/11 bombings in the USA and the July 2005 transport attacks in London. Al-Qaeda, for instance, seems itself to be constituted by a network of loosely affiliated groups and sympathizers rather than forming a centrally controlling organization. Its agents are often people who are citizens or residents of countries far from the caves of Afghanistan or the hinterland of Pakistan, and their planning for attacks may have little to do with co-ordinated direction from those areas. The more general point is that existing grievances exacerbated by continuing political and/or military actions that are viewed as aggressive or persecutory by a sufficient number of members of widespread ethnic, religious, or political groups will tend to recruit for terrorist acts in widely diverse environments. Preventive war makes no sense as a way of dealing with such a phenomenon.

FURTHER REJOINDERS AND AN ALTERNATIVE APPROACH

There are two possible responses to this criticism. One is to urge the merits of attacking states that harbor or in some way sponsor terrorism, the other is to retreat from all-out war and argue the merits of targeted assassination. As to the first, many of the points already made about the dangers of preventive war apply, perhaps with even more force. Not only are there the risks of mislocating the sponsors as happened with the Bush administration's belief that Iraq was a sponsor, or a directing agent, of the 9/11 attacks, but there is a serious danger of mistaking support for a political or revolutionary program with support for terrorist tactics in advancing that program. (Here, I understand terrorist acts in the fashion of the tactical definition discussed above.) Moreover, the waging of a war against a state whose government is believed to be supporting sub-state terrorism or has allowed some organization that plans sub-state terrorism to operate within its boundaries is highly likely to produce countervailing results, as the invasion of Afghanistan has surely demonstrated. The United States and its dwindling Allies have found themselves in a protracted conflict not only with the handful of Al-Qaeda operatives, but with a revived Taliban and a large number of nationalist insurgents who fiercely resent the damage caused by the invasion of a Western power. This even extends to those who appear to be supporters of the Allied troops as the periodic killing of those troops by their Afghan colleagues illustrates most dramatically. Some of this is no doubt specific to the circumstances of Afghanistan, but many of these points have general applicability as indicated by Israel's enduring difficulties with Lebanon.

As for targeted assassination, the theoretical possibility of its effectiveness in preventing future resort to terrorism is vastly outweighed by the practical realities. (In fact, in the case of targeted assassination, the motive is often retaliation or punishment for acts done, as well as, or rather than, prevention of future acts, but it can be instructive to consider its possible preventive justification.) Osama bin Laden's assassination is often treated as a form of extra-judicial punishment, but it is sometimes justified as prevention of further terrorism by the removal of a significant terrorist leader. Such preventive assassination is somewhat distant conceptually from preventive war in that figures like bin Laden are already engaged in directing a sort of war, or, in the case of Afghanistan, parts of an actual war. So, it is not as though they have directed no violent attacks but may pose a potential threat for the relatively remote future. Even so, it is worth noting the defects of assassination as a technique for preventing future terrorist attacks by groups that have perpetrated them in the past. The first problem is that the piecemeal killing of leaders is as likely, perhaps more likely, to increase terrorist activity rather than decrease it. This is because there are usually plenty of people waiting to step into the fallen leader's shoes and where their cause is ideological, their commitment is likely to be intensified by the way their leader has been dispatched. If the leader was charismatic or inspirational his influence on followers will survive his death and he will be elevated to the status of martyr, with all the propaganda benefits likely to accrue from that claim. So the principal effect of targeted killing is likely to be the encouragement of more terrorism rather than its prevention.

A second point is that the risks of wrongly identifying the target and of harming innocent bystanders compound the difficulties of assassination and can bring the perpetrators into disrepute. The record of Israeli assassination operations against the terrorist leaders Mossad has identified should be instructive here. Not only have the killings failed to produce any sort of solution to the political mess that breeds terrorism in the occupied territories, but the occasional killing of wrongly identified "terrorist leaders" and the incidental killing of bystanders has contributed to the widespread alienation of support for Israel in the Western world. The recent revelations that the United States' targeted killings in Pakistan proceed by classifying all military-age adults in an identified area as legitimate targets makes a nonsense of the idea that drone attacks are "morally clean," and is bound to increase resentment and anger against the United States amongst populations that would otherwise be unsympathetic to terrorists.[26]

Moreover, if we imagine a "pure case" of preventive war (or assassination) to ward off future attacks by agents who have committed none in the past, then many of these objections apply with even greater force. Where planning and initial operational implementation have proceeded far enough to constitute the sort of imminence of attack envisaged in the justification for preemption, then a case can of course be made for a military recourse, subject to the other prudential constraints of just-war theory such as last resort and proportionality. But where such imminence and gravity of risk are lacking, a strictly preventive attack is not legitimate. Indeed, the circumstances of supposed "wrongful imposition of dire risk" (to echo Buchanan) that could be cited in such circumstances would not only demonstrate that those attacked were innocent of any wrongful acts at the time, but would inevitably create sympathy for the victims of attack and garner support for their political objectives. This in turn would surely raise the probability of actual terrorist attacks. By contrast, the circumstances cited might reasonably have been addressed in other ways, such as police arrest and subsequent testing by a court of alleged criminal intent or practice.

The fact is that prevention of terrorist attacks, whether in the rare "pure" circumstances imagined above or in the more common circumstances, is much better sought through civil rather than military methods. There are basically four of these civil methods: (1) domestic policing, legal, and regulatory measures; (2) international policing, legal, and regulatory measures; (3) diplomatic measures; (4) removing, mitigating, or at least confronting the grievance. There is some overlap between the categories but it is still useful to distinguish them. All of them point to the usual superiority of policing, legal, and political measures over military measures, especially warfare, for preventing terrorism in most circumstances. Of course, nothing is guaranteed to work and there are problems with

---

[26] See Becker and Shane, "Secret 'Kill List' Proves a Test of Obama's Principles and Will." As they report, "Mr. Obama embraced a disputed method for counting civilian casualties that did little to box him in. It in effect counts all military-age males in a strike zone as combatants, according to several administration officials, unless there is explicit intelligence posthumously proving them innocent."

anti-terrorism laws and their implementation, as indeed with each of the categories mentioned. But these problems are dwarfed by the costs of preventive war. Let me say something very briefly about each of these (a full discussion would take us well beyond the limits of this chapter). Re (1), this is principally aimed at uncovering terrorist planning and plotting in the home nation circumstances, but could be (and has been) expanded to take in the planning in other countries by cooperation with policing and legal agencies in those countries. It therefore has something of the flavour of (2) but it is complementary to explicit international legislation and regulatory measures. Problems with this approach are mostly to do with the way in which alarm about terrorist threats tends to make governments extend police powers and suspend or restrict long-established legal rights often beyond what is necessary to combat the threat.

As for (2) and (3), the outlawing of terrorism and the cooperation of state jurisdictions and political regimes in preventing terrorist attacks are clearly good things in principle, even if in practice there is reason not to be over-confident about their effectiveness. Some of the techniques available are outlined in UN documents relating to what is called R2P (abbreviating the "Responsibility to Protect") and include a "preventive toolbox." These originated in the Report of the International Commission on Intervention and State Sovereignty entitled "The Responsibility to Protect" where the toolbox was discussed in the chapter on "The Responsibility to Prevent." The implements in the toolbox are primarily addressed to humanitarian intervention but also secondarily address terrorism. In the ICISS report they include military measures, though as a last resort, but the UN's later endorsement of R2P principles in 2005 departed in several respects from the ICISS report, most significantly in placing even less emphasis on military intervention. As for (4), it would seem obvious that ways of addressing the grievance that generates terrorism would offer some prospects of eliminating or reducing the terrorist threat. If the grievance is a legitimate one, then steps should be taken to remove it; if it is not considered legitimate, there may still be ways of making the issue in question less of a grievance or producing sensible compromises around it. If the perceptions of grievance that fuel terrorist acts are so misguided or perverse that no compromises are possible or desirable, then open discussion of the grievance and demonstration that it is unreasonable should at least be tried. This might lead, at a minimum, to increased understanding and might even induce some degree of changed perception and practice.

It may be said that the sceptical approach argued for here constitutes a reasonable warning against too much confidence in preventive war against terrorists, but that it cannot amount to a total prohibition. This response raises an interesting question concerning what considerations could amount to "a total prohibition." Those philosophers who adopt a consequentialist or utilitarian outlook will usually think, as a matter of principle, that no rule can be without exception; indeed, most contemporary moral philosophers will follow them (whatever their basic moral theory) in insisting that only moral "fanatics" (in Richard Hare's phrase) will hold to total or absolute prohibitions.[27] For some time it appeared that there was a complete impasse between the majority of philosophers who insisted that no moral prohibition or rule could be without exceptions and those who held that some prohibitions should be total. The former would support their position by citing real or (mostly) highly imaginary situations in which our intuitions told us that adherence to an absolute rule was unreasonable (remember McMahan's Paralysis case) and the latter would resist the intuition, redescribe the scenario, or reject it as unrealistic. But more recently, there are signs of a sort of rapprochement. Some philosophers have used basically rule-consequentialist arguments to arrive at absolute condemnations of a number of categories of public wrongs. So, for example, Bob Brecher has used only utilitarian arguments (though he is not a consequentialist himself) to argue that torture should be absolutely prohibited morally, and Stephen Nathanson is a utilitarian philosopher who rejects terrorism out of hand on rule-utilitarian grounds.[28] And these are purely moral objections. When it comes to legal prohibition, there is an even stronger case for an absolute ban in these areas.[29] It seems plausible therefore that the same strategy applies to a ban on preventive war against terrorism, if the arguments I have produced are persuasive.

PREVENTIVE INTERVENTION FOR HUMANITARIAN REASONS

Let me now turn briefly to humanitarian intervention. Again the standard objections rehearsed earlier apply, particularly to the point that a case may be available for preemption that is not available for prevention. There is

[27] Richard Hare, *Freedom and Reason* (Oxford: Clarendon Press, 1963).
[28] Bob Brecher, *Torture and the Ticking Bomb* (Oxford: Blackwell, 2007); Stephen Nathanson, *Terrorism and the Ethics of War* (Cambridge University Press, 2010).
[29] Jeff McMahan is one prominent non-consequentialist philosopher who thinks that the prohibition on targeting non-combatants cannot be absolute as a matter of deep morality, but must be held absolute in law and international regulation of war. Since this forms part of the tactical definition of terrorism (which McMahan seems to support) then his position on terrorism seems to be that there should be a strong but not absolute moral prohibition on it, but a total legal ban. See Jeff McMahan, *Killing in War* (Oxford: Clarendon Press, 2009).

also the fact that the broad argument for armed humanitarian intervention (of a non-preventive kind) is widely considered less persuasive, on both legal and moral grounds, than the case for self-defensive war, especially where it is unauthorized by the United Nations.[30] An additional consideration against preventive violence on behalf of humanity is that such an intervention runs the considerable risk that the animosity motivating the preparations or policies that present a case for preventive violence will be fanned to greater intensity by the outside attack so that a failed or indecisive intervention will be likely to increase the harm to the innocent potential victims. The minority that are at risk will then be seen, or can be portrayed, as allied to foreign invaders. In that event, potential severe persecution may turn to outright ethnic cleansing or genocide beyond the power of the interveners to prevent. On the home front of the interveners, the sort of political support required both practically (and even morally) is bound to be less available for a preventive war of humanitarian protection based on predictions than for humanitarian intervention to deal with an actual attack.

It may be objected that all this may be true but there is surely a case for short, "surgical" violent strikes that can head off a humanitarian disaster. There is, for instance, the UN's military representative in Rwanda, General Dallaire's argument that his troops could have prevented the ghastly massacre in Rwanda in 1994 by raiding the arms supplies that were about to be used by the mostly Hutu killers.[31] This may have involved some killing of guards and potential killers but would have been a small price to pay. Ignoring empirical problems with his solution (much of the slaughter was carried out with primitive weapons such as hatchets), we should note that this intervention would have been in the category of the preemptive rather than preventive since he was moved to request permission to act when the attack was imminent and no other resort was available. Other plausible candidates are likely to be in the same category. One such is the multi-state intervention in Libya on behalf of civilians at risk from the threats and actual behavior of Muammar Gaddafi in the civil war then raging. Gaddafi's forces were actually attacking civilians, apparently uninvolved in the war, and threatening to do more of it. Even so, the case for the intervention is by no means decisive since it killed many civilians,

---

[30] Though see David Rodin, *War and Self-Defense* (Oxford University Press, 2002). Rodin argues that the case for self-defense is less robust than often believed and claims instead that there may be a better case for altruistic war.

[31] Romeo Dallaire, *Shake Hands with the Devil: The Failure of Humanity in Rwanda* (New York: Carroll and Graf, 2003).

probably prolonged the conflict, and contributed to the perception of Western powers as military meddlers in Middle Eastern affairs. Interestingly, it was criticized strongly even by those who support humanitarian intervention in some circumstances, most notably by Michael Walzer.[32]

This intervention may well have been justified, and was authorized by the UN Security Council, though there are doubts that its practice was as restricted as that justification and endorsement required. In any event, we should be wary of the temptation to treat "surgical strikes," "no fly zones," and so on as far less morally problematic than outright war. The idea recalls Michael Walzer's attempt to construct a softer version of warfare and the morality appropriate to it with his concept of "force-short-of-war." The "short-of-war" description seems meant to cover interventions such as rocket strikes or bombing raids to punish, rescue, or deter, though Walzer uses it, *inter alia*, for more sustained violence such as the American "no-fly zone" bombing of Iraq carried out as part of the "containment" system imposed after the Gulf war.[33] Walzer also uses the example and the idea of the proposed category to argue that "force-short-of-war" is easier to justify than war itself.[34]

The example of the "no-fly zone" intervention is relevant to the case for preventive war we are considering here because its ostensible purpose was to prevent Saddam Hussein from using his military capacity against the Kurds in the north or the Shi'a in the south. We may well doubt that this was the primary purpose of the intervention, especially in its later stages, but Walzer portrays the exercise in altogether too mild a fashion. The bombing (which was a primary part of the exercise of "force-short-of-war") covered 60 percent of Iraq, and it was estimated in 2002 that the US had averaged more than 34,000 military sorties per year since 1991. Confidential UN reports are said to put the number of civilian casualties between 1998 and 2002 at over 300, though other estimates are higher.[35] In addition

---

[32] Michael Walzer, "The Case Against our Attack on Libya," *The New Republic*, March 20, 2011. Or see www.tnr.com/article/world/85509/the-case-against-our-attack-libya (accessed June 26, 2012).

[33] Michael Walzer, "Regime Change and Just War," *Dissent* 53 (2006), 106–108. This article was taken from the new introduction to the 2006 edition of Walzer's *Just and Unjust Wars: A Moral Argument with Historical Illustrations* (New York: Basic Books, 2006).

[34] Walzer, "Regime Change and Just War," 106.

[35] Jeremy Scahill, "No-Fly Zones over Iraq: Washington's Undeclared War on 'Saddam's Victims'," (2002) at www.IraqJournal.org claims the figure of 300 as a "UN statistic" and cites Hans von Sponeck, the coordinator of the UN Humanitarian Program in Iraq from 1998–2000 as claiming that in 1999 alone 120 civilians were killed. Von Sponeck is also quoted to similar effect by Susan Taylor Martin, "'No-fly' Zone Perils were for Iraqis, Not Allied Pilots" in the American paper, *The St. Petersburg Times*, October 29, 2004. Scahill is the source for the estimate of 34,000 sorties and the 60 percent area and he cites as his authority the Washington Institute for Near East Policy.

there were many Iraqi military deaths and much property destruction, though reliable estimates of these are hard to come by. Moreover, this protracted exercise over more than a decade was not authorized by the UN though its justification was couched in terms of enforcing UN Security Council resolution 688 that called on Iraq to cease repression of its civilian population. It might not matter too much in some contexts whether we call this "war" or not, but in the context of the moral assessment of resort to sustained political violence and Walzer's attempt to relax the conditions for that assessment, it does matter. Let us define war, as I have suggested elsewhere, following, but adapting, that provided by Clausewitz in his classic treatise *On War* as follows: "War is the resort by an organized group to a relatively large-scale act of violence for political purposes to compel an enemy to do the group's will."[36] This allows for small wars that are nonetheless large scale compared, for instance, to an individual or small group sniper attack on a hated political figure.[37] The no-fly bombing clearly counts as war on this definition.

Of course the duration and expected duration of a violent conflict and the scale of its costs are relevant to the moral assessment of it, but this does not entail that different, essentially weaker conditions for justification apply. Walzer does allow that considerations parallel to just-war principles should govern force short of war, and this surely indicates that it is a phenomenon of the same kind, but he insists that the just-war condition of "last resort" and perhaps other conditions are much easier to satisfy than in the case of war proper.[38] He believes we need a new theory of *jus ad vim* to supplement *jus ad bellum*; the new theory should not be "overly tolerant or permissive" but "more permissive" than just-war theory.[39] But we need no such theory and the talk of such a weaker theory flies in the face of the background to just-war thinking that I outlined at the beginning of this chapter. The last resort condition, to which Walzer makes explicit reference, cautions against too hasty a resort to war and embodies a genuine reluctance to shed blood. It should apply to any war, short or long, and no matter how extreme the devastation. Of course, a short war that has a just

---

[36] See Clausewitz, *On War*, chapter 1, section 2, 75. My reasons for departing somewhat from Clausewitz are given in Coady, *Morality and Political Violence*, 5.

[37] There will also be grey areas created by the definition, such as bloodless wars where one side is so overwhelmed as not to require bloodletting and not to respond with it. These are rare enough to ignore, and, in any case, probably should count as a marginal form of war just because the coercive occupation is effected by soldiers and their armaments with palpable violence imminently threatened and always available for use against resistance.

[38] Walzer, "Regime Change and Just War," 106.   [39] Ibid.

cause and involves relatively few killings and injuries on both sides is more likely to satisfy the proportionality requirement of the *jus ad bellum* than a protracted conflict with massive casualties. But it still needs to satisfy the same conditions, including last resort, as the larger war. To think otherwise is to demean the value of the lives of the soldiers and civilians who are killed or wounded in the conflict. Walzer confuses possible differences in applying rules or measures with differences in the nature of the rules or measures themselves. It is easier to measure the dimensions of a small book than the dimensions of a large room, but the same measure and measuring device can be applied to both. So it is with different sorts of war.

I conclude that the case for preventive war against potential terrorism or anticipated humanitarian persecution faces overwhelming difficulties. Instead of a war on potential terror or a war on prospective persecutors we do much better to seek other methods for preventing these grave evils. There are plenty of alternatives. In the case of terrorism: policing, surveillance, diplomacy, education, international cooperation, recognizing and meeting genuine grievances; in the case of government persecution of its citizens: diplomatic pressure, non-violent coercive measures including carefully developed sanctions aimed at the rulers rather than the ruled, economic and financial measures aimed at dictators, and legal sanctions against powerful persecutors. None of these are guaranteed to work and involve complex difficulties in practice, but the same applies more emphatically to the resort to preventive warfare. Beating swords into ploughshares was always good advice, and in the case of prevention it applies even more so to the modern equivalents of those contrasting implements.

CHAPTER 12

Enough about just war, what about just peace? The doctrine of preventive non-intervention

Deen K. Chatterjee

> We can admit the grain of truth in the cynical slogan, "If you want peace, prepare for war," but the surer path to a more tranquil world is to prepare for peace directly.
>
> C. A. J. Coady[1]

> Preventive war short-circuits nonmilitary means of solving problems.
>
> Neta C. Crawford[2]

The increasingly common "preventive" use of military force and the tragic dilemmas of recent military operations have severely challenged international law in regard to the justification of waging preventive wars for self-defense and under the guise of international peace and security. Also, the growing trend of justifying preventive use of force by invoking principles of the just-war doctrine has left the just-war theorists wondering whether the theory itself is in need of a fundamental shift. This chapter responds to these concerns by placing the debate in the wider discourse of global justice. By invoking the concept of just peace, I discuss prevention from a non-interventionist perspective and show how it can be an effective measure for national security as well as for humanitarian policies. I call this approach "preventive non-intervention" and explain how it is intimately tied to human rights concerns. The best way to prevent a crisis is to ensure justice and fair representation in global governance, for which other means than the use of military force are more prudent and effective. An emphasis on global justice underscores the need for a preventive approach that is non-interventionist; it calls for rooting out the underlying causes of conflict, injustice, and humanitarian crises by a collaborative system of just governance through institutional implementation of rights. The focus

---

[1] C. A. J. Coady, "War for Humanity: A Critique," in Deen K. Chatterjee and Don E. Scheid, eds., *Ethics and Foreign Intervention* (Cambridge University Press, 2003), 274–295; 293.
[2] Neta C. Crawford, "The Slippery Slope to Preventive War," *Ethics and Inernational Affairs* 17:1 (2003), 30–36; 35.

is on being proactive by getting involved in issues of economic justice and inclusive democratic-political processes both within countries and especially in the global order.

Promotion of real-world justice is the best guarantee against human-rights abuse and can be the most effective strategy for national defense. It is also far less costly in the long run than the use of military force. Peace is not just an absence of military conflicts. Peace with justice, or "just peace," is the true foundation for an enduring peace. Though the just-war doctrine has been around for many centuries – in its early days primarily intended for securing peace and order by limiting if not eliminating war – the concept of just peace is a relatively recent one, indicating an emerging awareness that the broader issues of global justice transcend the confines of just-war concerns in promoting peace. Accordingly, the emphasis should be on just peace rather than on just war as a more lasting solution to global conflicts. In this chapter I explicate the just-peace concept in some detail to provide substance to my idea of preventive non-intervention.

The views of the major just-war theorists in the sixteenth and the seventeenth centuries were a notable departure from the early tradition. Alberico Gentili, the late sixteenth-century legal scholar who drew from the just-war tradition, included offensive war as part of justified self-defense in response to anticipated dangers, even if they are remote or merely probable. Unlike Augustine's moral injunction against anticipatory wars, Gentili's prescription vastly expanded the idea of just war by construing self-defense on prudential – almost Machiavellian – grounds. Hugo Grotius, who came after Gentili and whose ideas profoundly shaped international law, disputed Gentili's construal of what counts as acceptable ground for going to war. For Grotius, offensive wars cannot be justified in response to uncertain and remote dangers. Justified self-defense allows reasonable preventive measures of force in response to real and credible danger that is imminent, not when the threat is remote, probable, or merely possible because that could create false pretext for war.

Grotius lived through the long period of warring states in Europe that ended with the Treaty of Westphalia in 1648, creating agreement among nations to respect mutual sovereignty as the norm of international relations. This norm, along with Grotius' limited prescription of what constitutes justified warfare, has long been the guiding principle of international law. Emer de Vattel, another seminal figure in the founding of international law who lived a century after Grotius, was working within the broad Grotian tradition even as he expanded the Grotian limits on preventive war. The blurring of the distinction between preemption and prevention, depending on whether imminent danger is understood as certain and irrevocable or speculative but likely, is at the heart of this debate. Grotius' guidelines leave room for such blurring, and Vattel made good use of it. Emphasizing prudence and caution but not going to the extent of Gentili, Vattel famously said that if a sovereign has reasonable grounds for suspicion of danger based on the evidence of a neighboring state showing signs of dominance beyond its border, then the sovereign is justified in taking appropriate steps in forestalling the perceived danger even if the danger is not forthcoming or imminent. But Vattel showed moderation in noting that the use and extent of force should be in direct proportion to the likelihood and seriousness of the danger.

Vattel's reliance on reasonable suspicion of danger as justification for measured use of preventive force is a nod to the Grotian legacy of caution and moderation in international law. In contrast, Gentili's vastly expanded construal of precaution where even fear for a remote danger can be taken as a justification for offensive war has been deemed too dangerous. No wonder, then, that today's prominent just-war theorists are mindful of the Grotian tradition even as they espouse an expanded version of self-defense that construes the idea of imminent danger not necessarily as immediate but as a sufficiently serious risk of high probability. This expanded reading gives them a broader latitude in justifying first strike. Predictably they move closer to Vattel and away from Gentili, finding the latter's ideas rather far-fetched. For the same reason, most of these just-war theorists find the United States National Security Strategy of September 2002 – the so-called Bush doctrine – too broad and therefore unacceptable.

The Bush doctrine of 2002, largely in response to the September 11, 2001, terrorist attacks on the United States, contains the most expanded strategy declaration of national defense to date. However, the doctrine's blurring of the distinction between preemption and prevention may not seem to be all that radical. As noted above, the trend can be traced in the modern just-war tradition. What may seem brazen about the doctrine is its self-proclaimed authority to use unilateral preventive military measures for self-defense under the broad rubric of global security, in which the hegemonic interests of the United States are tied to the peace and security of the global order on US terms.

Even this seeming brazenness of unilateralism for the sake of global safekeeping may not seem to be a radical departure from the recent trends of warfare and international law. Though the United Nations Security Council prohibits unilateralism in humanitarian military interventions, the slippery transition from multilateralism to unilateralism is implicitly left open in the practice, if not in the mandate, of the Security Council. Chapter 7 of the United Nations Charter permits multilateral use of force with the Council's authorization in response to threats to international peace and security. Breach of human rights is not mentioned in the directive, but because humanitarian emergencies involving egregious violation of human rights challenge international peace and security, coalitions of nations have undertaken rescue wars in cases of egregious human rights abuses, even at times without the sanction of the Security Council. But while collective self-defense can be taken to be an important part of international peace and security, providing distinct sets of guidelines in practice by separating self-defense and humanitarian intervention can be difficult.[3] The broad mandate of the Bush doctrine effectively makes the idea of "global safekeeping" an important part of national security strategy, giving the United States an open-ended unilateral license to respond militarily, in the name of "war on terror," to any acts or events in the world based solely on the internal perception of the United States. Thus, it should not come as a surprise that the Security Council's implicit inclusion of the provision of (collective) self-defense to its authorization of multilateral military operations for peace and security has given the United States a convenient opening for claiming a global mandate in the name of national security.

Though most contemporary political and legal theorists advocating preventive use of force find the Bush doctrine too broad, they feel compelled to respond to the challenges of the changing nature of warfare in the twenty-first century. Consequently, the traditional debates of just war have become a major focus of controversy in these defining years of unconventional warfare. A similar major turn in rethinking the just-war concerns occurred during the Second World War where the distinction between combatants and non-combatants blurred, making that war the first truly "total war." It compelled the Allied forces to navigate across a moral divide in deciding whether to undertake massive bombing of German civilian targets for military and strategic reasons. "I see this idea of just killing civilians and targeting civilians as being unethical – though the most unethical act in World War II for the Allies would have been allowing themselves to lose," says military historian Conrad Crane, quoted in the 2010 PBS Television's American Experience segment titled "The Bombing of Germany." We find the echo of Crane's words in Michael Walzer's

---

[3] In fact, as Michael Doyle has noted, "Security Council practice . . . has [practically] merged the two," in Michael Doyle, *Striking First: Preemption and Prevention in International Conflict* (Princeton University Press, 2008), 36.

classic restatement of the just-war doctrine. He writes: "But if there was no other way of preventing a Nazi triumph, then the immorality [of creating massive terror by targeting the non-combatant] ... was also, simultaneously, morally defensible."[4] For Walzer, in cases of "supreme emergency," rules of war can be breached "when we are face-to-face not merely with defeat but with a defeat likely to bring disaster to a political community."[5]

The just-war dilemma of the Allied leaders over bombing the German civilians was prompted by the German bombers attacking London for fifty-seven consecutive nights, which indicates that the Allied response was directed at a "face-to-face" situation of dire catastrophe. The quandary facing today's political theorists who draw from the just-war tradition is provoked by a new set of challenges unique to the new century. The question now is not only justifying first strike but deciding on how much in advance of the perceived threat, given the potential for catastrophic consequences if the threat is given the time to be carried out. The certainty factor of an imminent danger, already compromised in the Grotian tradition of expanded preemption, is now put to severe test in view of this new challenge.

However, contemporary political theorists espousing preventive war as justified self-defense remain mindful of the Grotian plea for caution and moderation. In fact, Walzer is highly reluctant to call his expanded preemptive guidelines "preventive," lest the term is taken as a permissive license for speculative military measures against uncertain dangers. For Walzer, at one end of a spectrum of anticipation is preemption, which is "like a reflex action ... necessary and determined; at the other end is preventive war, an attack that responds to a distant danger, a matter of foresight and free choice."[6] Walzer's initial moral idealism gets less rigid when faced with the reality of "threats sufficiently serious" in considering preemptive strike. Discussing the 1967 six-day war between Israel and Egypt, Walzer stipulates a set of conditions under which anticipatory strike would be justified to counter "sufficient threat." Though Walzer admits that the phrase is "necessarily vague," he intends it to cover three items: "a manifest intent to injure, a degree of active preparation that makes that intent a positive danger, and a general situation in which waiting, or doing anything other than fighting, greatly magnifies the risk."[7] Instead of a strict standard of imminence that would demand "moral

---

[4] Michael Walzer, *Arguing about War* (New Haven, CT: Yale University Press, 2004), 34–35.
[5] Michael Walzer, *Just and Unjust Wars* (4th edn., New York: Basic Books, 2006), 268.
[6] Ibid., 75.   [7] Ibid., 81.

necessity of rejecting any attack that is merely preventive in character,"[8] these guidelines leave the standard of imminence sufficiently open. As Walzer puts it: "The line between legitimate and illegitimate first strikes is not going to be drawn at the point of imminent attack but at the point of sufficient threat."[9] Evidently, Walzer's moral high ground gives in to the demands of necessity at the midpoint of the spectrum of anticipation.

In Walzer's discussion of the dire risks of "supreme emergency," the moral absolutism of non-combatant immunity so passionately defended by Walzer himself is especially compromised. Though for Walzer "supreme emergency" is a "face-to-face" situation where the way of life of a political community is in danger of obliteration, the understanding of a "face-to-face" danger in today's world could take a whole new meaning in view of the unconventional nature of warfare and the specter of WMD. It could come eerily close to the former US Vice President Dick Cheney's "one-percent doctrine," which proclaimed that even a one-percent possibility of being attacked with weapons of mass destruction poses an unacceptable risk, warranting a massive "preemptive" measure. We see here how Walzer's slippery spectrum of anticipation can push us toward the other extreme, paving the way toward the Bush doctrine's unilateralism and blurring of the distinction between prevention and preemption. Ironically, though the Bush administration's espousal of self-defense actually embraces far-fetched prevention similar in tone to Gentili's assertions, the document's language calls the move preemption! Even here we find a nod to the Grotian spirit in international law, but also a crafty move to unilateralism in the guise of preemptive self-defense.

In fact, the idea of supreme emergency is elastic enough to give any state the excuse to go beyond the legitimate limits of the just-war doctrine or international law. C. A. J. Coady rightly observes that "supreme emergency is . . . so elastic, indeed, that whenever you are engaged in legitimate self-defense and seem to be losing, you will be able to produce plausible reasons of supreme emergency for attacking the innocent."[10] Neta Crawford's observation is worth noting here: "In sum, a preemptive-preventive doctrine moves us closer to a state of nature than a state of international law."[11]

I'll briefly sketch here the views of three prominent contemporary political and legal theorists who advocate preventive war for justified self-defense. Their concern is to stay within the spirit of international

---

[8] Ibid., 80.   [9] Ibid., 81.
[10] C. A. J. Coady, *Morality and Political Violence* (Cambridge University Press, 2008), 289.
[11] Crawford, "The Slippery Slope to Preventive War," 35.

law and devise means of accountability in offensive wars, with the goal of finding ways to respond to the new threats to peace and security posed by unconventional warfare and unconventional weapons systems. In contrast to these views, I intend to show below why advocacy of preventive war, however constrained, is not the way toward peace and security. Preventive non-intervention is the way.

In his recently published important study on preemption and prevention in international conflicts, titled *Striking First*, Michael Doyle critiques the Bush doctrine for its go-alone approach that defies the carefully set standards and procedures of multilateralism stipulated in the United Nations Charter. Unilateralism in preventive ventures based on subjective and open-ended assessment of security threats can go horribly wrong in its calculations of anticipatory events and developments, Doyle notes, and because it lacks political legitimacy and legal authority, it sets a dangerous precedent. Doyle's provision for preventive use of force is primarily multilateral, guided by his carefully worked-out "jurisprudence of prevention" based on four guidelines collectively held together: severity of threat, the likelihood of its occurrence, just-war criteria of legitimacy, and the legality of the threat and the proposed response.[12] Dubbed both substantive and procedural, the approach is a mix of the just-war criteria and legal propriety, putting emphasis on collaboration whenever possible, and citing the UN Security Council as the venue for open arbitration and debate for procedural legitimacy. Doyle points out that there are carefully set procedural remedies for global crises at the UN Security Council. But Doyle leaves room for multilateral preventive response without the approval of the Security Council if warranted, or even unilateral action by individual states in rare cases of extreme emergency, as long as these moves meet his carefully construed jurisprudence of prevention. For him, the guidelines provide "both substantive and procedural standards in order to decide upon the *rare circumstances* in which we will want to authorize unilateral prevention."[13] Accordingly, Doyle's critique of the Bush doctrine is not directed to the doctrine's license to use force preventively, nor even to its unilateralism *per se*, but to its *reckless* unilateralism.

Commenting on the Bush doctrine, Doyle observes: "Subjective and abstract standards of prevention are subject to unverifiable claims that are very difficult to contest. They are much too likely to be self-serving, promoting narrow partisan advantages."[14] Ironically, Doyle's own guidelines for prevention that include provisions for a broad range of

---

[12] Doyle, *Striking First*, 43–64.   [13] Ibid., 43 (emphasis added).   [14] Ibid., 29.

anticipatory measures are also open-ended and can be misused. His just-war legitimacy criteria such as proportionality, necessity, and last resort are matters of disputation and prone to subjective interpretation, especially if a go-alone provision is allowed in the guidelines.[15] The assessment of severity and likelihood of threat in anticipatory circumstances is no less subjective and open to mistakes or abuse. And the idea of legality is a moot question in claims of existential threat. As Walzer has famously stated: "necessity knows no rules."[16] Thus, Doyle's "jurisprudence of prevention" leaves open the possibility that a powerful nation with global hegemony can construe his guidelines as an open-ended license to respond militarily, in the name of self-defense, to any emerging or anticipatory events in the world based on its own perception.

However, if the standards in matters of preventing conflict and danger were construed not on the principles of just war but on the premise of just peace, then the claims of moral mandate in the slippery transition from preemption to prevention in the name of peace and security would be hard to justify. The just-peace approach relies on the normative prerogatives of justice in global affairs. In contrast, Doyle on the whole adopts a realist, practical/political approach in matters of conflict and international rela-tions. His method is not significantly framed by normative guidelines, though he notes at times the relevance of Kantian liberalism. Just peace, on the other hand, is primarily a normative initiative of globalism where the norm is egalitarian justice for all. Today's entrenched global order affects all nations, especially the poor ones, and thus indirectly their citizens. It is well documented that the pervasive state-failure to respond to citizens' broader human needs is linked to the inequity in the global order itself. Any theory of international justice must address this entrenched inequity in the global order. Mitigating the "global democracy deficit"[17] consists primarily of ensuring an equitable global structure, along with domestic democratic reforms in individual countries. The latter is mostly ineffective, and often hard to achieve, without the former. Amartya Sen and Joseph

---

[15] In challenging the legitimacy of the concept of "just war," R. J. Myers notes that the doctrine's major flaw is that it allows self-interested interpretation by the contesting parties. "Whose justice are we talking about?" he asks, in "Notes on the Just War Theory: Whose Justice, Which Wars?," *Ethics and International Affairs* 10:1 (2006), 115–130.

[16] Walzer, *Just and Unjust Wars*, 254. David Rodin notes that even the question of whether there exists a right of preemptive self-defense in international law is "by no means" a settled issue. See Rodin, "The Problem with Prevention," in Henry Shue and David Rodin, eds., *Preemption: Military Action and Moral Justication* (Oxford University Press, 2007), 143–170; 145.

[17] Benjamin Barber, "The War of All against All: Terror and the Politics of Fear," in Verna V. Gehring, ed., *War After September 11* (Lanham, MD: Rowman and Littlefield), 75–91.

Stiglitz, among others, have been providing a conceptual framework for the slowly emerging trend of this democratization of globalization.[18]

This two-prong process of democratization is the foundation for just peace, which is the goal of global justice where the debate is placed within the broader discourse of the normative and institutional challenges of globalization, with a focus on human development and well-being. Normative pronouncements, empirical findings, and strategies of enforcement work together to make viable the theories of global justice and human rights. This collective approach consists of taking advantage of existing international organizations and tribunals, promoting international legal frameworks, shunning ineffective methods such as food embargoes, working to influence public opinion in all relevant nations, and taking the reins of suggesting how to alleviate poverty and injustice and other root causes. Obviously, a non-interventionist approach is not simply refraining from doing anything. It calls for proactive engagement in promoting just governance both within countries and especially in the global order through acts and policies carried out routinely in order to diminish crises and emergencies requiring the need for military and humanitarian interventions. This prospect is far more achievable and less costly than the current practice of perpetual war for perpetual peace. Benjamin Barber sums it up best:

The call today for the globalization of democracy, the globalization of law, the construction of strong international institutions that allow genuine participation, is no longer simply a romantic call of irrelevant world federalists for an impossible utopia. It has become an issue of national security, an imperative of a new realism.[19]

Favoring a general ban on preventive war, David Luban in a recent study makes preventive war an exception to the general no-first-use rule in international law.[20] For Luban, the "narrow exception" is when basic rights of people are at stake, and the likelihood of that scenario is the "high probability" of danger posed by rogue states. This construal of the doctrine of preventive war merges the idea of prevention with preemption by taking the idea of imminence in probabilistic rather than temporal terms. Thus, by recasting a preventive war as a preemptive operation in

---

[18] Amartya Sen, *The Idea of Justice* (Cambridge, MA: Harvard University Press, 2009) and *Development as Freedom* (New York: Knopf; Oxford: Clarendon Press, 1999); Joseph Stiglitz, *Globalization and its Discontents* (New York: W. W. Norton, 2002).

[19] Barber, "The War of All against All," 87.

[20] David Luban, "Preventive War," *Philosophy and Public Affairs* 32:3 (2004), 207–248; 219 n. 21.

cases of high probability of threats, a first strike is made to seem more like self-defense than aggression, thus giving it moral legitimacy and making it permissible in international law. In cases of high probability of danger, for Luban, the distinction between preemption and prevention "thins to the vanishing point."[21]

Though construed as a rare exception, in reality Luban's provision of prevention against rogue states is rather open-ended in a predictably one-sided fashion due to the dominance of powerful states in the global order. These states could use it – and often have done so – as a convenient excuse for legitimacy in taking anticipatory military measures against a "rogue" state for the sake of promoting their own hegemonic interests, often garbed in the rhetoric of concern for security and the common good.

However, unlike Doyle whose approach is primarily practical/political, Luban raises the important normative question of moral acceptability in matters of international law. For instance, by questioning the idea of sovereign equality of the post-Westphalian order in today's radically changed international order marked by clear US dominance, Luban addresses the issues of political morality in assessing the idea of American exceptionalism. For Luban, claims of American exceptionalism should not be judged as morally unacceptable if the claims are indeed valid in a world of US supremacy, not only in power but also in its stated global mission of securing democracy, free markets, and human rights. But Luban thinks that the heavy burden of defending such a tall claim of moral hegemony cannot be established. In that case, the United States would not be justified in launching unilateral preventive war against the enemies of cosmopolitan values in the name of self-defense, "unfettered by rules that should rightly bind non-leader nations."[22] Thus, without a credible moral theory of international politics that can justifiably validate the morality of US global hegemony, Luban would hold that the Bush doctrine of American exceptionalism cannot give the United States the moral (or legal) right to launch a preventive strike against a distant threat under the broad banner of "War on Terror."

This critique of the Bush doctrine, based on the principles of political morality embedded in Henry Kissinger's advice about translating intervention into terms of "general applicability for an international system",[23] is markedly different from Doyle's construal of the critique on strategic

---

[21] Ibid., 230.   [22] Ibid., 244.
[23] Henry Kissinger, "Our Intervention in Iraq," *Washington Post*, August 12, 2002, cited in Luban, "Preventive War," 236.

grounds. This universal doctrine, for Luban, is a general ban on preventive war, with the "narrow exception" of permitting anticipatory war for all states only in the rare cases of preventing extreme danger of high probability posed by rogue states. Like Walzer, Luban construes a normative argument of international morality based on the demand of the legalist paradigm of sovereign equality, though his argument is different from Walzer's. Questioning Walzer's defense of sovereign equality predicated on ensuring autonomy of peoples, which Luban thinks equal sovereignty cannot guarantee, Luban offers his defense based on the normative implications of the legalist paradigm of general applicability.

Luban's moral theory of international relations has the imprint of "soft normativity," which is not the robust egalitarian model of human equality that for Luban doesn't apply to state relations. However, sovereign equality is a statist paradigm that is contingent and arbitrary, so a theory of justice built on a statist paradigm would also be arbitrary, especially in today's world where human associations breach political boundaries. Liberal egalitarianism, on the other hand, is about human equality, not sovereign equality, and necessarily has a globalist tilt. If the contingency of the political arrangements is allowed to reflect the normative scope of equality in a manner that favors a paradigm of state borders, then the statist tilt enters at the outset of the debate, making the burden of proof rest on the side of the globalists. But if liberal egalitarianism is to be taken seriously, then it seems that the burden of proof should be the other way around. The point of this argument is that the idea of political morality based on the general applicability of sovereign equality, though normatively more promising than political realism, is still not robust enough to withstand the charges of contingency and arbitrariness. In other words, political morality does not go far enough, normatively speaking. But one cannot defend this shortcoming by pointing out that we should not expect full-fledged normativity in politics. As will be discussed below, if morality is compromised in the name of politics, then the broader and more foundational questions of justice would be hard to decide.

Walzer, Doyle, and Luban are decidedly not globalist or cosmopolitan theorists – their imperatives are based on the legal paradigm of sovereign equality. However, the foundational issues of peace and security have to respond to the challenges of global justice in today's interconnected, interdependent, densely populated, and radically unequal world with contested and shifting boundaries and identities. The statist paradigm has to be transcended in favor of a global paradigm. The global world needs an adequate and expanded theory of global justice.

One recurring theme in political and international legal theories is that of group and political membership in deciding the question of allocation of rights. The realists rightly point out the shortcomings of the liberal egalitarians of various stripes in their inability to devise an adequate theory of membership, but they (the realists) do not give this important issue the attention it deserves. They brand the cosmopolitan thrust of robust egalitarianism as unrealistic, if not "inherently chimerical," based on the lack of plausible institutional mechanism in international enforcement.[24] Yet given the global nature of today's politics, commerce, and institutions, and the many existing measures in the current international system that are designed to enforce order and human rights, it is imprudent to dismiss so easily the global paradigm of justice and political legitimacy. Indeed, it is imperative to seriously explore potential alternatives to nation-state politics and justice. For instance, one can legitimately question the moral justification for dividing the world into nation-states.[25] Even some communitarians, for whom group rights usually trump individual political rights, are open to the idea that national membership need not be the basis for politics.[26] In general, non-cosmopolitan liberal political theorists do not give good reasons when they have a strict standard for domestic liberal justice but a less demanding standard for justice beyond borders. John Rawls' stated reasons for holding onto a version of the legalist paradigm of sovereign equality in moving from his political liberalism to the law of peoples have been critiqued by the democratic theorists for not being democratic enough and by the liberal cosmopolitans for not being robustly liberal. In fact, questioning Walzer's defense of sovereign equality predicated on ensuring autonomy of peoples, even Luban (who is not a cosmopolitan liberal) thinks that equal sovereignty cannot guarantee self-determination – individual or collective – and may in fact facilitate the fostering of entrenched inequality and human-rights violations behind the veil of sovereignty. This critique can be extended to Rawls' law of peoples.

---

[24] Ian Shapiro, *The Moral Foundations of Politics* (New Haven: Yale University Press, 2003), 221; cf. Thomas Nagel, "The Problem of Global Justice," *Philosophy and Public Affairs* 33:2 (2005), 113–147; Chandran Kukathas, "The Mirage of Global Justice," *Social Philosophy and Policy* 23:1 (2006), 1–26.

[25] Entrenched social hierarchy such as a caste system is an affront to the liberal conscience, yet many of the same liberals are silent on the de facto illiberalism of entrenched statism in international law. (I am grateful to Arvind Sharma for pointing this out to me.) For an innovative and insightful analysis of citizenship and global inequality, see Ayelet Shachar's recent study of citizenship-as-inherited-property analogy. Shachar argues for enhancing citizenship's enabling dimension domestically and extending its redistributive obligations globally to mitigate the moral luck of "birthright lottery." See Ayelet Shachar, *The Birthright Lottery: Citizenship and Global Inequality* (Cambridge, MA: Harvard University Press, 2009).

[26] Shapiro himself points this out in *The Moral Foundations of Politics*, 220.

In view of concerns about powerful regimes using "the rogue-states rhetoric" in a self-serving manner to target vulnerable states, Luban's provision for the "narrow exception" of preventive war against the "certain danger" posed by a rogue terrorist state should be taken with due caution. Epithets like "rogue" and "terrorist state" can be abused in a highly charged world where the "politics of fear" in the name of self-defense are being manipulated as an open-ended license to bolster power and dominance. Luban's provision unfortunately gives undue credence to such a possibility. Rawls at least stipulates that an international organization rather than single states should authorize intervention, but with Luban, the possibility of unilateralism is left open.

Ironically, Luban himself raises the concern of "the incredible disparity in power between the United States and other nations" in asking whether "it makes sense any longer to ask about appropriate 'general doctrines'." He states: "To put it another way: should we continue to think of just-war theory as a collection of rules or principles that apply to all states, or is this legalistic model of political morality inapplicable in the dramatically altered political constellation we inhabit?"[27] Based on the imperatives of the just-war doctrine, he concludes that Kissinger's "general applicability" rule is a good guide for construing the morality of international relations that would mitigate the misuse of incredible disparity in power. However, his argument for allowing aggressive use of force against rogue states leaves open the very possibility of misuse that his moral doctrine is meant to guard against. After all, the radical inequity in the world order and the penchant of the powerful nations for using military means to sustain it is itself a form of global terrorism that causes perpetual deprivation for the majority of the world's population. But the rhetoric of terrorism is framed by the dominant nations in a tilted fashion that is predictably to their advantage.

Political realists tend to think that the vision of global justice by liberal egalitarians is empty idealism with no place in international politics. But this need not be true. As vital as it is to make vivid the need for a realistic assessment of moral pronouncements, it is also necessary to continually emphasize the importance of moral imperatives in world affairs. Normative claims of justice and fairness serve both in setting the ideal and in practice. For instance, though international relations are usually guided by power and self-interest, the concept of fairness is invariably brought in when there is a dispute. This is evident in international trade agreements,

---

[27] Luban, "Preventive War," 210.

environmental policies, and other mutually agreed-upon treaties, as well as in military ventures. Nonetheless, liberal globalists have been critiqued for offering normative ideals of justice that have been routinely deemed utopian and impractical. Political realists seem reluctant to speculate about normative ideals that prevail nowhere; instead, they would rather evaluate political theories by reference to mechanisms of collective decision-making that actually prevail in the world, imperfect as they are.

Though the critique of liberal egalitarianism – that it suffers from excessive abstraction – is not entirely unfounded, it is not evident that a political approach favoring the status quo should be viewed as having a better prospect of practical imperative in critical international issues or humanitarian emergencies than the normative demands of justice in international affairs. Consider, for instance, as an example of the ideal in practice, the NATO bombing of Yugoslavia in 1999, which was a clear violation of international law as well as contrary to NATO's own charter. The United States was careful to pitch the action as justified in terms of "moral imperatives" and not in terms of standards of international law.[28] European leaders made similar statements.[29] Accordingly, to distill ideal theories of their normative imperative for ready strategies of enforcement is to misunderstand the role of the ideal in practice. The crucial issue seems to hinge on the task of showing how a normative theory can be conceptualized within an institutional and political setting so that it is workable as a guiding moral principle. For instance, the US-led invasion of Iraq, which happened despite strong opposition by the international community and without the approval of the United Nations, highlights the importance of a viable theory of international justice, while also making vivid the need for a realistic assessment of moral pronouncements.

From this perspective, Luban is partly right in claiming that "[t]he right test for a moral norm should not be whether the norm will be efficacious, but rather whether it would be efficacious if states generally complied with it."[30] If moral norms were measured on the basis of whether states would comply with them, then something unique about morality is left out: its normativity. Moral norms are not legal rules. As noted above and as Luban himself agrees, "states so frequently disregard moral and legal norms."[31] So, though it is important that normative guidelines are realistic and acceptable for moral

---

[28] Then-US President Bill Clinton in a TV speech on March 24, 1999.
[29] Former British Prime Minister Tony Blair, "A New Generation Draws the Line," *Newsweek*, April 19, 1999, 40.
[30] Luban, "Preventive War," 226.   [31] Ibid.

efficacy, it is also imperative that the idea of normative legitimacy embedded in claims of justice and fairness are given their due in the affairs of the world. The challenge should be to bring the idea of moral efficacy and claims of normative legitimacy closer together where both sides are receptive to each other. A focus on just peace moves in that direction, as will be shown below.

In a later publication, Luban admits that the "phrase 'rogue state' was perhaps an unfortunate choice," but his attempt to assign the phrase a "nonpropagandistic meaning" fares no better because Luban does not discuss the deeper issues of entrenched power and dominance in the global order.[32] In contrast, Allen Buchanan, another contemporary just-war theorist who advocates a narrow range of preventive use of force for human rights and security, addresses the broader issues of a justice-based international legal order by drawing attention to the deeper structural forces that shape the world, such as human rights, rules of warfare, environmental protection, and trade policies, along with global distribution of resources.[33] Buchanan proposes a modified cosmopolitan approach, where states are the de facto agents of distributive justice yet the model is not state-centric, in an attempt to conceptualize a viable global order that places an urgent premium on basic human rights. He stipulates the required institutional reconfiguration in global governance that would make the ideal a practicable concept. This ideal is the notion of a justice-based international order that calls for the priority of justice over international peace, in contrast to the dominant realist idea that the goal of the international system should be peace among nations, which may leave room for injustices within states or in the international order itself.

Within the backdrop of this moderate cosmopolitan setting, Buchanan calls for a reform of international law to permit morally legitimate preventive use of force for the sake of justice and human rights. I argue below that Buchanan's provision of preventive intervention does not go well with his just-peace approach. Preventive non-intervention is the direction of just peace.

In another publication Buchanan, along with co-author Robert Keohane, reaffirms a limited justifiability of preventive military measures by devising an institutional framework of democratic decision-making for ensuring better judgment and improved accountability in such moves.[34] For them,

---

[32] David Luban, "Preventive War and Human Rights," in Henry Shue and David Rodin, eds., *Preemption: Military Action and Moral Justification* (Oxford University Press, 2007), 171–201; 189–190.

[33] Allen Buchanan, *Justice, Legitimacy, and Self-Determination: Moral Foundations for International Law* (Oxford University Press, 2004).

[34] Allen Buchanan and Robert Keohane, "The Preventive Use of Force: A Cosmopolitan Institutional Approach," *Ethics and International Affairs* 18:1 (2004), 1–22.

the permissibility of preventive war should be based on a "contingent contract" that applies both to the states proposing preventive measures and states opposing them. The contract is meant to ensure enhanced accountability and institutional safeguards *ex ante* and *ex post* through the deliberative channel of the UN Security Council and, in addition, through the mediation of a democratic coalition of states. Doyle cites their ideas with approval in devising his own "jurisprudence of prevention," though Buchanan and Keohane's approach is different from Doyle's in that they look at the issues primarily from a normative perspective, adopting a broad-based egalitarian human-rights yardstick even as they, like Doyle, provide a judicious analysis of the legal, empirical, and policy issues that accompany an appropriate institutional framework. While Doyle pursues a modified version of Hobbesian realism that is tinged with Kantian liberalism, Buchanan and Keohane engage in a normative enterprise that is heavily invested in Kantian liberalism, including universal human rights and mutual respect among nations.

My proposal for preventive non-intervention shifts the discourse in the direction of just peace. But unlike the approach stipulated by Buchanan and Keohane, my idea of just peace does not seek legitimacy for prevention by invoking just war. I construe the idea of prevention not in military terms but through the normative lens of non-interventionist global justice. If peace is understood as hegemonic status quo of the political realists, then preventive war is always a lurking possibility. Just peace should be pursued from a justice-based cosmopolitan human-rights perspective. Though Buchanan and Keohane move in this direction in their normative cosmopolitan approach, their concern for security in the name of right to self-defense trumps the idea of preventive non-intervention. Claiming that their proposal for justified prevention is only in response to those wrongful acts that would be "*sudden and will cause massive violations of human rights*"[35], they put forward institutional arrangements "so that preventive action can become a more useful tool of policy" in their justice-based normative cosmopolitanism.[36] I claim that this move compromises their otherwise promising approach.

Buchanan and Keohane miss a good opportunity for emphasizing the need for preventive non-intervention as a prioritized principle sufficiently embedded in their normative human-rights approach. Though they show the direction for just peace, they get derailed by an interventionist take on just war. If one does not place a principled premium on a proactive and

---

[35] Ibid., 7 (emphasis in the original).   [36] Ibid., 10.

comprehensive non-interventionist policy, then the option of preventive war, however constrained, could gain undue legitimacy.[37] Buchanan's stipulation of preventive use of force in his "institutional approach to just war theory"[38] undermines his just-peace approach. To be sure, institutional provisions, not ad hoc judgments, are needed for ensuring procedural legitimacy in matters of war and peace, but legitimizing prevention can lead to more war and less peace.

My approach is not meant as a fool-proof solution because there is nothing in the murky issues of war and peace that is fool-proof. About his own prescribed guidelines, Doyle himself says that they are "far from cure-alls." And he adds: "There are no perfectly satisfactory outcomes."[39] Buchanan and Keohane have this to say about their project: "The cosmopolitan accountability regime should be attractive … not only to those wishing to constrain states bent on preventive action but also to those seeking to engage in it. This is not to say that we regard our proposal as feasible in the short run."[40]

It seems that on matters of individual and collective self-defense in a high-risk world, there is no fool-proof answer. But we need to see if some direction other than preventive intervention, even when as judiciously framed as Doyle's "jurisprudence of prevention" and especially Buchanan and Keohane's "cosmopolitan institutional proposal," is at least as promising, if not more so. After all, anticipatory use of force can go horribly wrong, as recent military engagements in Iraq and elsewhere amply attest. If accountability is an important factor in construing legitimacy, I propose that we need to construe accountability not for legitimacy in preventive intervention but for preventive non-intervention. If "(e)ven the most powerful states wish others to view their actions as legitimate," as Buchanan and Keohane note,[41] then let us make the criterion of legitimacy go in the direction of just peace with a principled ban on preventive use of force. Otherwise, legitimizing principled preventive war, however constrained, can give a powerful nation the moral license to expand the

---

[37] In a similar vein, in commenting on the frequent use of unmanned drones in today's US military combat overseas, Peter W. Singer writes: "And now we possess a technology that removes the last political barriers to war. The strongest appeal of unmanned systems is that we don't have to send someone's son or daughter into harm's way. But when politicians can avoid … the impact that military casualties have on voters and on the news media – they no longer treat the previously weighty matters of war and peace the same way." ("Do Drones Undermine Democracy?," *New York Times* Sunday Review, January 22, 2012.)

[38] Allen Buchanan, "Justifying Preventive War," in Shue and Rodin, eds., *Preemption*, 126–142; 133.

[39] Doyle, *Striking First*, 96.   [40] Buchanan and Keohane, "The Preventive Use of Force," 21.

[41] Ibid.

principle by pushing it in the direction of its own convenience. Even with *ex post* standards of Buchanan and Keohane's matrix of accountability, the damage is already done. And no specter of a "contingent contract" of *ex ante* accountability would deter a powerful state from trying to manipulate legitimacy in its own favor so long as the idea of preventive intervention is in the vocabulary of legitimacy. Given all this, it seems that even a limited and measured permissibility of preventive war, regardless of how well it covers the needed legal, empirical, and policy issues, is in the end an exercise in futility.

Buchanan and Keohane's choice of the phrase "contingent contract" is indicative of their presumed awareness that the democratic institutional arrangements for deliberation among a diverse group of states for *ex ante* and *ex post* decisions regarding preventive military actions are at best ad hoc provisions in our uncertain and contingent world. In view of this, their use of such phrases as "rational persuasion" and "impartial commission" in stipulating the requirements for deliberative and fact-finding phases is wishful thinking. Of course, as noted above, these authors do not consider their proposal to be "feasible in the short run." However, it is doubtful whether even in the long run their proposal would be feasible. In a later publication, Buchanan still hopes for "a critical, impartial evaluation of the criteria and the evidence" by the international institutional framework for determining prospects for forcible democratization in places like Iraq.[42] Again he notes that there is no guarantee that his proposed institutional approach would find wide acceptance in the real world, especially by the powerful states who prevail on such decisions. But this time Buchanan goes a step beyond by stating that he doesn't know whether his proposal is feasible even in the future. He concludes that if the stipulated institutional safeguards "cannot be realized," then the just-war ban on such measures as preventive self-defense and forcible democratization should stand.

However, the future is an indefinite time frame, and one wonders how many horribly failed preventive military measures nations must go through, either for putative self-defense or for initiating political reforms abroad, before realizing that the future is now. As opposed to the *speculative* prospect of sudden and massive violations of human rights of innocent civilians due to the possibility of WMD falling in the wrong hands, preventive wars bring *guaranteed* violations of human rights on a sudden and massive scale to the other side. Accordingly, the Augustinian ban on preventive war should still stand as a reasonable normative prescription.

---

[42] Allen Buchanan, "Institutionalizing the Just War," *Philosophy and Public Affairs* 34:1 (2006), 2–38; 35.

Such a ban should not be compromised by threats of hypothetical scenarios or conditions of modern warfare made into a presumed reality by powerful states and by their continued disregard for proactive non-interventionist policies toward the weaker and vulnerable states and peoples.

Political and legal theorists are currently debating relaxation of the ban on torture as a national policy. Luban has expressed his steadfast opposition to any exception to this ban on both moral and prudential grounds, yet curiously, as noted above, he has proposed a policy of preventive war – even unilateral – that would go against the ban on prevention, though such a ban has been a normative if not a legal guideline enshrined in the tradition for centuries. The just-war doctrine has been the guiding force in this opposition to prevention, yet the ambiguities of some of the doctrine's criteria have prompted scholars, policy-makers, and political and military leaders to espouse what they think is a morally permissible policy in favor of prevention, based on the conditions of the just-war doctrine itself, in view of contemporary challenges.[43] Accordingly, to seek guidance in the just-war doctrine for working out the path toward peace and justice carries the risk of looking for ways to sanction preventive intervention, whereas my idea of just peace as preventive non-intervention takes the focus away from just war, though it supports the just-war doctrine's normative injunction against preventive military intervention.

To build a culture of just peace as preventive non-intervention takes time and political will, and is never complete or fool-proof. But, as I have argued above, the policy of preventive intervention cannot guarantee feasibility or total security either, even by the admission of its own proponents. The espousal of such policies, even when carefully constrained, has given leaders of powerful states a convenient excuse to assume a global military mandate in the name of peace and security, most often leading to untold suffering and mass violation of human rights. It is high time that we shift our discourse from finding security in resorting to just war to building security via just peace. In any case, I do not see how putting in practice preventive non-intervention as a serious and sustained policy directive could be any worse than the horrors of failed experiments with preventive intervention.

In a later publication where he attempts to "strengthen the institutional approach" to preventive war, Buchanan notes that the grave risks of

---

[43] On a similar note, see David Luban, "War as Punishment," *Philosophy and Public Affairs* 39:4 (2011), 299–330 for an excellent account of how some of the ambiguities of the just-war doctrine have led to the mistaken view of war as punishment.

justifying preventive war "can only be adequately addressed through the construction of novel institutions, not through the mere extension of traditional methods of decision-making through the perilous domain of preventive action."[44] My claim is that if we were to give peace a chance, then we need to move away entirely from the "perilous domain of preventive action" and try something really novel and bold. Preventive war has been with us for a long time but we still find peace and security as elusive as ever. In fact, one can make the case that the permissibility of preventive use of force can make war all too tempting and frequent.[45] Accordingly, in looking for a bold and novel approach that bears as much promise as preventive intervention, if not more, I propose preventive non-intervention as the path toward peace. The mindset of preventive war perpetuates the anxiety of living under the shadow of war, whereas "the stress of living in fear should be assuaged by true prevention – arms control, disarmament, negotiations, confidence-building measures, and the development of international law."[46] These preventive measures are instances of proactive non-intervention that use the soft power of diplomacy and democratic collaboration. This may be a long and hard road that promises no quick results but, then, if we're looking for a fail-safe quick path to peace and security in today's murky and uncertain world, nothing can take us there. Here too we should pay heed to Grotius who said: "Human life exists under such conditions that complete security is never guaranteed to us."[47]

In sketching my idea of preventive non-intervention as a policy guide for moving toward just peace in the real world, I start with a recent report on whether Israel will attack Iran to prevent Iran from acquiring nuclear weapons.[48] Based on Israeli Defense Minister Ehud Barak's three criteria for such a possible attack – namely, whether Israel has the capability to successfully launch such an attack, a coalition of international legitimacy, and last resort – the report says that some of Israel's most powerful leaders

---

[44] Buchanan, "Justifying Preventive War," 142.
[45] Luban in "Preventive War" himself makes this point quite forcefully by adopting a consequentialist approch to preventive war, though he makes a narrow exception to this general observation that I have critiqued above. See also Stephen Nathanson's chapter in this volume for his arguments that rule consequentialism leads to a rejection of preventive war. For an interesting discussion on the implausibility of the consequentialist approach to war, see Rodin, "The Problem with Prevention."
[46] Crawford, "The Slippery Slope to Preventive War," 36.
[47] Hugo Grotius, *De Jure Belli ac Pacis*, trans. Francis W. Kelsey (Oxford: Clarendon Press, 1925), 184, cited by Larry May in his chapter in this volume.
[48] Ronen Bergman, "Will Israel Attack Iran?," *The New York Times* Sunday Magazine, January 25, 2012.

believe that the response to all these questions is yes. Added to this is
Israel's perception that a nuclear-armed Iran is an existential threat
to Israel. So, according to Doyle's proposal and even Buchanan and
Keohane's normative guidelines, Israel's use of force to prevent a nuclear
Iran would be justified. Yet, the *New York Times* report says that Meir
Dagan, then head of Mossad in January 2011, "sharply criticized the
heads of government for even contemplating 'the foolish idea' of
attacking [Iran]." Rafi Eitan, one of Mossad's most seasoned and well-
known operatives, agreed with Dagan. The report states: "Asked if it was
possible to [militarily prevent] a determined Iran from becoming a
nuclear power, Eitan replied: 'No. In the end they'll get their bomb.
The way to fight it is by changing the regime there. This is where we
have really failed. We should encourage the opposition groups who turn
to us over and over to ask for our help, and instead, we send them away
empty-handed.'"

Eitan's reply goes in the direction of my idea of preventive non-
intervention. Instead of military strikes, a more effective – and far more
peaceful – approach is to create a world where less drastic means than force
would prove to be more efficacious. However, one has to be careful:
military strikes are not the only coercive interventions. There are so many
seeming non-interventions that are really interventionist in nature. Trying
to isolate Iran or any other country through embargoes and sanctions is
an instance of applying coercive preventive force. Such actions create
panic, resentment, and hardship among the target nation's population
and thus can be counterproductive.[49] In a recent study, Trita Parsi and
Natasha Bahrami note: "The evidence is clear: imposing sanctions to
promote democracy is foolish – in Iran and elsewhere. The policymakers
responsible for these measures either are ignorant of or are simply ignoring
the evidence."[50] In a *New York Times* op-ed, Hooman Majd writes: "If
America wants Iranians to overthrow their government, sanctions won't
help. Only when Iran's people are no longer hungry will they seek political
change."[51]

My justice-based approach addresses the underlying causes of global
tension and crises. Deprivation and humiliation in our inequitable global
order are the two chief reasons for tension and resentment, creating

---

[49] See Robert F. Worth, "Iran's Middle Class on Edge as World Presses In," *The New York Times*,
February 7, 2012.
[50] Natasha Bahrami and Trita Parsi, "Blunt Instrument: Sanctions Don't Promote Democratic
Change," *Boston Review*, February 14, 2012.
[51] Hooman Majd, "Starving Iran Won't Free It," *The New York Times*, op-ed, March 3, 2012.

hostilities. Confronting deprivation through economic development and responding to humiliation through political recognition would go a long way toward mitigating tension and resentment and diminishing the global democracy deficit.[52] Studies have shown that non-military measures can be more effective in confronting terrorism than military actions, which may even prove to be counterproductive.[53] The then United Nations Secretary General Kofi Annan, in a report released on May 1, 2005, observed that the ingredients of enduring global security lie not necessarily in deploying a nation's military force for global safekeeping but, more importantly, in promoting just development and comprehensive human rights.[54] A report on the mission of Dutch soldiers in Afghanistan seems to corroborate this proactive approach. While the United States and British troops were conducting sweeps and raids, the Dutch-led task force had mostly shunned combat and confrontation. Instead, they were helping the locals to build bridges and set up schools for children. As the Dutch commander put it: "We're not here to fight the Taliban ... We're here to make the Taliban irrelevant."[55]

Amos Yadlin, a former chief of Israeli military intelligence, while commenting on a possible Israeli strike on Iran's nuclear facilities, notes: "Mr. Obama will ... have to shift the Israeli defense establishment's thinking from a focus on the 'zone of immunity' to a 'zone of trust'." However, he construes the "zone of trust" in terms of preventive military intervention. He writes: "What is needed is an ironclad American assurance that if Israel refrains from acting in its own window of opportunity – and all other options have failed ... Washington will act to prevent a nuclear Iran while it is still within its power to do so."[56] In contrast to this

---

[52] See Lloyd Dumas, "Is Development an Effective Way to Fight Terrorism?," in Verna V. Gehring, ed., *War After September 11* (Lanham, MD: Rowman and Littlefield, 2003), 65–74 and Barber, "The War of All against All."

[53] Alistair Macleod, "The War Against Terrorism and the 'War' Against Terrorism," in Steven P. Lee, ed., *Intervention, Terrorism, and Torture* (Dordrecht: Springer, 2007), 187–202.

[54] Annan reportedly said, referring to the potential genocidal conflict in Kenya that was averted through diplomatic initiatives led by Annan himself in 2008: "When we talk of intervention, people think of the military ... But under R2P, force is a last resort. Political and diplomatic intervention is the first mechanism. And I think we've seen a successful example of its application." (Reported by Roger Cohen in "African Genocide Averted," *The New York Times* op-ed, March 3, 2008.) This reasoning is a clear example of just-war thinking where military option is the last resort and Annan apparently was in favor of it, even as a preventive means in averting truly horrible prospects, as was evident in the R2P report in 2001 that was strongly backed by Annan. However, in cases of collective security in the form of self-defense, Annan was less clear about preventive military initiatives, speaking mostly on comprehensive non-interventionist preventive measures.

[55] "Dutch Soldiers Stress Restraint in Afghanistan," *The New York Times*, April 6, 2007.

[56] Amos Yadlin, "Israel's Last Chance to Strike Iran," *The New York Times*, op-ed, March 1, 2012.

expanded just-war military approach, my idea of just peace would construe the "zone of trust" in terms of preventive non-intervention. Creating a zone of trust among nations through collaborative proactive measures, with an emphasis on recognition, dialogue, and assistance, makes the need for preventive military measures obsolete.

The idea of a democratic world order is not that premature. Global trends indicate that the process of moving in that direction is already underway. The slowly emerging global recognition of endemic poverty and systemic inequity as serious human rights concerns has put pressure on individual countries for internal democratic reforms and made vivid the need for more just and effective international institutional directives. The demands of the developing countries in various world summits for democratic reform of the international global order are getting progressively vocal. Likewise, global socioeconomic issues are increasingly dominating the agenda of the rich countries in their G-8 meetings, paving the way to the recent G-20 summits. All this shows that an effective move toward a just world that can be acceptable to the global community yet be a compelling normative guide must demonstrate the importance of human rights in world affairs and should also have a realistic institutional account of fair representation in the global governance. Accordingly, it is the task of an empirically informed liberal theory to conceptualize how to promote the democratic norms of equality and fair political participation in the global governing institutions and rules. At the least, it would call for an institutional rearrangement in the international order that would be democratically responsive and reflect the fluid dynamics of collaboration and interdependence in today's global world.

The gradual move in this direction is the move toward just peace, which I have dubbed preventive non-intervention. Unlike the principled anti-interventionist arguments of the pacifists, this stance is anti-interventionist in a contingent sense. It is not necessarily against intervention *per se* (as for instance when intervention is the only option for preemptive reasons); it is against the way it usually takes place or against its feasibility in a complicated and interdependent world. But this limited provision for preemption, when construed on the premise of just peace but not just war as argued above, would not provide the moral mandate in the slippery transition to preventive military measures in the name of peace and security. In other words, a just-peace approach sanctifies the traditional Augustinian just-war ban on anticipatory military measures in a way that the premise of just war cannot. A just-peace initiative allows measured military response, if needed as the only option for self-defense or humanitarian reasons, either after an attack has occurred or when an attack is imminent, in the strictest sense of imminence requiring interception when the offense is evidently irrevocable. Augustine's just-war provision for limited and moral warfare (if not complete elimination of war) was not for ensuring just peace but for what Coady has dubbed "earthly peace," meaning mostly stability and order in this world among us fallen creatures.[57] Just peace for Augustine is only to be found in the City of God.

I share Kant's critique of Grotius and Vattel's doctrines of just war in that the doctrines provide the pretext for justifying wars.[58] My idea of global democracy as the foundation for just peace is quite similar to Kant's vision of a global federation of democratic (republican) states – like a universal civil society held together for peace and collective security where each state retains all its sovereign rights except the right to wage war. In such a justice-based global democracy that strives toward inclusion, participation, and empowerment, no member state would be considered an outlaw state, hence there would be no rogue states that could be targeted for preventive military strikes. This democratic global order would vastly increase the prospect of internal democratic reform within states in a peaceful manner, with initiatives generated by the states themselves. Because of the privilege of recognition and membership in the global body, they would not like to compromise this position through a failure of granting democratic rights to citizens. For inept states, there would be help from a common pool of funds for development assistance, along with the needed institutional support, without coercive conditions attached. In such a collaborative global order, the rhetoric of military intervention for imposing democracy from without would ring hollow. Also, the idea of a military strike against a group of subversive non-state actors in remote areas who are about to be shipping lethal virus for release in populated areas – Buchanan's hypothetical scenario for justifying preventive intervention – would be an empty argument. If the actors are domestic terrorists, then the question of intervening in a sovereign state does not arise, and if they are known foreign terrorists, then in a collaborative global order the idea of intervention goes against the thrust of collaboration. There are numerous collaborative avenues for responding to such distant threats.

---

[57] Coady, *Morality and Political Violence*, 264–270.
[58] Immanuel Kant, *Perpetual Peace and Other Essays*, trans. T. Humphrey (Indianapolis: Hackett Publishing, 1983).

Pondering over the prospects of international civil society and the kind of governmental agencies needed in the age of globalization, Walzer writes: "We will strengthen global pluralism only by using it, by seizing the opportunities it offers. There won't be an advance at any institutional level except in the context of a campaign or, better, a series of campaigns for greater security and greater equality for groups and individuals across the globe."[59] So, for Walzer, though "the level of participation in international civil society is much too low," we can make a difference through our participation and grassroots movements. For a liberal nationalist, this is liberal internationalism at its best.[60] Even a global egalitarian like Sen who is likely to question Walzer's statist paradigm would find Walzer's recipe a step in the right direction.[61]

In stark contrast to the promotion of a global civil society, in the move from preemption to prevention in the rhetoric of the just-war premise of the Bush doctrine, "the vocabulary of foreign policy was being militarized."[62] And, symbolically, at a certain point it gets hard to square the image of the militarized state with the ideals of peace and understanding. In fact, in today's tilted global order that is far from democratic, "preventive war privileges the already powerful."[63] For instance, militant non-state actors in inept or failed states are routinely condemned in the West as subversive agents bent on a terrorist mission against Western nations and their allies – an overly simplified and one-sided approach to a complex issue. Especially in the increasingly escalating use of drone attacks in the name of just war where drones are often termed "moral predators," thus making obligatory their uninhibited use, unresolved questions of peace and justice abound.[64] But when it comes to powerful non-state actors such as multinational corporations in today's unregulated global market who are undermining political and economic sovereignty of poor countries, similar rhetoric and moral outrage do not surface and preventive measures are not contemplated. This tilted global order is not conducive to just peace.

The gradual emergence of the global human rights culture in the last fifty years has achieved a certain level of international recognition for

---

[59] Walzer, *Arguing about War*, 191.

[60] Another liberal internationalist, Richard Miller, sees similar hope in the global social movements clamoring for a more just and equitable world. See Miller, *Globalizing Justice: The Ethics of Poverty and Power* (New York: Oxford University Press, 2010), chapter 9.

[61] See Deen Chatterjee, "Veiled Politics: The Liberal Dilemma of Multiculturalism," *The Monist* 95:1 (2012), 127–150 and "Reciprocity, Closed-Impartiality, and National Borders: Framing (and Extending) the Debate on Global Justice," *Social Philosophy Today* 27 (2011), 199–216.

[62] Hugh Strachan, "Preemption and Prevention in Historical Perspective," in Shue and Rodin, eds., *Preemption*, 38.

[63] Crawford, "The False Promise of Preventive War," 123.　　[64] See note 37 above.

justice when there is an egregious violation of negative human rights, but severe poverty and radical inequity in the socioeconomic arena are still not properly recognized as urgent human rights concerns. This "holocaust of neglect"[65] perpetuates deprivation, destabilization, and violence, creating the presumed need for preventive intervention, whereas preventive non-intervention, if practiced as a systemic antidote to the inequity and neglect in the world, can take us beyond the need for preventive use of force.

Understanding the idea of just peace can help us understand the seeming paradox of indifference leading to intervention, and proactive engagement leading to non-intervention.[66]

---

[65] Henry Shue, *Basic Rights: Subsistence, Affluence, and U.S. Foreign Policy*, 2nd edn. (Princeton University Press, 1996), 42.

[66] An earlier version of this chapter was presented as the keynote at the 2012 Graduate Conference on Global Justice and Ethics at New York University. I thank the members of the responding Faculty Panel – Patty Chang and Vasuki Nesiah of NYU and Joel Rosenthal of the Carnegie Council and NYU – as well as the conference director Lynette Sieger of NYU, for their valuable comments.

Bibliography

Arend, A. C. *Legal Rules and International Society*. Oxford University Press, 1999.

Arend, A. C. and Beck R. J. *International Law and the Use of Force: Beyond the United Nations Paradigm*. London: Routledge, 1993.

Azimi, Negar. "Hard Realities of Soft Power," *New York Times*, June 24, 2007.

Bacevich, A. *The New American Militarism*. New York: Oxford University Press, 2005.

Bahrami, N. and Parsi, T. "Blunt Instrument: Sanctions Don't Promote Democratic Change," *Boston Review*, February 14, 2012.

Barber, B. "The War of All against All: Terror and the Politics of Fear," in Verna V. Gehring, ed., *War After September 11*. Lanham, MD: Rowman and Littlefield, 2003, 75–91.

Becker, J. and Shane, S. "Secret 'Kill List' Proves a Test of Obama's Principles and Will," *New York Times*, May 29, 2012.

Begby, E. "Liberty, Statehood, and Sovereignty: Walzer on Mill on Non-Intervention," *Journal of Military Ethics* 2:1 (2003), 46–62.

Beitz, C. R. "Human Rights and the Law of Peoples," in Deen K. Chatterjee, ed., *The Ethics of Assistance: Morality and the Distant Needy*. Cambridge University Press, 2004, 194–214.

"Human Rights as a Common Concern," *American Political Science Review* 95:2 (2001), 269–282.

Bellamy, A. *Responsibility to Protect: The Global Effort to End Mass Atrocities*. London: Polity Press, 2009.

Benbaji, Yitzhak. "A Defense of the Traditional War Convention," *Ethics* 118:3 (2008), 464–495.

Bergman, Ronen. "Will Israel Attack Iran?," *The New York Times*, Sunday Magazine, January 25, 2012.

Bernstein, A. R. "Democratization as an Aim of Intervention: Rawls's Law of Peoples on Just War, Human Rights, and Toleration," *Proceedings of the 21st IVR World Congress*. Stuttgart: Franz Steiner Verlag, 2004, 23–35.

Betts, R. K. "Striking First: A History of Thankfully Lost Opportunities," *Ethics and International Affairs* 17:1 (2003), 17–24.

Blainey, G. *The Causes of War*. London: Macmillan, 1973.

Blake, M. "Reciprocity, Stability, and Intervention: The Ethics of Disequilibrium," in Deen K. Chatterjee and Don E. Scheid, eds., *Ethics and Foreign Intervention*. Cambridge University Press, 2003, 53–71.

Bluth, C. "The British Road to War: Blair, Bush and the Decision to invade Iraq," *International Affairs* 80:5 (2004), 871–892.

Boot, M. *The Savage Wars Of Peace: Small Wars and the Rise of American Power*. New York: Basic Books, 2003.

Bradford, W. C. "The Duty to Defend Them: A Natural Law Justification for the Bush Doctrine of Preventive War," *Notre Dame Law Review* 79 (2004), 1365–1492.

Brandt, R. "Utilitarianism and the Rules of War," in M. Cohen et al., eds., *War and Moral Responsibility*. Princeton University Press, 1974, 24–45.

Brecher, B. *Torture and the Ticking Bomb*. Oxford: Blackwell, 2007.

Bronfenbrenner, U. "The Mirror Image in Soviet-American Relations: A Social Psychologist's Report," *Journal of Social Issues* 17:3 (1961), 45–56.

Brown, C. "Practical Judgement and the Ethics of Preemption," in Brown, *Practical Judgement in International Political Theory: Selected Essays*. London: Routledge, 2010, 236–249.

  Practical Judgement in International Political Theory: Selected Essays. London: Routledge, 2010.

  "The 'Practice Turn', *Phronesis* and Classical Realism: Towards a *Phronetic* International Political Theory," *Millennium: Journal of International Studies* 40:3 (2012), 439–456.

  "Selective Humanitarianism: In Defence of Inconsistency," in Deen Chatterjee and Don Scheid, eds., *Ethics and Foreign Intervention*. Cambridge University Press, 2003, 31–50.

Brownlie, I. *International Law and the Use of Force by States*. Oxford: Clarendon Press, 1963.

Buchanan, A. "Institutionalizing the Just War," *Philosophy and Public Affairs* 34:1 (2006), 2–38.

  Justice, Legitimacy, and Self-Determination: Moral Foundations for International Law. Oxford University Press, 2004.

  "Justifying Preventive War," in Henry Shue and David Rodin, eds., *Preemption: Military Action and Moral Justification*. Oxford University Press, 2007, 126–142.

Buchanan, A. and Keohane, R. "The Preventive Use of Force: A Cosmopolitan Institutional Approach," *Ethics and International Affairs* 18:1 (2004), 1–22.

Bundy, M. *Danger and Survival: Choices About the Bomb in the First Fifty Years*. New York: Vintage Books, 1990.

Burke, A. "Against the New Internationalism," *Ethics and International Affairs* 19:2 (2005), 73–89.

Chatterjee, D. "Reciprocity, Closed-Impartiality, and National Borders: Framing (and Extending) the Debate on Global Justice," *Social Philosophy Today* 27 (2011), 199–216.

"Veiled Politics: The Liberal Dilemma of Multiculturalism," *The Monist* 95:1 (2012), 127–150.

Chatterjee, D. and Scheid, D., eds. *Ethics and Foreign Intervention.* Cambridge University Press, 2003.

Cicero, *Works, vol.* XIV. *Loeb Classical Library.* London and Cambridge MA: Harvard University Press, 1979.

Clausewitz, C. *On War,* ed. and trans. Michael Howard and Peter Paret. Princeton University Press, 1976.

Coady, C. A. J. "How New Is the 'New Terror'?," *Iyyun: The Jerusalem Philosophical Quarterly* 55:1 (2006), 49–65.
    Morality and Political Violence. Cambridge University Press, 2008.
    "War for Humanity: A Critique," in Deen K. Chatterjee and Don E. Scheid, eds., *Ethics and Foreign Intervention.* Cambridge University Press, 2003, 274–295.

Coates, A. J. *The Ethics of War.* Manchester University Press, 1997.

Cohen, J. "Minimalism About Human Rights: The Most We Can Hope For?," *The Journal of Political Philosophy* 12:2 (2004), 190–213.

Cohen, Roger. "African Genocide Averted," *The New York Times,* op-ed, March 3, 2008.

Cook, M. L. *The Moral Warrior.* Albany, NY: State University of New York Press, 2004.

Coppieters, B. "Legitimate Authority," in B. Coppieters and N. Fotion, eds., *Moral Constraints on War.* Lanham, MA: Lexington Books, 2002.

Cote, O. R. "Weapons of Mass Confusion," *Boston Review* 28:2 (2003), 26–27.

Crawford, N. "The False Promise of Preventive War," in Henry Shue and David Rodin, eds., *Preemption: Military Action and Moral Justification.* Oxford University Press, 2007, 89–125.
    "The Slippery Slope to Preventive War," *Ethics and International Affairs* 17:1 (2003), 30–36.

Dallaire, R. *Shake Hands with the Devil: The Failure of Humanity in Rwanda.* New York: Carroll and Graf, 2003.

Daly, E. and Sarkin, J. *Reconciliation in Divided Societies: Finding Common Ground,* Philadelphia: University of Pennsylvania Press, 2007.

DeCosse, D., ed. *But Was It Just? Reflections on the Morality of the Persian Gulf War.* New York: Doubleday, 1992.

Dershowitz, A. M. *Preemption: A Knife that Cuts both Ways.* New York: W. W. Norton, 2006.

Dinstein, Y. *War, Aggression, and Self-Defense.* 3rd edn., Cambridge University Press, 2001.

Doyle, M. *Striking First: Preemption and Prevention in International Conflict,* ed. Stephen Macedo. Princeton University Press, 2008.

Draper, Kai. "Defense," *Philosophical Studies* 145:1 (2009), 69–88.

Drumbl, M. *Punishment, Atrocity, and International Criminal Law.* New York: Cambridge University Press, 2007.

Dumas, L. "Is Development an Effective Way to Fight Terrorism?," in Verna V. Gehring, ed., *War After September 11.* Lanham, MD: Rowman and Littlefield, 2003, 65–74.

Eckert, A. and Mofidi, M. "Doctrine or Doctrinaire – The First Strike Doctrine and Preemptive Self-Defense Under International Law," *Tulane Journal of International and Comparative Law* 12:1 (2004), 117–151.

Ellsberg, D. *Secrets: A Memoir of Vietnam and the Pentagon Papers.* New York: Penguin Books, 2003.

Elshtain, J. B. "A Just War?," *Boston Sunday Globe*, October 6, 2002.

"International Justice as Equal Regard and the Use of Force," *Ethics and International Affairs* 17:2 (2003), 63–75.

Entous, A. "US Spies: Iran Split on Nuclear Program," *The Wall Street Journal*, February 17, 2011.

Evans, G. and Sahnoun, M. "The Responsibility to Protect," *Foreign Affairs* 81:6 (2002), 99–110.

The Responsibility to Protect: Report of the International Commission on Intervention and State Sovereignty. Ottawa: International Development Research Centre, 2001.

Falk, R. "The Challenge of Genocide and Genocidal Politics in an Era of Globalization," in Tim Dunne and Nicholas J. Wheeler, eds., *Human Rights in Global Politics*. Cambridge University Press, 1999, 177–194.

Falk, R. and Krieger, D. *The Path to Zero: Dialogue on Nuclear Dangers.* Boulder, CO: Paradigm Publishers, 2012.

Farer, T., Archibugi, D., Brown, C., Crawford, N., Weiss, T., and Wheeler, N. "Roundtable: Humanitarian Intervention after 9/11," *International Relations* 19:2 (2005), 211–250.

Fathi, Nazila. "Ahmadinejad Sees Nuclear Energy in Iran by 2009," *New York Times*, January 31, 2008.

"Iranian Leader Calls Report US Confession of 'Mistake'," *New York Times*, December 6, 2007.

"Iran's New President says Israel 'Must Be Wiped Off the Map'," *New York Times*, October 27, 2005.

Feinstein, L. and Slaughter, A. "A Duty to Prevent," *Foreign Affairs* 83:1 (January–February 2004), 136–150.

Fletcher, G. *A Crime of Self-Defense: Bernhard Goetz and the Law on Trial.* New York: The Free Press, 1988.

Franck, T. M. *Fairness in International Law and Institutions.* Oxford: Clarendon Press, 1995.

Galston, W. "The Perils of Preemptive War," *Philosophy and Public Policy Quarterly* 22:4 (2002), 2–6.

Gentili, A. *De Jure Belli (1598)*, trans. John C. Rolfe, in *The Classics of International Law*, vol. II. Oxford: Clarendon Press, 1933.

Giglio, M. "Interview: Pervez Musharraf," *Newsweek* , May 16, 2011.

Glennon, M. J. *Limits of Law, Prerogatives of Power: Interventionism After Kosovo.* London and New York: Palgrave Macmillan, 2001.

Goldberg, J. "Baghdad Delenda Est, Part Two," *National Review*, April 23, 2002.

Goodin, R. E. "Nuclear Disarmament as a Moral Certainty," *Ethics* 95:3 (1985), 641–658.

"Toward an International Rule of Law: Distinguishing International Law-Breakers from Would-Be Law-Makers," *The Journal of Ethics* 9:1/2 (2005), 225–246.

Gordon, M. and Trainor, B. *Cobra II: The Inside Story of the Invasion and Occupation of Iraq*. New York: Atlantic Books, 2006.

Gray, C. *International Law and the Use of Force*. New York: Oxford University Press, 2004.

Greenblum, B. M. "The Iranian Nuclear Threat: Israel's Options Under International Law," *Houston Journal of International Law* 29:1 (2006), 55–112.

Gross, M. L. *Moral Dilemmas of Modern War*. New York: Cambridge University Press, 2010.

Grotius, H. *De Jure Belli ac Pacis* (1625), trans. Francis W. Kelsey. Oxford: Clarendon Press, 1925.

Gutmann, A. and Thompson, D., eds. *Ethics and Politics: Cases and Comments*. Chicago: Nelson Hall, 2005.

Hare, R. *Freedom and Reason*. Oxford: Clarendon Press, 1963.

Hehir, J. B. "The Ethics of Intervention: Two Normative Traditions," in Peter G. Brown and Douglas MacLean, eds., *Human Rights and U.S. Foreign Policy*. Lexington Books, 1979, 121–139.

Held, D. "Law of States, Law of Peoples: Three Models of Sovereignty," *Legal Theory* 8:1 (2002), 1–44.

Hendrickson, D. "Towards Universal Empire: The Dangerous Quest for Absolute Security," *World Policy Journal* 19:3 (2002), 2–10.

Hersch, S. *Chain of Command*. New York: HarperCollins, 2004.

Hobbes, Thomas. *Leviathan* (1651), ed. Richard Tuck. Cambridge University Press, 1996.

Holmes, S. and Sunstein, C. R. *The Cost of Rights: Why Liberty Depends on Taxes*. New York: Norton & Co., 1999.

Hosein, Adam. "Are Justified Aggressors a Threat to the Rights Theory of Self-Defense?," in Helen Frowe and Gerald Lang, eds., *How We Fight*. Oxford University Press, forthcoming.

Hurka, Thomas. "Liability and Just Cause," *Ethics and International Affairs* 21:2 (2007), 199–218.

IAEA, Board of Governors. "Implementation of the NPT Safeguards Agreement and relevant provisions of Security Council resolutions 1737 (2006) and 1747 (2007) in the Islamic Republic of Iran," GOV/2007/58, November 2007.

"Implementation of the NPT Safeguards Agreement and relevant provisions of Security Council resolutions 1737 (2006), 1747 (2007), 1803 (2008) and 1835 (2008) in the Islamic Republic of Iran," GOV/2009/74, November 16, 2009.

"Implementation of the NPT Safeguards Agreement and relevant provisions of Security Council resolutions in the Islamic Republic of Iran," GOV/2011/29, May 24, 2011

"Implementation of the NPT Safeguards Agreement and relevant provisions of Security Council resolutions in the Islamic Republic of Iran," GOV/2012/23, May 25, 2012.

Ignatieff, M. *The Lesser Evil: Political Ethics in an Age of Terror.* London: Penguin Books, 2004.

Iklé, F. *Every War Must End,* revised edn. New York: Columbia University Press, 1991.

Johnson, D. *Overconfidence and War.* Cambridge, MA: Harvard University Press, 2004.

Johnson, J. T. "The Just War Idea and the Ethics of Intervention," in J. Carl Ficarrotta, ed., *The Leader's Imperative.* West Lafayette, IN: Purdue University Press, 2001, 107–125.

    Morality and Contemporary Warfare. New Haven: Yale University Press, 1999.

    The War to Oust Saddam Hussein: Just War and the New Face of Conflict. Massachussetts: Rowman and Littlefield, 2005.

Kant, I. *Perpetual Peace and Other Essays,* trans. T. Humphrey. Indianapolis: Hackett Publishing, 1983.

Kaufman, W. "What's Wrong With Preventive War?: The Moral and Legal Basis for the Preventive Use of Force," *Ethics and International Affairs* 19:3 (2005), 23–38.

Kissinger, H. "Our Intervention in Iraq," *Washington Post,* op-ed, August 12, 2002.

    "The Rules on Preventive Force," *Washington Post,* op-ed, April 9, 2006.

Klare, M. *Rogue States and Nuclear Outlaws: America's Search for a New Foreign Policy.* New York: Hill and Wang, 1995.

Korsgaard, C. "The Right to Lie: Kant on Dealing With Evil," *Philosophy and Public Affairs* 15:4 (1986), 325–349.

Krieger, D. *The Doves Flew High.* Santa Barbara, CA: Artamo Press, 2007.

Kukathas, C. "The Mirage of Global Justice," *Social Philosophy and Policy* 23:1 (2006), 1–25.

Kuper, A. *Democracy Beyond Borders: Justice and Representation in Global Institutions.* New York: Oxford University Press, 2004.

Lee, S., ed. *Intervention, Terrorism, and Torture.* Dordrecht: Springer, 2007.

Litwak, R. *Rogue States and U.S. Foreign Policy: Containment After the Cold War.* Washington, DC: Woodrow Wilson Centre Press; Baltimore: Distributed by the Johns Hopkins University Press, 1999.

Love, M. C. "Global Problems: Global Solutions," in Love, ed., *Beyond Sovereignty: Issues for a Global Agenda,* 2nd edn. Belmont, CA: Wadsworth, 2003, 1–42.

Luban, D. "Preventive War," *Philosophy and Public Affairs* 32:3 (2004), 207–248.

    "Preventive War and Human Rights," in Henry Shue and David Rodin, eds., *Preemption: Military Action and Moral Justification.* New York: Oxford University Press, 2007, 171–201.

    "War as Punishment," *Philosophy and Public Affairs* 39:4 (2011), 299–330.

Lucas, G. R. "Defense or Offense? The Two Streams of Just War Tradition," in Peter French, ed., *War and Border Crossings: Ethics When Cultures Clash.* Lanham, MD: Rowman & Littlefield, 2005, 45–57.

    "From *jus ad bellum* to *jus ad pacem:* Re-thinking Just-War Criteria for the Use of Military Force for Humanitarian Ends," in Deen K. Chatterjee and

Don E. Scheid, eds., *Ethics and Foreign Intervention*. Cambridge University Press, 2003, 72–96.

"'Methodological Anarchy': Arguing about Preventive War," in Roger Wertheimer, ed., *Empowering our Military Conscience: Transforming Just War Theory and Military Moral Education*. London: Ashgate Press, 2010, 33–56.

"Methodological Anarchy: Arguing about War, and Getting it Right," *Journal of Military Ethics* 6:3 (2007), 246–252.

"The Reluctant Interventionist," in Lucas, *Perspectives on Humanitarian Military Intervention*. Berkeley, CA: University of California Press/Institute for Intergovernmental Studies, 2001.

"The Role of the International Community in the Just War Tradition: Confronting the Challenges of Humanitarian Intervention and Pre-emptive War," *Journal of Military Ethics* 2:2 (2003), 141–148.

Macleod, A. "The War Against Terrorism and the 'War' Against Terrorism," in Steven P. Lee, ed., *Intervention, Terrorism, and Torture*. Dordrecht: Springer, 2007, 187–202.

Majd, Hooman. "Starving Iran Won't Free It," *The New York Times*, op-ed, March 3, 2012.

Margalit, Avishai and Walzer, Michael. "Israel: Civilians and Combatants: An Exchange," *The New York Review of Books* 56:8, May 14, 2009, 21–22.

Martin, S. T. "'No-fly' Zone Perils Were for Iraqis, not Allied Pilots," *The St. Petersburg Times*, October 29, 2004.

May, Larry. *After War Ends: A Philosophical Perspective*. Cambridge University Press, 2012.

Aggression and Crimes Against Peace. Cambridge University Press, 2008.

Mazzetti, M. "US Finds Iran Halted Its Nuclear Arms Effort in 2003," *New York Times*, December 4, 2007.

McMahan, Jeff. "Comment," in Michael Doyle, *Striking First: Preemption and Prevention in International Conflict*, ed. Stephen Macedo. Princeton University Press, 2008, 129–147.

"The Ethics of Killing in War," *Ethics* 114:4 (2004), 693–733.

"Innocence, Self-Defense, and Killing in War," *Journal of Political Philosophy* 2:3 (1994), 193–221.

Killing in War. Oxford University Press, 2009.

"The Morality of War and the Law of War," in David Rodin and Henry Shue, eds., *Just and Unjust Warriors: The Moral and Legal Status of Soldiers*. New York: Oxford University Press, 2008, 19–43.

"Preventive War and the Killing of the Innocent," in Richard Sorabji and David Rodin, eds., *The Ethics of War: Shared Problems in Different Traditions*. Aldershot: Ashgate, 2006, 169–190.

"Self-Defense Against Justified Threateners," in Helen Frowe and Gerald Lang, eds., *How We Fight: Issues in Jus in Bello*. Oxford University Press, forthcoming.

"Self-Defense and Culpability," *Law and Philosophy* 24:6 (2005), 751–774.

"What Makes an Act of War Disproportionate?" Annual Stutt Lecture, US Naval Academy, Annapolis MD, 2008.

Mearsheimer, J. *The Tragedy of Great Power Politics*. New York: W. W. Norton, 2001.

"Why We Will Soon Miss the Cold War," *The Atlantic Monthly* 266:2 (1990), 35–50.

Mill, J. S. "A Few Words on Non-Intervention" [1859], reprinted in *Dissertations and Discussions*, 3 vols. London: Longmans, Green, Reader, and Dyer, 1867, vol. III, 153–178.

Miller, R. *Globalizing Justice: The Ethics of Poverty and Power*. New York: Oxford University Press, 2010.

Montesquieu, C. de. *The Spirit of the Laws* (1748), trans. A. M. Cohler, B. C. Miller, and H. S. Stone. Cambridge University Press, 1989.

Myers, R. J. "Notes on the Just War Theory: Whose Justice, Which Wars?," *Ethics and International Affairs* 10:1 (2006), 115–130.

Myers, S. L. and Cooper, H. "Bush Insists Iran Remains a Threat Despite Arms Data," *New York Times*, December 5, 2007.

Nagel, T. "The Problem of Global Justice," *Philosophy and Public Affairs* 33:2 (2005), 113–147.

Nathanson, S. "Kennedy and the Cuban Missile Crisis: On the Role of Moral Reasons in Explaining and Evaluating Political Decision-Making," *Journal of Social Philosophy* 22:2 (1991), 94–108.

"Patriotism, War, and the Limits of Permissible Partiality," *Journal of Ethics* 13:4 (2009), 401–422.

Terrorism and the Ethics of War. Cambridge University Press, 2010.

National Conference of Catholic Bishops. *The Challenge of Peace*. Washington, DC: US Catholic Bishops Conference, 1983.

The Harvest of Justice is Sown in Peace. Washington, DC: US Catholic Bishops Conference, 1993.

National Intelligence Estimate. "Iran: Nuclear Intentions and Capabilities," National Intelligence Council, November 2007.

Nussbaum, M. "Women and Theories of Global Justice: Our Need for a New Paradigm," in Deen K. Chatterjee, ed., *The Ethics of Assistance: Morality and the Distant Needy*. Cambridge University Press, 2004, 147–176.

O'Connell, M. E. *The Myth of Preemptive Self-Defense*. Washington: American Society of International Law Task Force on Terrorism, August 2002.

Pagden, A. and Lawrance, J. eds. *Vitoria, Political Writings*. Cambridge University Press, 1992.

Parfit, Derek. *On What Matters*, vol. 1. Oxford University Press, 2011.

Pogge, T. "An Institutional Approach to Humanitarian Intervention," *Public Affairs Quarterly* 6:1 (1992), 89–103.

Ramsey, M. "Reinventing the Security Council: the UN as a Lockean System," *Notre Dame Law Review* 79:4 (2004), 1529–1562.

Rawls, J. *A Theory of Justice*. Cambridge MA: Harvard University Press, 1971.

The Law of Peoples. Cambridge MA: Harvard University Press, 2001.

Reichberg, G. M. "Is There a 'Presumption against War' in Aquinas's Ethics?," *The Thomist* 66:3 (2002), 337–367.

"Preventive War in Classical Just War Theory," *Journal of the History of International Law* 9:1 (2007), 3–33.

Reiter, D. *Preventive War and its Alternatives*. Carlisle, PA: Strategic Studies Institute, 2006.

Ricks, T. *Fiasco: The American Military Adventure in Iraq*. New York: Penguin Press, 2006.

Rodin, D. "The Problem with Prevention," in Henry Shue and David Rodin, eds., *Preemption: Military Action and Moral Justification*. Oxford University Press, 2007, 143–170.

War and Self-Defense. Oxford University Press, 2001.

Rodin, D. and Shue, H., eds. *Just and Unjust Warriors: The Moral and Legal Status of Soldiers*. Oxford University Press, 2008.

Rogin, J. "Exclusive: New National Intelligence Estimate on Iran Complete," *The Cable*, February 15, 2011.

Sagan, S. "How to Keep the Bomb From Iran," *Foreign Affairs* 85:5 (September–October 2006), 45–59.

Sanger, David E. "Rice Says Iran Must Not Be Allowed to Develop Nuclear Arms", *New York Times*, August 9, 2004, A3.

Scahill, J. "No-Fly Zones: Washington's Undeclared War on 'Saddam's Victims'," (2002) at www.IraqJournal.org.

Schlesinger, A. "Unilateral Preventive War: Illegitimate and Immoral," *Los Angeles Times*, August 21, 2002.

Scott, J. B. *The Classics of International Law*. Washington, DC: Carnegie Institution, 1916.

Segev, T. *1967: Israel, the War, and the Year that Transformed the Middle East*. New York: Henry Holt and Company, 2007.

Sen, A. *Development as Freedom*. New York: Knopf; Oxford: Clarendon Press, 1999.

The Idea of Justice. Cambridge, MA: Harvard University Press, 2009.

Shachar, A. *The Birthright Lottery: Citizenship and Global Inequality*. Cambridge, MA: Harvard University Press, 2009.

Shapiro, I. *The Moral Foundations of Politics*. New Haven: Yale University Press, 2003.

Shue, H. *Basic Rights: Subsistence, Affluence, and U.S. Foreign Policy*, 2nd edn. Princeton University Press, 1996.

"Let Whatever is Smouldering Erupt? Conditional Sovereignty, Reviewable Intervention, and Rwanda 1994," in A. J. Paolini, A. P. Jarvis, and C. Reus-Smit, eds., *Between Sovereignty and Global Governance: The United Nations, the State, and Civil Society*. London: Macmillan, 1998, 60–84.

"Limiting Sovereignty," in Jennifer Welsh, ed., *Humanitarian Intervention and International Relations*. Oxford University Press, 2004, 11–28.

"War," in Hugh LaFollette, ed., *The Oxford Handbook of Practical Ethics*. Oxford University Press, 2003, 734–761.

"What Would a Justified Preventive Military Attack Look Like?," in Henry Shue and David Rodin, eds, *Preemption: Military Action and Moral Justification*. New York: Oxford University Press, 2007, 222–246.

Shue, H. and Rodin, D. eds. *Preemption: Military Action and Moral Justification*. Oxford University Press, 2007.

Sidgwick, Henry. "The Morality of Strife," in his *Practical Ethics*. London: Swann Sonnenschein and Co., 1898, 47–62.

Practical Ethics. London: Swann Sonnenschein and Co., 1898.

Simms, B. *Unfinest Hour*. London: Penguin, 2002.

Singer, Peter. "Do Drones Undermine Democracy?," *New York Times*, Sunday Review, January 22, 2012.

Sinnott-Armstrong, Walter. "Preventive War, What is it Good For?," in Henry Shue and David Rodin, eds., *Preemption: Military Action and Moral Justification*. Oxford University Press, 2007, 202–221.

Slocombe, W. "Force, Pre-emption, and Legitimacy," *Survival: Global Politics and Strategy* 45:1 (2003), 117–130.

Smith, M. B. E. "Is there a Prima Facie Obligation to Obey the Law?," *Yale Law Journal* 82:5 (1973), 950–976.

St Augustine. *The City of God*, ed. Henry Bettenson. New York: Penguin, 1972.

Steinberg, James. "The Use of Preventive Force as an Element of US National Strategy," www.wws.princeton.edu/ppns/papers/Steinberg_Preemption.pdf.

Stephens, R. *Nasser: A Political Biography*. New York: Simon and Schuster, 1971.

Stiglitz, J. *Globalization and Its Discontents*. New York: W. W. Norton, 2002.

Strachan, H. "Preemption and Prevention in Historical Perspective," in Henry Shue and David Rodin, eds., *Preemption: Military Action and Moral Justification*. Oxford University Press, 2007, 23–39.

Sunstein, C. *Laws of Fear: Beyond the Precautionary Principle* Cambridge University Press, 2005.

Suskind, R. *The One Percent Doctrine: Deep Inside America's Pursuit of its Enemies Since 9/11*. New York: Simon and Schuster, 2006.

Swaine, J. and Greenwood, P. "Obama: I will not hesitate in using force to block Iran's nuclear threat from Iran," *The Telegraph*, March 4, 2012.

Tetlock, P. *Expert Political Judgement*. Princeton University Press, 2005.

Toulmin, S. *Cosmopolis: The Hidden Agenda of Modernity*. University of Chicago Press, 1990.

Thompson, E. P. "Notes on Exterminism: The Last Stage of Civilization," in Thompson et al., *Exterminism and Cold War*. London: Verso, 1982.

Trachtenberg, M. "Preventive War and US Foreign Policy," in Henry Shue and David Rodin, eds., *Preemption: Military Action and Moral Justification*. Oxford University Press, 2007, 40–68.

"Preventive War and U.S. Foreign Policy," *Security Studies* 16:1 (2007), 1–31.

Uniacke, S. "On Getting One's Retaliation in First," in Henry Shue and David Rodin, eds., *Preemption: Military Action and Moral Justification*. Oxford University Press, 2007, 69–88.

United Nations. *A More Secure World: Our Shared Responsibility: Report of the Secretary-General's High-level Panel on Threats, Challenges and Change*. New York: United Nations, 2004.

Walzer, M. *Arguing about War*. New Haven: Yale University Press, 2004.

"The Case Against our Attack on Libya," *The New Republic*, March 20, 2011.

Just and Unjust Wars: A Moral Argument with Historical Illustrations. 4th edn. New York: Basic Books, 2006.

"No Strikes: Inspectors Yes, War No," *The New Republic*, September 19–22, 2002.

"Regime Change and Just War," *Dissent* 53 (2006), 106–108.

Weigel, G. "The Development of Just War Thinking in the Post-Cold War World: An American Perspective," in Charles Reed and David Ryall, eds., *The Price of Peace: Just War in the Twenty-First Century*. Cambridge University Press, 2007, 19–36.

Woodward, B. *State of Denial*. New York: Simon & Schuster, 2006.

Worth, Robert F. "Iran's Middle Class on Edge as World Presses In," *The New York Times*, February 7, 2012.

Yadlin, Amos. "Israel's Last Chance to Strike Iran," *The New York Times*, op-ed, March 1, 2012.

Yoder, J. H. *When War is Unjust: Being Honest in Just-War Thinking. Revised edn*. New York: Orbis Books, 1996.

Yoo, J. and Delahunty, R. "The 'Bush Doctrine': Can Preventive War Be Justified?," *Harvard Journal of Law and Public Policy* 32:3 (2009), 843–865.

Index